FORECASTING

FORECASTING
AN APPRAISAL
FOR POLICY-MAKERS
AND PLANNERS

WILLIAM ASCHER

THE JOHNS HOPKINS UNIVERSITY PRESS
BALTIMORE AND LONDON

The Johns Hopkins University Press, Baltimore, Maryland
21218
The Johns Hopkins Press Ltd., London

Originally published, 1978
Second printing, 1979

Johns Hopkins paperback edition, 1979

Library of Congress Catalog Card Number 77-21423
ISBN 0-8018-2035-9 (hardcover)
ISBN 0-8018-2273-4 (paperback)

Library of Congress Cataloging in Publication data will be
found on the last printed page of this book.

CONTENTS

FIGURES

TABLES

FOREWORD

Professor Ascher's volume is a unique and pathbreaking treatment of a fundamental component of public and private policy-making. The topic is the theory and practice of forecasting. The treatment is distinctive because of the number of past forecasts that are reviewed for success or failure, and for method. The forecasts are classified in groupings that are large enough to have a substantial number of instances spread over enough time to warrant appraisal. The three principal categories are energy, transportation, and technology, the last including nuclear energy and computer forecasting.

The appraisal has been executed with great analytic proficiency and in a remarkably calm tone of voice. The field has been, and still is, full of emotionalized differences over basic theory and technique; and these controversies have important implications for the choice of policy and for the investment of billions of dollars.

I shall not summarize the findings further than to say that Professor Ascher's results are the most comprehensive and able judgement that we have yet had of the validity of forecasts, and of the relationship between methods and results. Perhaps the most striking demonstration is that core assumptions are more crucial than the sophistication of technique. The improvement of technique does not compensate for erroneous core assumptions, as shown, for example, in population forecasting in the 1930s and 1940s, and in the forecasts of demand for electricity in the 1960s.

Ascher formulates an important theory of "assumption drag," linking it, among other factors, with the distinctive symbolic characteristics of many sociopolitical processes. The significance of the theory is that it identifies a series of problems that can be overcome by further effort to create organized scenarios and to improve the availability and use of social indicators. Ascher's estimate of the probable future of forecasting is that developments will take place in three areas: modeling, surprise-sensitive forecasting, and normative forecasting.

Professor Ascher's volume will become a classical contribution to the field of forecasting, and is therefore welcomed by all serious students of every dimension of the policy process. The prose and the tables are so clear that the nonspecialist user of forecasts may momentarily doubt its profundity. But on reflection he will gladly give up any "assumption drag" that obscurity guarantees truth.

HAROLD D. LASSWELL
Ford Foundation Professor Emeritus of Law and the Social Sciences
Cochairman of The Policy Sciences Center, Inc., New York City

ACKNOWLEDGMENTS

This study grew out of the intellectual stimulation of the *policy sciences,* an approach to linking "politics" and "policy analysis" by focusing on the modes of policy formulation. The promise of this approach lies in its potential both for the analysis of social process and for prescribing improvements in the policy process. Whatever success this book may have in connecting the forecasting task to its complex environment is due to what I have learned from the leading developers of this approach: Harold Lasswell, Ronald Brunner, and Garry Brewer. The reactions of many forecasting theorists aided in this project, most notably those of Joseph Martino, A. Donald Bender, and Donald Pyke. My colleagues Matthew Crenson and Francis Rourke provided invaluable insights into "bureaucratic politics," which are crucial for understanding how forecasts are used. Lawrence Lundgren, Marc Blum, and Louis Maccini lent their considerable expertise in making some of the substantive fields of forecasting understandable.

Inasmuch as this study is based on the analysis of hundreds of forecasts, it rests on the painstraking efforts of many individuals who took the trouble to collect and compile them. In particular, I wish to gratefully acknowledge the efforts of the Battelle Memorial Institute, the Edison Electric Institute, the Atomic Industrial Forum, the National Bureau of Economic Research, Resources for the Future, Inc., the Federal Aviation Administration, and the Federal Power Commission.

Able research assistance was provided by Georgina Guernica and F. David Levenbach. The artwork of John S. Spurbeck, the copy-editing of Penny Moudrianakis, and the editorial guidance of Michael Aronson are responsible for making this book intelligible. My wife, Barbara, deserves credit for making this book even conceivable.

ABBREVIATIONS

AEC	Atomic Energy Commission
AIME	American Institute of Mining Engineers
API	American Petroleum Institute
ASA	American Statistical Association
BEA	Bureau of Economic Analysis
CAA	Civil Aeronautics Administration
CAB	Civil Aeronautics Board
DRI	Data Resources, Inc.
ERDA	Energy Research and Development Administration
EW	*Electrical World*
FAA	Federal Aviation Administration
FEA	Federal Energy Administration
FPC	Federal Power Commission
FRB	Federal Reserve Bank
MIPS	millions of instructions per second
MTE	minimum typical error
NBER	National Bureau of Economic Research
NPA	National Planning Association
NPN	*Natural Petroleum News*
NRPB	National Resources Planning Board
OBE	Office of Business Economics
OECD	Organisation for Economic Cooperation and Development
OMB	Office of Management and Budget
OPEC	Organization of Petroleum Exporting Countries
PPBS	Planning-Programming-Budgeting System
RMSE	root-mean-square error
SSRC	Social Science Research Council

FORECASTING

CHAPTER I

INTRODUCTION

Because of past failures to foresee or acknowledge trends, many of the problems now facing the United States seem worse than they might otherwise have been. The energy crises emerged as a result of unanticipated shortages of fuels and inadequate recognition of the implications of the continually growing demand for energy. City streets are clogged with too many cars. Colleges that suffered from overcrowding in the late 1960s, and expanded reactively, face bankruptcy in the present era of dwindling enrollments and economic downturn. Air and water pollution persist because of the failure to take remedial and preventative action years ago. Some of the anticipated "solutions" to these problems—electric cars, unlimited and clean nuclear energy, automated teaching machines—have failed to materialize, and indeed may have hindered problem-solving by holding out false hopes of easy solutions. All the technological sophistication of our public and private sectors has not produced an enviable record of forecasting future problems and events.

This conclusion, however, is as much a recognition of the difficulties of forecasting as it is a criticism of attempts to forecast. Of all the information used by policy-makers, projections are the least rooted in discoverable facts. Diligence may reward efforts to choose among past patterns and existing relationships, and even to choose among alternatives on the basis of firm information, but projections depart from the currently knowable.

The art of forecasting, therefore, is intrinsically difficult. The challenge facing a policy-maker is to decide whether and how to use the projections supplied by forecasting specialists, in light of the problematical nature of forecasting. Policy-makers continually use forecasts. Whether they use their own informal, rule-of-thumb projections or the forecasts provided by specialists depends on how well they can appraise these expert forecasts. Are the forecasts worth heeding at all? Of all available forecasts, which are the most likely to be accurate and useful? What are the forecasts' limitations? Is it possible to correct expert forecasts for likely biases?

In some respects the appraisal of forecasts puts a greater burden on the policy-maker than the original task of forecasting itself. The accuracy of current forecasts is, of course, yet to be determined. Evaluation of the methodology of various forecasts may require technical sophistication at least as great as, and perhaps greater than, that of the specialists in forecasting. Yet the policy-maker is rarely a specialist in forecasting techniques, nor is he often an authority on the phenomena being projected. Moreover, for the frequent case in which numerous forecasts of the same trend are available, the selection of a "most likely" forecast is in itself an act of forecasting, since the policy-maker chooses the forecast which reflects assumptions and methods that appear most reasonable to him. The policy-maker thus tacitly chooses a set of assumptions about the future and methodology for projecting the essence of those assumptions.

THE APPRAISAL TASK APPLIED TO FORECASTS

Any aspect of the policy process can benefit from an appraisal of its performance. This is particularly true for the uncertain undertaking of forecasting, whose contribution to policy outcomes is inevitably problematic. Appraisal requires that a given procedure or outcome be evaluated in terms of whatever criteria are considered relevant, and then be compared to alternative procedures or outcomes. Considering the difficulty of evaluating a large set of forecasts according to any single standard of performance, it is disconcerting that the choice of appraisal criteria is itself a thorny problem. Often one criterion is used without the realization that many other criteria are available and are valid in terms of particular goals.

Without specifying the goals of forecasting, one cannot identify appropriate performance criteria. The choice of appraisal standards is difficult because there are multiple and sometimes contradictory goals of forecast formulation and use. For example, if the real goal is to provide an image of technical sophistication for the policy-maker using a forecast, the methodological elegance of the forecast would be a more important criterion than its accuracy. The full range of goals includes enhancing the reputation of the forecaster or forecast-user, sensitizing policy-makers to future opportunities or dangers (regardless of whether or not they are the most likely outcomes), and improving the quality of decisions, however quality is defined. The goals of forecasting vary according to the perspectives of the primary actors in the policy process—namely, the forecaster, the policy-maker, and the analyst of the policy process.

The forecaster's perspective centers on how useful and successful he can be in his dealings with his clientele, as well as with the fundamental problem of prediction. Numerous manuals on "how to forecast" emphasize the goal of maximizing accuracy. These works also demonstrate how to present forecasts in striking and memorable formats. Taking advantage of graphic displays and other eye-catching devices, they maximize the impact of the forecasts, but without manipulating the content of the forecasts themselves.

Recently, a new line of thought has emerged from the forecaster's perspective (particularly in the field of technological forecasting) which shifts the focus to the overall *usefulness* of forecasts in policy-making. The introduction of "normative" forecasting, which is the use of projections to systematically explore and select goals and alternatives, is the most prominent indication of the effort to transform the forecast from an isolated piece of information into a decision-making process in its own right. According to this more ambitious outlook, the status of a forecast as an accurate piece of information becomes less important than its utility in producing "good" decisions or policies. Accuracy is sacrificed for greater comprehensibility, availability, or forcefulness. Conceivably, a deliberately exaggerated forecast (e.g., one that predicts dire consequences of pollution, beyond what is actually probable) could be justified within this point of view, if it goaded people into taking the appropriate measures to solve the actual problem. By exaggerating the crisis confronting decision-makers—a strategy employed in gaming simulations under the name "scenario goad"—more forceful actions are encouraged, but at the risk of sacrificing credibility.[1] The danger is that a quite legitimate concern, such as that over the environmental side effects of industrialization, may be discredited as a result of the repudiation of a forecasting effort that became prominent through exaggerated claims. The Jay Forrester studies for the Club of Rome, discussed in chapter 2, may very well have had this effect. Usefulness thus entails an amalgam of the impact of the forecast and its compatibility with appropriate decisions and policies. Advocacy of this position politicizes the forecaster's role in the policy process, inasmuch as manipulation of the content of the forecast and of the behavior of the policy-makers becomes an option for the forecaster.

The policy-maker's perspective emphasizes the forecast's usefulness in helping him to arrive at decisions that maximize *his* goals, and in supporting his decisions once they have been made. From the policy-maker's point of view, the utility of the forecast lies in its comprehensiveness and comprehensibility, but most importantly in its accuracy. If the policy-maker actually relies on experts' forecasts to guide his deliberations, he will not appreciate any attempt by the forecasters to increase their own impact and influence, or to achieve their own programmatic goals, through the sacrifice of forecast accuracy. Once a decision is made or a policy formulated, the contribution of the forecast lies in how authoritative, attention-getting, and credible it is in the service of the policy-maker's position. Hence forecasting serves as both "intelligence" and "promotion" for the policy-maker.

The analyst of the policy process is concerned with what forecasting adds to the overall complex mechanism of policy formulation. This mechanism is highly variable, and the role of forecasting in it can be minimal or crucial. The analyst may focus on how important forecasting is to a specific policy-making sequence, how the decisions that emerge are affected by the presence or absence of distinct efforts to forecast, or how forecasts serve as assets or liabilities for actors seeking to achieve their preferred outcomes. All aspects of forecast performance are thus important *per se* or as indicators of why and how forecasts enter into the decision-making process. The ultimate accuracy of forecasts is generally of less concern to the policy-process analyst than are the importance of the forecasts and the specifics of their impact on the decision-making process.

ACCURACY AS A CRITERION OF APPRAISAL

The criterion of accuracy in the appraisal of forecasts has its critics. In view of the many functions of forecasting that are relevant to each perspective on forecasting, however, opposition to this criterion is not surprising.

The first criticism of the accuracy criterion is simply that a forecast's accuracy is an *incomplete* appraisal of its worth and consequences. While this point seems indisputable, the real question is whether other criteria can be applied to the appraisal of broad sets of forecasts. The present study, which is designed to examine the *general* performance of forecasting and the *broad* principles of who and what produce relatively good forecasts, must emphasize the accuracy criterion because the potential for reaching general conclusions regarding other criteria is very limited. The limitations involve both problems of measurement and problems of establishing what factors or methods lead to "good" forecasts.

The problems of measurement arise from the fact that other relevant characteristics of forecasts—comprehensibility, persuasiveness, usefulness, authoritativeness, provocativeness, importance, and so on—pertain to the *impact* of the forecasts on diffuse audiences whose reactions usually cannot be observed or measured. Whereas a forecast's accuracy can be calculated more or less independently of the context in which it is made, its impact is profoundly embedded in its context. Yet even the audience of a given forecast is difficult to determine. Who has or has not read the Resources for the Future study *Resources in America's Future?* Who has read it carefully enough that the forecasts therein have had some impact? How did the forecasts strike these readers?

It is as difficult to estimate the importance of forecasts in a given decision-making process as it is to determine how important any piece of information is in influencing policy-makers exposed to many sources and types of information. There is first the problem of determining how much conscious attention is paid to forecasts, but there is also the problem of determining whether and to what extent the forecasts are discounted if they clash with the policy-maker's intuitive beliefs about the future or about what the proper policy should be regardless of what the forecasts imply about the validity of that policy. Forecasts are always presented along with other information about goals, conditions, trends, and alternatives that are not necessarily consistent with the forecasts themselves. Undoubtedly policy-makers themselves are generally unaware of how important the forecasts really are in

4

their ultimate decisions. The same difficulties hold for measuring the other aspects of a forecast's impact. Chapter 2 explores some of those factors, but also demonstrates the difficulties of generalizing from case studies to the performance of forecasting in general.

The second criticism of the accuracy criterion is that the demand for accuracy might encourage some forecasters to make vague or hedged forecasts in order to maintain their reputations for high accuracy. However, it seems quite unlikely that obfuscation would be tolerated when accuracy, and appraisability in terms of accuracy, are emphasized as criteria for evaluating forecasts. In fact, freeing forecasters from the imperative to be as accurate as possible would create great confusion in how the policy-maker should regard the forecast and its implications.

The third, and most complicated criticism of the accuracy criterion centers on the phenomena of self-fulfilling and self-defeating predictions. Predictions are self-fulfilling if the fact that they are made itself leads to actions that make them correct. Self-defeating predictions, which would have been correct if they had "fallen on deaf ears," become incorrect because of responses to the predictions. The criticism is that predictions may be "accurate" at the moment they are made, but become inaccurate by virtue of their very existence. Forecasts that are effective in averting the crises they predict become inaccurate *because* they are effective. Forecasters who try to adjust their predictions (to account for the reactions to the forecasts themselves) so that they become accurate, end up producing confusing forecasts of little relevance to policy-making.[2] "Poor" forecasts that prove to be self-fulfilling also are possible; for example, forecasts of low demand may prove accurate if supplies are discouraged by the forecast, even if potential demand is much higher than the forecast specified.

Forecast theorists have exaggerated the incidence and importance of self-fulfilling and self-defeating forecasts, however. First, the decision-makers for whom forecasts are developed generally do not control the pace of the trends involved. For example, forecasts of school-age children are useful for educators and for planners of school facilities, but they do not control the birth rate. There would be little sense in presenting these school planners and educators with forecasts of how many schools there will be, since *they* determine this. Thus, most of the forecasts utilized by various decision-makers consist of projections of trends which they must take into account *because* they do not control them.

Second, for those forecasts which do involve trends that are controllable by the audience of the forecasters, there is little sense in presenting absolute rather than conditional forecasts. Each conditional forecast can project a trend based on a different assumption of policy response. As long as such condi-

5

tional forecasts are linked up with the best available estimates of the probabilities of possible policy adoptions, the set of conditional forecasts is sufficiently precise and explicit for the appraisal of its accuracy.

Finally, the use of accuracy as the criterion for appraising forecasts can be strongly defended directly from the policy-maker's perspective, and indirectly from the forecaster's perspective insofar as the forecaster's usefulness and status depend on the credibility ultimately established by the forecasts' accuracy. From the policy-maker's perspective, accuracy for its own sake is *a priori* useful for rational planning (defining "rational" as "oriented toward the maximization of valued outcomes as defined by the participants"). While it is conceivable that in some cases true knowledge of the future would paralyze policy-makers and make them incapable of acting rationally, false knowledge seems just as likely to have this effect; on balance, accurate forecasts are more likely than inaccurate forecasts to improve the rationality of decision-making.

For forecasters interested in increasing the impact of their forecasts, accuracy is an asset because the utilization of forecasts requires, at a minimum, *credibility*. Although few studies have systematically evaluated the accuracy of past projections, unsystematic and particular appraisals have molded negative opinions about the credibility of the entire task of forecasting. Rarely is a dismissal of the importance of forecasting written without a short list of past projections that have failed miserably in terms of accuracy. Of course, the imperative of credibility also relates to the trade-offs of utilizing forecasts to accomplish goals that require deliberately inaccurate projections. "Scare tactics" may work in the short run to mobilize efforts or to inhibit certain behavior, but they run the risk of undermining the credibility and persuasiveness of further efforts at forecasting.

In short, the following conclusions can be drawn from the considerations outlined above: (*a*) there are numerous criteria by which a forecast can be legitimately appraised; (*b*) accuracy is one of the major criteria in this category; (*c*) a specific forecast (or very limited set of forecasts) can be usefully appraised in terms of these multiple criteria; but (*d*) accuracy is the only major criterion which can be applied to the appraisal of a large number of forecasts; and (*e*) accuracy is the only major criterion for which general propositions about the impact of various factors on forecast performance can be made.

A FRAMEWORK FOR IDENTIFYING
CORRELATES OF ACCURACY

Evaluating the accuracy of specific forecasts with hindsight is a modest accomplishment for specialists and nonspecialists alike. The challenge, of course, is to evaluate (and perhaps to adjust) forecasts which are of current importance. To identify which forecasts are likely to be more accurate than others, and to anticipate the biases of particular forecasts requires some means of identifying and testing the relevance of various characteristics of the forecasts' formulation. But which characteristics? And what constitutes a demonstration that a particular characteristic is relevant? One approach to these problems is theoretical, but another approach, which is more definitive from the perspectives of the policy-maker and the policy-process analyst, is basically empirical.

THE "INSIDER'S" APPROACH

Forecasts, or indeed any of the work of specialists, can be evaluated as the specialists themselves would appraise them. When the focus is thus "inside" the forecasting problem, relevant factors are the basic scientific information and techniques at the forecaster's disposal. One may evaluate the adequacy of the data, the *a priori* validity of the assumptions, the biases that are likely to stem from the *formal* characteristics of the techniques (for example, the linear bias of methods that employ only linear relationships), and the context of the trends themselves. The accuracy of a forecast is thus estimated from its logical consistency, the plausibility of its assumptions, and the validity of its techniques for that specific application. The insider's approach limits the relevant factors to what a practicing forecaster is likely to emphasize: characteristics of techniques and aspects of the context which pertain to the trends rather than to the forecasting process itself. For example, the history of the trend, its stability and variability, and the nature of the phenomena underlying the trend may be relevant.

THE "OUTSIDER'S" APPROACH

An alternative to the insider's approach is to evaluate forecasts in terms of the *behavior* of forecasters. If one is "outside" the forecasting task as a scientific endeavor, and evaluates past projections in terms of their record of accuracy instead of their scientific validity, one can appraise and adjust current forecasts in light of the known behavorial biases of forecasters. For example, if a particular forecaster is known to be prone to overestimation, current forecasts may be regarded as *probably* too high, and the policy-maker can interpret them accordingly. The probability that a bias will surface will depend on the consistency of expression of that bias in the past and the similarity of the past and present contexts.

Use of the outsider's approach opens up a broad avenue of inquiry which is not relevant to the scientific validity of forecasting procedures, but comes closer to studying the sociology and psychology of the experts who formulate the forecasts. The forecasters' institutional affiliations, their training, and the climate of opinion in which they work all become potential explanations of why some forecasts are more accurate than others. Establishing the correct-

7

ness of these explanations by examining the actual record of forecast accuracy is the only way to go beyond theoretical speculation, which can establish only the plausibility of forecast propositions.

The outsider's approach has occasionally been used by insiders in command of great technical expertise. For example, a special technical committee advising the Federal Power Commission during its national power survey in 1964 deliberately disregarded indications that the electricity production projections they were endorsing were too high, on the grounds that, although a lower estimate was more likely to be technically correct, technical estimates in the past had been too low: "The Committee recognized the fact that almost invariably long-range utility forecasts are low. There is a historic pattern of new, ever increasing uses of electric energy which are not now envisioned."[3] What is significant about the committee's approach is that, although it tried to integrate the prospect of future innovations into the assumptions of its projections, these prospects were deductible not from the expert analysis of the situation, but rather from the examination of past forecasts.

It is reasonable to ask why forecasters themselves do not more often look back at the biases of their predecessors and adjust their own forecasts in a direction that would have rectify earlier forecasts. Why do insiders usually forego the outsider's approach when the record of past forecasts reveals some avoidable biases?

In addition to practical reasons, such as the difficulty of reviewing previous forecasts to detect bias, there is a good theoretical reason for specialists to remain insiders in making their forecasts. Presumably, they consider that they are using the best information, assumptions, and techniques at their disposal. It is reasonable for them to assume that the flaws of past assumptions have been taken into account in the prevailing conventional wisdom. Consequently, the forecast generated by the specialist is his "best shot," and from his point of view an alteration based on the errors of old forecasts would simply deflect his forecast from the most likely outcome.

QUESTIONS ON THE CORRELATES OF ACCURACY

The insider and outsider approaches provide numerous *potential* correlates of accuracy, i.e., plausible connections between accuracy and the characteristics of a formal forecasting technique or of the forecaster and his behavior. In practice these connections may or may not hold true; if they do, they may or may not be of sufficient importance to make a difference.

RELEVANCE OF METHODOLOGY

Because different formal methods are applied to different forecasting tasks, connections between methodology and accuracy must be examined in the context of a specific forecasting task. Nevertheless, some methodological options and contextual factors are relevant to almost all forecasts.

Components. One methodological choice that all forecasters face is whether to project a unitary trend or to separate the phenomenon into "components": other trends which in combination define the original trend. This so-called component approach is not really a specific method, however. Since most policy-relevant trends are aggregate measures (such as GNP, energy use, or national population), *all* of the alternatives for disaggregating each trend are potential components. Trends can also be cast in terms of "rates," in which case components become the rates and the bases to which they are applied. In some cases, such as population projection, the components used (e.g., fertility, mortality, and net migration rates) are so standard that the component method comes to mean the use of these particular components. In general, however, the choice of components is as important and difficult a task as the initial decision to use the component approach. Taking energy forecasting as an example, all of the following are possible components: (*a*) energy use for industrial, commercial, and residential purposes (*b*) energy use per unit of each component of the GNP; (*c*) energy use per mode or form of energy (electricity, fossil fuels, etc.); and (*d*) energy use per capita, accompanied by a population projection. Furthermore, each of these components may be further divided into more specific components, again with no obvious guidelines as to how far to go in disaggregation.

The use of a component breakdown, together with the specific choice of components, distinguishes among the methods applied to forecasting aggregate trends. The potential advantage of the component approach is that less aggregated trends may be less complicated, or more uniform, and hence easier to project accurately. Thus it is important to know whether the component approach generally pays off in terms of greater accuracy, and whether particular component breakdowns lead to greater accuracy than others.

Scope. Another general methodological option concerns the scope of the total forecasting effort in which a particular forecast is generated. "Systems theory," with its emphasis on the holistic analysis of all interacting factors in a system, calls for broad forecasting efforts that embed specific forecasts in the context of forecasts of related trends. This exercise of comprehensive forecasting, covering many aspects of the socioeconomic context, tends to impose consistency on individual projections. Consequently, forecasts included in comprehensive efforts may in theory be more accurate than isolated forecasts. A number of such comprehensive studies are included in the forecasts examined in this study, and it is my goal to determine empirically whether the projections emerging from these comprehensive efforts have indeed been more accurate than isolated forecasts made at the same time for the same trends.

Consensus. An attractive option for any forecaster with limited time, resources, or expertise at his disposal is to select an "average" or "typical" forecast from among the forecasts previously made by others. This consensus or multiple-opinion approach is thus adopted by forecasters who are unwilling to generate their own projections, but who have no particular reason to accept one forecast over another. In effect, the consensus strategy discards extreme forecasts and focuses on the center of opinion. Besides convenience, the rationale of this approach is that the center of expert opinion is more likely to be reliable than opinions at the extremes.

If all current forecasts were included in the compilations from which consensus forecasts are selected, their accuracy would be the same as that of each corresponding set of forecasts; the consensus is the average value of the other forecasts and therefore reflects the average error. However, depending on the usually implicit criteria used by the compilers in including *some* of the available forecasts, consensus forecasts may prove to be more accurate or less accurate, according to which of the total spectrum of forecasts are included. Moreover, in practice, multiple-opinion forecasts are based on at least a few rather dated original forecasts. The ultimate accuracy of such consensus forecasts can be examined empirically to determine how they fare in comparison with single, original forecasts.

Judgment. No explicit forecasting technique embodies all that the forecaster knows about the phenomena under consideration. Additional considerations, intuitions, and the unarticulated "wisdom of experience" may be employed in forecasting in lieu of a specific, explicit method. Or the results of an explicit method may be adjusted by the forecaster in light of what seems plausible to him beyond what the method dictates. All of these implicit considerations go under the heading of "judgment." The question is whether fully or partially judgmental forecasting improves forecast accuracy by bringing expert opinion and intuition into the forecasting process, or detracts from accuracy by introducing the errors of unexamined, perhaps incoherent, intuition.

Of course, all forecasting requires some judgment, regardless of explicit methodology (the choice of method is itself generally judgmental), but it is not always clear exactly how much judgmental adjustment has been introduced into a particular forecast. Nevertheless, it is possible to identify forecasting efforts which rely heavily on the judgmental input; some forecasters deliberately forego the explicit methods used by others in forecasting a particular trend. In these cases, not only can the judgmental approach be evaluated as an alternative method, but its results can serve as benchmarks for the performance of more explicit methods.

RELEVANCE OF CONTEXT

The insider's approach not only considers the relevance of methodological options, but it also takes into account the importance of contextual factors to the overall accuracy of forecasts and to the comparative advantages of various methods. When the policy-maker's concern is to establish the confidence limits of all forecasts of the same trend, the contextual factors affecting overall accuracy become relevant. Do some factors make the projection task inherently more difficult? When the policy-maker has to choose among different methods applied to the same forecasting task, to what extent is the context at that moment more amenable to prediction by one method than by another?

Remoteness of the Target Date. In essence, a forecast must account for the characteristics of a trend from the date the forecast is made to the target date. The longer the forecast period (i.e., the more remote the target date from the forecast date), the greater the chances any of the conditions affecting the trend may change. In other words, the certainty of prevailing conditions declines as the length of the forecast period increases. It is plausible, therefore, that more remote forecasts are intrinsically more difficult, and in general will be made with less accuracy. However, long-term forecasts do have the advantage of providing decision-makers more lead time and hence more flexibility in handling problems recognized well before they become urgent crises. Therefore, the sacrifice in accuracy that is likely to arise from greater remoteness of the target date (as most of the findings in this study show) may be offset by the simple fact that early forecasts sometimes provide a glimpse of the basic outlines of future conditions.

Usually, projections covering both short and long time periods are made by applying one forecast methodology to all the years covered by the forecast. In other words, once a methodology is chosen, the projections for successive years are spewed out by that method as far into the future as the forecaster believes it to be useful or likely to be accurate. However, the methods appropriate for short- and long-term projections of the same trend may differ. The assumptions on which short-term projections are based take advantage of current information and structures that would be irrelevant for long-term projections. For example, survey data on anticipated purchases of automobiles, airplanes, or electrical appliances can provide the information necessary to make short-term forecasts of the demand for these items, but would be inappropriate for long-term forecasts of this demand. Short-term forecasts of nuclear capacity can rest on plans and commitments already made, while long-term capacity projections must be linked to long-term trends in energy needs, cost comparisons, and so on.

Structural Stability. The "structure" in which a trend unfolds is imposed by the *relationships* of this trend to other factors. At any point in time, the structure links the trend to factors that "cause" it and hence can explain it. Consequently, an accurate characterization of the structure can account for—and predict—this trend. The problem is that structures are not necessarily stable. When the structure changes, the former relationships that allowed prediction may not hold. Factors that were not constraints before may become so (e.g., the price of energy). The growth of one activity may still influence the growth of another, but to a different extent.

The stability of structure has two implications for accuracy. First, instability (i.e., change in structures) presumably would result in less certainty and accuracy for any forecast, regardless of the method used. Thus, knowing the level of stability might help the policy-maker estimate the likely accuracy of available forecasts. Second, since some methods depend more heavily than others on the presumption of structural stability, the level of stability may be relevant for choosing the most appropriate method for each specific application. However, the use of expectations of stability or instability in gauging forecast accuracy and in selecting methods is complicated by the fact that one must also *predict* the level of stability itself.

Complexity of the Context. Trends do not develop in a vacuum; each is an aspect of a more-or-less interactive, more-or-less complex "configuration"[4] of factors. To the extent that other conditions and trends impinge upon the forecasted trend, it is more difficult to accurately specify the "equilibrium" of conditions and trends that will prevail at any future moment. Thus, if the context of a trend is complex in the sense that many different factors have some bearing on its development, the task of "taking into account all relevant variables" becomes more difficult, and hence the forecast's accuracy becomes more problematical.

The forecasters' answer to the problem of complexity has often been to broaden the scope of the forecasting effort, on the grounds that forecasting more trends brings more of the context into consideration. While this is a perfectly reasonable approach, assuming the resources for broad forecasting efforts are available, it does not dismiss the problem of understanding and coping with the complexity. The fact that many trends are considered does not mean that their interrelationships have been accurately specified. Mesarovic and Pestel, in presenting their elaboration of the type of world model developed first by Forrester et al. for the Club of Rome, point with pride to the fact that "in our model about 100,000 relationships are stored in the computer."[5] However, it would be much more reassuring to a policy-maker who is aware of the complexity of world patterns of economic growth, population, energy, and environmental trends to see some evidence that Mesarovic and Pestel had undertaken a careful "configurative analysis" to ensure that the assumptions underlying their model are valid.

RELEVANCE OF THE FORECASTER'S CHARACTERISTICS

The additional perspective of the outsider calls for an examination of the nature of the forecaster rather than the nature of the techniques used or the trends themselves. What sorts of forecasters make the best forecasts?

Institutional Base. One obvious characteristic of forecasters is their institutional base. The nature of the organization in which a forecaster works establishes the kind of information at his disposal, the organizational biases he is likely to hold, and sometimes the methodology employed, if it is traditional for that organization. Are the forecasts of government, private business, academia, or the consulting firms the best? How accurate are forecasts by prestigious governmental or foundation commissions? There are no clear *a priori* answers. Private-business forecasts, especially those released for use by the government and the public, are often suspected of deliberate biases. The oil companies' projections of energy supply and demand have been suspect for more than half a century, though very few critics have taken the time to see whether indeed the biases are revealed when the target years come around. Private-business biases could also result from the "wish-fulfillment" effect of businesses forecasting their own future successes.

On the other hand, other institutions generally lack the close familiarity with the data and the dynamics of the industry that the private sector has. Governmental forecasters readily admit that they are dependent on private sources for data and for insights into what is really going on in specific industries. With a few notable exceptions, academics and consultants often lack the years of experience of day-to-day contact with the subject matter; they are contracted to study a problem in a relatively short time and come up with a forecast. They are also pressured by the incentive system of academic promotion, or by the competition for contracts, to be "fancy," when simpler methods might be more appropriate. Since it cannot be assumed *a priori* that one type of forecaster is necessarily more accurate than another, only the historical record can show which institutional bases are most conducive to accuracy.

Forecaster's Training. Because every discipline views the world from a different perspective, forecasters trained within different disciplines may impart different biases. Some disciplines may provide forecasters with greater insight and hence with greater accuracy. However, very few forecasters have been trained *as* forecasters; most often, specialists in a particular field are part-time forecasters of trends that are relevant to several fields (e.g., nuclear power is of interest to nuclear physicists, engineers, energy administrators, economists, etc.). Forecasts of the same trend are often distinguishable in terms of the disciplines of their authors, which may be a useful tool for pinpointing those forecasts of greatest accuracy, and for adjusting for biases likely to arise from the forecasters' professional training and preoccupations.

THE PLAN OF THIS STUDY

To determine whether in fact these potential connections to forecast accuracy hold, this study examines the empirical record of forecasts of policy-relevant trends for target dates up to 1975. The success of the forecasts in terms of accuracy is appraised retrospectively, and, when possible, the relevance of the considerations discussed above is examined.

Three considerations dictated the choice of forecasting tasks covered in this study. First, the trends must be relevant to the deliberations of a broad spectrum of policy-makers. While any forecast is "policy relevant" to someone, few are of general importance.

Second, a large enough number of forecasts must exist in order for meaningful comparisons of forecast accuracy to be made according to the factors outlined above. This requirement eliminates a surprisingly large number of trends which in theory would be expected to receive a great deal of forecasting attention. Many important trends have not been forecast frequently simply because they are highly manipulable by policy decisions. For example, long-term projections of unemployment levels are very rare, since forecasters who are willing to venture a prediction of the economic future recognize that the unemployment level can be changed by discrete political decisions.

Third, calculations of accuracy require that the terms of the forecasts be compatible with the terms in which "actual" growth is reported. Incompatibilities are very common, however, and for good practical reasons. Data-gatherers require systematic and often large-scale methods to monitor current events. Often the only feasible monitoring mechanisms are the legal procedures that register actions or phenomena as "legal events." Automobile registrations provide a clear example; the operation of a car is recorded officially in automobile registration statistics. On the other hand, the forecaster is not restricted by the difficulties of measurement, but he is obligated to forecast items of greatest policy relevance. In the case of automobile forecasts, highway and pollution-control policy-makers would find the total number of automobiles in operation more useful than the total number of automobiles registered. In this and other cases the usefulness of the forecasts calls for definitions that are difficult to measure through normal means. Therefore, the forecasts examined here cover only those trends that are expressed in the same terms as available "authoritative" statistics or that can be straightforwardly converted into such terms.

The forecasting tasks examined in this study cover national trends in population, economic growth, transportation, and energy demands and resources. In addition, technological forecasting, which is often an aspect of other forecasting efforts as well as a distinct enterprise in its own right, is appraised in an examination of key predictions and the general results of broad forecasting efforts. There are, of course, many national trends within each of these areas. National economic trends include the growth of GNP, unemployment, inflation, and so on; transportation trends include such factors as the numerical growth of each type of conveyance, the mileage for each, and the number of facilities available. For each area, only a few of the most prominent of these trends are examined, to ensure that the maximum number of forecasts can be compared.

The forecasting records for most of these trends were appraised by compiling all available forecasts found after a fairly exhaustive search. Requests for past forecasts were made to public and private organizations likely to be engaged in forecasting these trends. With some exceptions, governmental agencies were more responsive to these requests than were private organizations, probably because the forecasts of private organizations are sometimes considered proprietary, whereas governmental forecasts are more frequently part of the public record. Some of the energy forecasts and most of the economic forecasts were obtained from existing compilations. For recent population forecasts, Census Bureau projections have been so predominantly authoritative that only these forecasts were examined for the post–World War II period.

Discrepancies (or errors) in forecasts were calculated in terms of the most current and authoritative statistics available as of early or mid-1976. Undoubtedly, there are some errors in the "official" statistics; and some of the most recent figures will be revised by official sources. However, these errors are generally quite small in comparison with the discrepancies that exist between forecasts and actual values.

Finally, the errors, either in percentage or in absolute-level terms, are examined in two ways. Forecasts of nearly equal length (e.g., five-year forecasts or ten-year forecasts) made in different years are compared. Such comparisons reveal whether forecast accuracy has improved over time and point out the comparative advantages of different methods and forecaster characteristics. Differences in the accuracy of forecasts of nearly equal length also indicate which historical periods have proved to be more difficult to forecast. Forecasts of different lengths, but with the same target date, also are examined in an attempt to determine the relationship between forecast length (or recency) and forecast accuracy. The "approach curve" of accuracy for forecasts made closer and closer to a particular target date is a crucial piece of information for establishing the confidence limits of a given forecast. It also permits examination of the importance of methods and forecaster characteristics, since it matches forecasts made in the same years and addressed to the same target dates.

CHAPTER 2

THE IMPACT OF EXPERT FORECASTING

The introductory chapter of this study emphasized the obstacles to appraising the impact—as opposed to the accuracy—of forecasts in any general or systematic way. However, some tentative insights into the general impact of forecasting, and what makes some forecasts more important or persuasive than others, have emerged in the course of reviewing hundreds of forecasting efforts and through contacts with forecasters and forecast-users.

It is a commonly stated truism that everyone makes forecasts. Every deliberate action, from the pettiest to the most significant, rests on the actor's expectations of the results of his action. Therefore, it is in practice impossible, and hardly meaningful, to determine the impact of *all* forecasts. The important questions on impact concern the effects of distinct, explicit forecasting efforts made available to decision-makers by people of specialized expertise. Thus, the impact of forecasting is usefully regarded as a special case of the general impact of experts, and the incorporation of expertise into decision-making.

There are two ways to study the impact of forecasting. One is to examine widely used decision-making procedures to see how they incorporate forecasts. Another approach is to examine specific forecasting efforts or forecasting institutions which have obvious records of success or failure. Both of these approaches fall short of being systematic, even if they are insightful. The cases discussed below are illuminating, but the conclusions reached must be regarded as tentative since their representativeness is open to question.

THE NATURE OF IMPACT

There is one fascinating difference in the forecaster's and forecast-user's evaluations of the importance of expert forecasting. Most of the forecasters contacted in the course of this study, particularly those with the greatest prominence and presumably the greatest access to policy-makers, were very skeptical about the impact of their efforts on relevant policy-makers. Yet the forecast-users in general seemed quite convinced of the utility and influence of experts' forecasts. At first glance this may seem to be a case of misperception by the forecasters, polite deference by the forecast-users, or both.

An explanation that seems more consistent with the realities of forecasting and policy-making is that the difference is due to different notions about what a forecast's impact can and ought to be. As indicated in chapter 1, the forecaster's perspective focuses on securely implanting the forecast in the decision-making routine, which is aided (but not guaranteed) by making consideration of expert forecasts a necessary step in the policy-making process. In contrast, the policy-maker's perspective calls for forecasts (and technical expertise in general) to be useful in his deliberations, but without reducing his flexibility in policy choice.

What does the "impact" of a forecast mean? There are really three dimensions of the impact of forecasts (or other technical inputs) in policy-making: (1) the attention received from policy-makers; (2) the explicitness of use; and (3) the decisiveness of the forecast in the choice of decision outcomes. These are related facets, since explicit use of forecasts as inputs can attract attention and connect forecasts decisively to decision outcomes; but, except in the extreme case, explicitness is neither necessary nor sufficient for decisiveness. Although explicit use *may* enhance the decisiveness of forecasts, a forecast may be decisive even if it is not explicitly used in decision-making deliberations. By the same token, prominent forecasts can be rejected by policy-makers, just as forecasts receiving little attention can turn out to be pivotal in determining policy choices.

Of these three aspects, explicitness of use is most easily determined, since it is embodied in the routines employed by decision-makers. Attention and decisiveness are much less tangible and hence are more difficult to detect and measure. Explicitness is somewhat revealing of the attention and influence of the forecast, but the connections between forecast use and ultimate impact are quite slippery.

The minimum form of explicit use occurs when a forecast (or other form of technical input) does not become a part of the informational base employed by policy-makers. A slightly more explicit use occurs when the forecast is *merely* a part of this base. Forecast use is more explicit when forecasts are directly linked to outcomes relevant to the organization's goal criteria (e.g., when energy price forecasts are used to calculate a future reduction in the sales of the company's high-energy-consumption applicances). More explicit yet would be a direct linkage of the "inputs" of technical information and goal specifications to policy recommendations emerging from systematic procedures. Numerous decision-making approaches are designed explicitly to calculate optimal policy choices (e.g., in terms of investment levels, project or product selections, or scheduling) on the basis of specified goal criteria and various elements of technical input, including forecasts. Operations research, systems analysis, decision theory, and econometric modeling are among the many overlapping approaches that provide "optimization" routines for this purpose. Finally, the most explicit (and ambitious) use of forecasts would be attained if the policy choices emerging from optimization procedures were regarded as binding on the policy-makers. In other words, the range of explicitness runs from the absence of a given forecast from the policy-maker's informational base to the "automatic" adoption of policies calculated on the basis of the forecast.

Obviously, each successively more explicit use draws the information comprised by the forecast farther into the policy-making sequence. The contrast between a forecast as a piece of background information and a forecast that directly enters into a binding policy-choice calculation is striking. If a forecast is totally absent from the informational base at the disposal of policy-makers, it can hardly have impact, whereas the most ambitious state of explicitness certainly can guarantee that the forecast will be decisive in the policy choice. But these cases are the logical extremes. Even the second most explicit form of use, the nonbinding optimization result, could in theory be totally disregarded by policy-makers. By the same token, forecasts that are "merely" informational can still strongly alter the decision-maker's perspective and hence structure his choices, by changing the focus of attention and the climate of opinion in which the decision-maker operates. Certainly, Rachel Carson's *Silent Spring* was never used to calculate optimal policies, but its impact in focusing attention on ecological concerns is undeniable.

Attention-focusing occurs both when forecasts attract attention to a particular set of issues by pointing out serious problems on the horizon, and when attention is deflected from issues by forecasts that in effect imply that things are going quite well. This capacity to focus attention, it turns out, is a surprisingly "political" aspect of forecast impact, since attention-focusing is so closely linked with priority-setting. The agenda of issues to be considered by an organization or by the body politic is not fixed; it varies with the preoccupations of the actors involved.[1]

The climate of opinion is influenced by forecasts to the extent that generalized moods are established by expectations as well as by experience.[2] Many forecasts can be interpreted as "good news" or "bad news"; consequently, they can establish moods of optimism or pessimism without being used explicitly in policy formation, and without necessarily being recognized as influential. Other dimensions of mood can be similarly influenced. Should the executives of a particular company feel that their company's market share is secure or vulnerable? Should foreign-policy analysts and decision-makers assume a stance of aggressive confidence or one of conciliation?

The climate of opinion also encompasses tacit assumptions on the nature of the world, which impinge on policy choices even if they are not articulated. Forecasts obviously can affect or alter these assumptions, but such effects are usually indirect and cumulative. World views are usually "stored" in the minds of policy-makers as broad, interconnected belief systems, rather than as discrete forecasts or specific technical observations. Therefore, the influence

18

of forecasts or other technical input cannot be traced definitively in their impact on the working assumptions that guide much of policy-making.

CORPORATE VERSUS GOVERNMENTAL CONTEXT

In examining the impact of various forecasting efforts, one important distinction must be kept in mind. The impact of forecasting on governmental decision-making must be considered separately from its impact on organizations in the private sector. The status of any element of technical input is fundamentally different in the corporate and governmental contexts; therefore, the same forecast may have quite different impacts on the public and private sectors. In the governmental setting all forms of expert input have an additional political facet that is less significant (but not completely absent) in the corporate setting. To a large extent this difference is manifested in the difference in status of corporate and governmental *planning*, which is one of the major vehicles for experts' forecasts and input in general.

Corporate planning is fundamentally different from governmental planning because corporate actors generally operate under the assumption that clearly delineated, consensual goals prevail—for instance, that of maximizing profits. In contrast, governmental planning (and policy-making in general) in a pluralist polity is as much a process of establishing goals as it is a mechanism for selecting the means to achieve the goals. A given forecast is usually consistent with only a limited portion of the available policy options. Therefore, while the corporate strategies implied by accepted forecasts do not challenge ultimate corporate ends (since, in theory, action is chosen to maximize these fixed ends on the basis of the forecast), forecasts may be controversial in the governmental setting because they imply priorities which may not be held by some policy-makers.

Because of the lack of goal consensus in the public arena, expert advice of any sort is suspect to the extent that the experts may be thought to be pushing their own goals. Robert Dahl and Charles Lindblom point out that one of the major obstacles to integrating expert advice closely into the process of public policy-making is the possibility that experts may impose their own goals through their greater mastery over technical aspects of prevailing conditions and policy choices: "How to delegate to experts choice of factual assumptions without granting them an unwanted choice of the very goals to be maximized is, however, a staggering problem. In this sense, delegation to experts is both an indispensable aid and an unremitting threat to rational calculation."[3]

In addition to fostering distrust, the lack of goal consensus increases the likelihood that forecasts will be regarded as *promotional* in the public arena. If a credible forecast underscores a particular future problem, it raises the priority of action on that problem. Governmental policy-makers may prefer to ignore forecasts that they regard as accurate but that promote priorities other than their own. They may disregard forecasts that emphasize more distant problems when the political significance of current concerns is more compelling. Thus, the acceptability of a forecast in the governmental setting depends not only on its perceived accuracy and plausibility, but also on the acceptability of the priorities it seems to promote.

Of course, this is not to say that corporations are apolitical.[4] The crucial point is that the lack of *overt* disagreement on ultimate goals enhances the acceptability of forecasts in the corporate setting simply as *intelligence*. It is hard to imagine that a believable forecast would be deliberately disregarded by corporate decision-makers. Governmental decision-makers may have quite good reasons for disregarding believable forecasts that conflict with their goal priorities. This difference explains why private businesses are often more eager consumers of forecasts.

IMPACT IN THE CORPORATE SETTING

The impact of expert forecasting in the corporate setting is not hampered by the antiplanning stance traditionally ascribed to American business. Whatever opposition there has been to "planning" pertains to governmental planning as it entails governmental intervention and regulation, not to planning in individual businesses. Surveys by the McGraw-Hill Economics Department showed that long-range (i.e., three-year or longer) corporate planning was undertaken by 90 percent of the companies surveyed in 1966.[5] Corporate planning of this sort naturally requires projections of the markets for relevant goods and services, and very often also includes projections of technological opportunities and forecasts of the broad economic context. Trend forecasting can be carried out either in-house by the company's own forecasters (sometimes organized as a separate unit), or externally by other firms or agencies. The more specific the trends are to the company's own activities, the more likely the forecasts will be produced within the company. For example, a firm manufacturing air conditioners may accept forecasts of national economic trends from an outside source (a subscription service like the Wharton Economic Forecasting Unit or a governmental agency like the Bureau of Economic Analysis), but will make its own forecasts of trends in the air conditioning market. Often the trade associations of each industry will provide specific market forecasts for the use of member companies.

The financial costs that corporations are willing to bear for expert forecasts are quite high. The conscientious corporate forecast-user typically subscribes to one or more outside econometric forecasting service (at an annual cost of $15,000 each) and an outside technological forecasting service (at a cost of $6,000 or more). Many corporations also sponsor sociopolitical studies by think tanks such as the Hudson Institute or the Institute for the Future. Many companies contract for special studies relevant to their own particular product lines. For every dollar spent to purchase outside forecasts, several must be devoted to in-house forecasting efforts, either to utilize and adapt the projections purchased from outside, or to generate in-house forecasts. To automate the retrieval and manipulation of forecasts and other technical data via "corporate planning models," a firm typically must spend an average of $80,000 for the model's initial development alone.[6]

A corporation's total investment in forecasting is extremely difficult to estimate, since forecasting efforts shade off into other aspects of analysis. Corporation executives and technical staff who do some "expert" forecasting usually are not designated as "forecasters." There are, however, some indications of what the magnitude of this investment might be. Erich Jantsch estimated that in 1966 each of the largest 500–600 U.S. firms spent about $100,000 annually on in-house technological forecasting, and an additional $25,000 for outside subscription services and contracted studies.[7] Considering the increase in costs in the 1966–76 decade (subscription to the Stanford Research Institute's technological forecasting service has increased in price from $4,000 to $6,500 annually [62.5 percent], and salaries of technical personnel have increased by about 70–75%[8]), a current estimate of $200,000 per firm for technological forecasting is reasonable.

It is generally acknowledged that expenditures in economic forecasting are at least as great as those for technological forecasting. A large firm's expenditure of over $200,000 annually for economic forecasting is consistent with the estimate of $40,000 for outside economic forecasts[9] and with the 4:1 ratio of in-house to outside expenditures that Jantsch presents as a conservative estimate for technological forecasting.[10] Thus, it is reasonable to assume that a large American corporation may spend more than $400,000 annually for the generation of explicit technological and economic forecasts. The costs of energy forecasting and operations forecasts for specific industries would probably bring the total to around half a million dollars. This does not include, of course, expenditures in analyzing and employing forecasts, for that would encompass all management personnel to some (unknown) extent.

Another indication of the importance of forecasts to corporate decision-making is the fact that many corporations jealously guard their internal forecasts. Instead of releasing these projections for their informational, promotional, or public relations value (as a small number of corporations do), most firms take the position that exclusive access to their own forecasts gives them a competitive edge. One aircraft corporation executive stated the prevailing position succinctly:

While our forecasting is a very important part of the way we conduct our business, we consider it to be one of the most private. We are in an extremely competitive business, and our forecasts serve almost as a ten-year roadmap for management. While some of the information developed for our forecasts finds its way to the public sector through speeches and other presentations by management, we have never made the information available in full context.[11]

Thus, there is strong evidence that, in the corporate setting, forecasts are considered to be a precious commodity. Corporations spend a great deal of money to purchase outside forecasts and to maintain internal forecasting operations. The secrecy of most corporate forecasts reinforces this conslusion. However, these indications of how forecasts are regarded do not speak to how they are *used*. Direct evidence on use is limited by secrecy, but is essentially inaccessible because of the very nature of decision-making as a process that cannot be entirely monitored through empirical methods. Only through the examination of explicit procedures for using forecasts can indirect inferences on the nature of use be made.

The status of explicit use of forecasts in corporations is illustrated quite well by a 1974 survey of 346 companies conducted by Thomas Naylor and Horst Schauland. Nearly two-thirds of the corporations surveyed were employing a "corporate planning model." Defined as some sort of formal procedure (i.e., ̦ sets of equations), this type of model is designed to project corporation performance for some period into the future (in the 1974 survey the average time horizon was eight years).[12] Two-thirds of the remaining firms were developing or planning to develop such models. These models are not only forecasting devices themselves, but, more importantly, are mechanisms for assessing the implications of projected trends of exogenous factors (such as macroeconomic trends) that impinge upon the corporation's performance.

Naylor and Schauland point out that the top-level management (corporate presidents, vice-presidents, treasurers, and controllers) often uses these models. In other words, "the right people are receiving and actually using the output generated by the models."[13] This should guarantee that the forecasts, or rather the implications of the forecasts, will come to the attention of top-level policy-makers. Thus, these models assure at least the level of explicitness of use provided by linking the forecasts to outcomes relevant to the organization's goal criteria.

However, Naylor and Schauland also point out that few of these models include optimization routines. "Most (76%) of the corporate planning models are *what if* models, i.e., models which simulate the effects of alternative managerial policies and assumptions about the firm's external environment. Only 4% of the models in our sample were optimization models ... [while] 14% of the models used both approaches."[14] "What if" models provide a structure of information (including forecasts) and relationships upon which to trace out the impact of alternative executive strategies. They can affect executive choice—and therefore impart to the decision whatever technical expertise underlies them—insofar as some executive strategies are shown to result in outcomes more preferable than others. Nevertheless, "what if" models are somewhat less definitive in forcing a choice onto the policy-maker, because these models reveal only the implications of policy options initially selected by the policy-makers; they do not establish that one strategy is better than all other alternatives. Thus, regardless of their heuristic value, the bulk of the models do not guarantee that recommendations consistent with the forecasts will be decisive, because the models stop short of calculating optimal policies.

But why are optimization routines lacking? Naylor and Schauland maintain that future corporate planning models will employ optimization techniques to a greater extent.[15] However, two considerations make this shift unlikely. First, from the point of view of corporate politics, it seems unlikely that managers will be willing to take the risks involved in commissioning technical optimization efforts. If the recommendations of optimization techniques are accepted, the managerial function of decision-making may be perceived by others as routine and if the policies fail, the managers will be open to criticism for employing and relying upon incompetent technicians. If the recommendations are not accepted, the managers will be open to criticism for squandering resources on technical functions that are not utilized and if the policies emanating from the managers' own judgments fail, they may be criticized for ignoring what might have been sound technical advice. In terms of the logic of the manager's position, he is far safer in using models as background information without allowing them to generate recommendations that may rival his own.

Second, from an empirical point of view, organizations that in the second half of the 1960s were the first to introduce explicit, mathematized planning and forecasting techniques have since shied away from the optimizing procedures that seemed to be "right around the corner" prior to 1970. It is revealing to trace the fate of the most ambitious of these procedures as cataloged by Erich Jantsch in his comprehensive study of technological forecasting. The early innovators, including 3M, Honeywell, North American Aviation, TRW-Aerospace Systems, and the advertising firm BBDO have downgraded or abandoned the decision-making components of their forecast utilization procedures. Honeywell's PATTERN technique, an "integrated decision scheme based on relevance trees," which was the most prominent and elaborate procedure of the mid-1960's, has given way to a much looser set of decision-making aids acknowledged to be informational rather than decisive. North American Aviation's SCORE technique apparently has suffered the same fate. Both 3M and BBDO had developed new-product selection models, which in their strongest form could rank potential products in terms of overall desirability, and hence provide strong recommendations as to which products should be selected. However, the BBDO model has been shorn of its optimization routines, and 3M has dropped the "figure of merit" routine designed to calculate an overall index of product (or project) merit. At TRW, where large-scale forecasting of technological breakthroughs (through multiple-expert panel exercises called PROBEs) was to be integrated into logical-network decision-making routines (called SOON-charts),[16] these very ambitious plans of the 1960's faded away as the individuals responsible for initiating the system went on to other tasks. In other words, the initiatives of the 1960's toward integrated forecasting and decision-making devices were not institutionalized even in the companies that led in developing the devices. Ralph Sprague and Hugh Watson emphasize that it has not been the absence or inadequacy of such devices, but rather the lack of utilization, that has kept them from being implemented:

Despite the plethora of decision models that have been developed, they have not been as operationally useful as one might expect. There are far too many examples in which well developed, carefully tested models have fallen into misuse. It is not that the models lack mathematical rigor or sophistication. Rather, it seems that too little attention has been devoted to data sources *and the subsequent use of the model's output.*[17]

This has been found to be the case even for the selection of research-and-design projects, to which much of the development of decision-making routines has been devoted. As Edward Roberts reported in 1969,

In their excellent review of formal project selection procedures, Baker and Pound found that few organizations of the 50 studied were employing the formal selection processes that were described in published papers by their employees. . . . In a study by the author of about 100 R & D contractor selection decisions, informal person-to-person factors were found to influence the awards far more than did formal evaluation procedures. . . . When major decisions are to be made it appears that management needs to consider factors other than those generally included in formal complex evaluation procedures. . . . Evidence gathered in a series of other studies also argues that real decisions are not made in the manner suggested by the formal, complex decision-aiding systems in R & D.[18]

In summary, it appears that the corporate policy-maker values expert forecasts, utilizes them to some extent in explicit decision-making procedures, but stops short of incorporating forecasts or other technical input into explicit procedures that would guarantee their decisiveness. This use, though inadequate from the perspective of many forecasters, is nonetheless considerably more advanced than the use of forecasting in the public sector.

IMPACT IN THE GOVERNMENTAL SETTING

In 1975 the Congressional Research Service undertook a study for the House Committee on Science and Technology to see what governmental decision-making could learn from the private sector's experiences in planning and forecast utilization.[19] The impetus behind this effort reflects the general belief that technical input is not as closely knit to decision-making in government as it is in the private sector. This can be illustrated by examining three examples of forecast-generating governmental institutions: the National Resource Planning Board of the 1930s and 1940s, the Planning-Programming-Budgeting System of the 1960s, and the Census Bureau's population forecasting efforts from the 1940s to the present. The first two illustrate the obstacles to the explicit use of forecasts in an antiplanning environment. The last case, which is a success story in terms of the prominence and general use of Census Bureau forecasts, nevertheless reveals that this success was achieved only by minimizing the specificity of the forecasts.

THE NATIONAL RESOURCES PLANNING BOARD

The first interesting case of governmental reaction to forecasting was the National Resources Planning Board, established in 1934 as a coordinating agency for the executive branch.[20] The NRPB issued numerous reports on energy, population, public works, and natural resources, many of which contained forecasts of future supplies and demands. The NRPB employed notable experts on its technical committees and as consultants, making it the foremost channel for the expression of expert opinion under governmental auspices. Reports by economists John Kenneth Galbraith and Alvin Hansen, demographers Pascal Whelpton and Warren Thompson, and sociologists William Ogburn and S. C. Gilfillan were published by the board or by the National Resources Committee, which the NRPB absorbed in 1939.

The NRPB was certainly prominent in academic circles, but its impact on policy-makers was another question. While it is impossible to measure the impact of its specific forecasts, the impact of the agency itself can be assessed. The NRPB came under very heavy criticism. Its existence, and many of its recommendations, were vigorously attacked, not so much because the quality of the effort was questioned, but rather because of opposition to the potential power of the agency to *plan*. Some opposition came from other executive agencies, whose power was supposedly jeopardized by the position of the NRPB as the overall coordinator—a position it never really attained. The ideological opposition was borne of hostility to the idea of governmental intervention. It was assumed that a systematic investigation of future resources and needs might promote the government's predisposition and authority to further control the public and private uses of resources.

In the early 1940s the NRPB was attacked in Congress as "extravagant and useless" "harmful and even vicious."[21] To many anti–New Dealers, and to some officials in agencies competing with the NRPB for power, the board's studies were not worth the government's expense (less than a million dollars annually for a staff of over 170) and the presumed threat the board posed to established governmental decision-making procedures. It was dismantled in 1943, and the rejection of the principles behind the NRPB was later reinforced by the anticommunism of the late 1940s and 1950s, which managed to equate planning with totalitarianism.

At first glance it appears that the NRPB's studies (i.e., its technical input) and its role as a coordinating agency may be separated. Conceivably, its forecasts could have been applied to policy-making without the policy-makers granting them any legitimacy in the formal policy-making process itself. This separation, however, misses the point of the opposition to the NRPB. The opposition to the planning function of the NRPB entailed the rejection of some of the major applications of forecasts. The anti-interventionist position was that forecasts—or any other technical information—should not be applied to the formulation of policies that might lead to greater governmental control. Obviously, any analysis of what the future holds paves the way for some sort of action, since action is more likely to be taken under the presumption that a situation is well understood than when it is uncertain. Opponents of planning as overall coordination (i.e., critics of centralization) would probably balk at global analysis. Hence, they would oppose the use of a forecast, portrayed as "scientific," to constrain all governmental bodies to comply with an overall policy. Thus, the opposition to planning limits the impact of forecasts by limiting their permissable policy uses.

THE PLANNING-PROGRAMMING-BUDGETING SYSTEM

In the 1960s another broad effort to incorporate forecasting into explicit governmental decision-making was undertaken with the ill-fated Planning-Programming-Budgeting System, which was introduced into the federal budgetary process from 1965 to 1971.[22] The PPBS was developed originally for the Defense Department, but was extended to other executive agencies by order of the Office of Management and Budget. It required each agency to submit multiyear, program-by-program analyses of problems and efforts under the agency's jurisdiction, as well as the impact of proposed programs. Forecasting was required to project the magnitude of problems and the contextual factors affecting the implementation of programs. Moreover, conditional forecasting (i.e., projections made under explicit assumptions of specific future constraints, such as governmental policies) was necessary in the PPBS to anticipate the impact of proposed programs. Thus, in order to comply with the requirement to formulate budgets according to the PPBS, numerous forecasts were essential. The PPBS was, in a sense, the government's counterpart to corporate planning models; it had the potential to integrate forecasts and other technical input into an explicit decision-making routine. Alain Enthoven and K. Wayne Smith point out how PPBS was to have been a vehicle for technical input:

A final basic idea underlying PPBS was that of open and explicit analysis; that is, each analysis should be made available to all interested parties, so that they can examine the calculations, data, and assumptions and retrace the steps leading to the conclusions. Indeed, all calculations, data, and assumptions *should* be described in an analysis in such a way that they can be checked, tested, criticized, debated, discussed, and possibly refuted by interested parties.[23]

To the obvious dismay of governmental policy analysis professionals, the PPBS never got off the ground outside the Defense Department, and even there its success was controversial. In the Defense Department PPBS left its mark, but for the rest of the federal agencies ample evidence indicates that PPBS reports never had much effect on the real budgetary process, which continued in its traditional, incremental, bureaucratic-political fashion. In 1971 the OMB quietly announced that these reports were no longer a required part of the budget application process. The system that was then dismantled had never provided a useful vehicle for technical input or comprehensive planning. As Allen Schick concluded in 1973, "Budgeting is the routinization of public choice by means of standardized procedures, timetables, classifications, and rules. PPB failed because it did not penetrate the vital routines of putting together and justifying a budget. Always separate but never equal, the analysts had little influence over the form or content of the budget."[24]

According to the post-mortems on PPBS, the system failed for numerous reasons, including insufficient understanding, insufficient personnel at the Budget Bureau to coordinate and analyze PPBS reports coming in from the various agencies, and antagonism toward a procedure seen as alien and imposed from the outside.[25] These explanations have little to do with forecasting *per se,* and certainly the presence or absence of forecasting in PPBS was not the crucial factor in determining its fate. But this is not an atypical problem for the incorporation of technical expertise into policy-making. The inclusion of technical input is rarely the determining factor in whether a particular policy or policy-making procedure is adopted. Policies and procedures that serve as *vehicles* of technical analysis usually are not accepted or rejected *because* of this function; more often, their adoption depends on other factors, such as the overall acceptability of the likely outcomes or the configuration of political forces involved. The value of technical expertise is often ignored when weightier political issues preoccupy the participants of the policy-making process.

Two fundamental weaknesses of PPBS do relate to the use of forecasts. As in the case of the studies produced by the NRPB, the PPBS forecasts were tied to *planning.* The rationale behind analyzing the context of three or five years into the future was to formulate programs that would be coherent over the time span of the analysis. Yet the OMB continued to make budgetary decisions in the traditional way—through incremental decisions based on the one-year time frame. The unwillingness or inability to utilize the PPBS reports for longer-term planning in individual agencies, or for the coordination of governmental programs, reduced the value of the forecasts for the OMB as well as for the specific agencies.

While there is some debate over why the OMB was unwilling to engage in the sort of planning that would have made the PPBS reports meaningful, there is agreement that close analysis of whether each governmental program "is worth it" would arouse much open conflict. The reason for the conflict is, again, that goals are not pre-established and consensual. Whether planning is decried or applauded for bringing this conflict out into the open, and whether it is attacked or defended for its tendency to replace incremental bargaining with global analysis, the fact remains that the usefulness of planning as a vehicle for expert forecasts and other technical input is limited in circumstances where goal consensus is lacking.

The second problem lies in the capacity of PPBS analysts within the various agencies to competently apply sophisticated, technical, and yet "wordly" analysis to the vast amounts of information required for the system to work. After all, the whole rationale of PPBS (and, incidentally, the rationale of "zero-based budgeting") is to bring into consideration the overall merits of all programs. Of course, to compare the costs and benefits of all programs requires both a comprehensive grasp of priorities and constraints *and* a detailed grasp of program specifics. Add to this the technical skill requirements of cost-benefit analysis, operations research, etc., and the result is that the PPBS analyst is called upon to be a combination generalist-specialist-mathematician-computer expert. So taxing is this requirement that David Novick has concluded: "Recruiting and training analysts and building an analytical capability has been the largest single problem in applying program budgeting."[26] Harper, Kramer, and Rouse, who evaluated PPBS in sixteen federal agencies in the Johnson era, concluded: "There were simply not enough professionals in government (or outside of it) with the skills deemed necessary for successful PPB analysts—at least not enough professionals with such skills were placed on the formal PPB staffs."[27]

From this perspective, the unwillingness of OMB to pay much attention to PPBS can explained—without invoking the notion of power struggles—by the opinion held by many in OMB, as well as in the agencies using PPBs, that the actual application of this shiny new device was simply inadequate. As Jack W. Carlson of OMB put it:

> The Program Memoranda (PMs) or comparable documents also have been of uneven quality. . . . In the early years, about 25 percent and since 1968, about 50 percent, could be judged as adequate to excellent. Most of the others did not identify major alternatives, concentrate on policy decisions, or present a multiyear strategy directed

toward specific objectives and outputs. Many of the PMs were descriptive, verbose, nonanalytic accounts of existing and proposed programs, usually coupled with an impassioned plea for funding at the full request.[28]

At issue here is the matching of technical input to the capacities of policy-makers and their analysts. At the agency level, analysts simply could not digest the flood of input relevant to the task at hand—comprehensive planning. Two conclusions have been reached on this problem. The optimistic interpretation of Novick and others is that PPBS failed in large part because of the lack of synchronization between the rate of introducing the method and the rate of training the analysts. If PPBS had spread more slowly, the problem of utilizing information could have been alleviated, as well it could be in the future, if PPBS is gradually reintroduced along with programs of careful analyst training. A more pessimistic conclusion was anticipated by Charles Lindblom well before the specific outlines of PPBS were formulated. According to Lindblom, the goal of comprehensive or "synoptic" analysis is unrealistic in any context; there is simply too much formation for any individual or coordinated collectivity to comprehend.[29] However, the attainment of a comprehensive perspective and the incorporation of a broad range of technical input are not "all or nothing" matters. While the ideal of "rational comprehensive" policy-making may never be achieved in practice, the possibilities of achieving *more* comprehensive understanding and *more* useful incorporation of technical input are not precluded by the impossibility of the ideal.

Some insights into these propositions can be gained from the relative success of PPBS in its first governmental setting, the Defense Department. PPBS was successful in the Department of Defense only insofar as PPBS analysts and their reports comprised one important element in internal Defense Department decision-making and in appropriations to the department. However, even this accomplishment constitutes "success," relative to the experiences in most other federal agencies, where PPBS did not reach the status of one important factor among many.[30]

The accomplishments of PPBS in the Department of Defense must be understood in the context of the strong support given PPBS by Secretary of Defense McNamara and the fact that PPBS was designed by its Rand Corporation developers specifically for defense procurement problems. On the other hand, the Defense Department has always faced the unique problems of interservice competition and the rivalries between civilian and military analysts.

To an important degree, the experience with PPBS in the Defense Department reflected the nature of the defense problems handled by PPBS—military procurement. During the 1960s the nuclear arms race and the Vietnam build-up focused much of the Defense Department's policy-making on the problem of designing, purchasing, and evaluating weapons systems. The military procurement problem has two important characteristics: it is quantifiable in terms of dollars, weapons payloads, defense capabilities, aircraft speeds, and so on; and it has, at least in theory, a single overarching objective or criterion—national security. Organizational consensus on the ultimate goal, despite interservice rivalries, is an advantage that the Defense Department holds over the multiple-function agencies such as the Department of Health, Education, and Welfare. Along with the overall increased defense spending during the 1960s, which managed to provide new weapons systems to each of the services, consensus on ultimate objectives spared PPBS from the paralysis it suffered in other agencies. This is consistent with the argument that lack of goal consensus is a major obstacle to the incorporation of technical input like forecasting via mechanisms of planning. The quantifiability of military procurement considerations was facilitated by the clarity of ultimate goals, inasmuch as the single metric of "national security per dollar" could be applied. This made it easier for quantitatively trained analysts to employ mathematical methods and to avoid those vaguely defined, elusive problems involving both means and ends which Ralph Strauch has wisely labeled "squishy problems."[31]

Finally, the accomplishments of the PPBS in the Defense Department also rest on the high caliber of the personnel who conducted it. The qualifications, dedication, and *esprit de corps* of PPBS personnel in the Defense Department were unmatched in subsequent applications of PPBS, and undoubtedly the prominence of PPBS was enhanced by this unique collection of individuals. At first glance this fact seems of little general significance, since it does relate to a unique occurrence. Yet the difficulty of successfully installing PPBS in other agencies of the federal government is simply one instance of the general problem of "institutionalizing" a practice that is successful in it first application in part *because* it was the first application. The PPBS under development at Rand and in its first practical application in the Defense Department was attractive to a cadre of innovative, imaginative, and well-trained experts who may have been much less interested in the more mundane prospect of replicating an already established method in subsequent applications. Many *prototypes* of decision-making techniques are successful to an extent that is misleading in terms of the probable success of normal applications because the prototypes benefit from the enthusiasm and the special skills of the pioneers.[32]

CENSUS BUREAU POPULATION FORECASTS

Beyond the successes and failures of specific forecasting efforts are the experiences of institutions which regularly produce forecasts. Probably the most notably successful governmental forecasting institution, the Census

Bureau has had a virtual monopoly on producing "authoritative" demographic forecasts. Other institutions (such as the National Planning Association and the Population Reference Bureau) also produce population projections, but it is usually taken for granted that Census Bureau forecasts are the most definitive estimates.

Four explanations can be given for the prominence of the Census Bureau forecasts. First, the initial prestige of these projections, first published in the 1940s, was in large part due to the collaboration of Pascal Whelpton.[33] Along with his colleague Warren Thompson, Whelptom was the most prominent demographer of the 1930s. His participation in the initial Census Bureau efforts carried with it his personal prestige and the considerable scientific respectability of the Scripps Foundation for Research in Population Problems, the base of Whelpton's research.

Second, once the Census Bureau had entered the field of population forecasting, it had first access to the sort of information that is crucial to making detailed demographic projections. The Census Bureau has the funds to conduct surveys and spot censuses to determine family size plans and actual fertility.[34] Since the Census Bureau is the national clearinghouse for demographic information, its forecasts are generally regarded as both the most current and the most official. Many policy-makers regard the Census Bureau as the "natural" place for making population predictions. Yet it should be noted that it would be just as "natural" for the Commerce Department's Bureau of Economic Analysis to monopolize economic forecasting, or for the Patent Office to monopolize technological forecasting. In reality, of course, many private and public institutions engage in economic or technological forecasting of at least as much prominence as that of the BEA and the Patent Office. Thus, the Census Bureau's monopoly should not be regarded as obvious; rather, it reflects the success of the bureau in capitalizing on its access to information.

Third, except for the nascent and still relatively minor field of population control policy, policy choices are rarely connected *directly* with specific population forecasts. Occasionally, population projections fit in directly with decisions on the size of future service facilities such as schools, airports, or sanitation systems. But, in general, population projections do not correspond to particular alternatives to the extent that acceptance of a specific projection narrows the range of reasonable alternatives. The fact that population projections are usually far removed from the point of decision means that they are less threatening to policy-makers guarding their own policy preferences.

Finally, but perhaps most importantly, the format of Census Bureau projections enhances their acceptability by minimizing the perception that the forecasters are imposing any assumptions on the forecast-user. The multiple-series format of the Census Bureau projections can flatter the forecast-user by allowing him to choose the particular projection series that best fits his own expectations. Thus, the forecasts are modest, uncontroversial (since the range of assumptions underlying the range of projections generally covers the whole spectrum of defensible positions), and "informational," though the range still can convey what the forecasters believe the future will bring (see chapter 3).

The success of the Census Bureau's forecasts has been protected by the fact that the Bureau does not make a *single* population projection. The multiple-projection approach forestalls not only the criticism of being "wrong," but also the possibility of rejection for political reasons. A policy-maker can often legitimate his own opinion by invoking one of the Census Bureau's series, without having his opinion challenged by "the" Census Bureau projection. Of course, the extent to which Census Bureau demographers are really providing technical input for policy-making is thereby limited. A set of forecasts that are consistent with a very wide range of plausible assumptions accomplishes little of what technical expertise can add to policy-making—namely, the experts' specifications of which assumptions are viable and which are not. This also suggests the discouraging possibility that insofar as forecasts or other technical input can have meaningful impact, their acceptability may be diminished. By the same token, forecasters may be tempted to water down their projections in order to enhance their acceptability.

SOME GENERAL-AUDIENCE FORECASTING EFFORTS

Besides the in-house forecasting efforts of private business and government, and the subscription services that can be obtained by policy-makers, many "public" studies have been made available to a potentially wide audience of policy-makers and the general public. These studies vary in their vision of the future, the specificity of their projections, and the tone of their presentation (ranging from highly popularized to highly academic).

The impact of a general-audience forecast is particularly difficult to trace. The generality of the audience itself makes the impact of a broadly accessible forecast equally diffuse. Moreover, explicit decision-making procedures can rarely translate forecasts coming from outside an organization into policy choices. General-audience forecasts necessarily have their influence through shifts in the focus of attention and through other changes in the broad climate of opinion in which decisions are made.

At any point in time an immense number of alternative images of the future are competing for attention. There is no way to sum up their collective impact except to conclude that prevailing, general expectations influence decision-making. Beyond this obvious point, however, only specific cases of prominent forecasting efforts can be usefully examined.

America's Needs and Resources VERSUS *Resources for Freedom*

In the decade after World War II, two massive studies projected a vast number of trends in national resource needs and supplies. The Twentieth Century Fund sponsored *America's Needs and Resources,* prepared under the direction of J. Frederic Dewhurst in 1947, and updated in 1955.[35] In 1952 the President's Materials Policy Commission, headed by William S. Paley, authored *Resources for Freedom.*[36] Covering essentially the same material, these studies were regarded in academic circles as of roughly equal quality and significance.

Yet Paley's *Resources for Freedom* appears to have had considerably more impact than the Dewhurst studies. *Resources for Freedom* is probably the most frequently cited forecasting study of the post–World War II period. Its projections were still being utilized in the 1960s, despite the availability of much more current forecasts. Its recommendation that an ongoing natural resource research institute be set up led to the creation of Resources for the Future, Inc.

Considering its greater impact, it is surprising and revealing that the Paley Report did not surpass the Dewhurst study in sales or in press coverage at the time of publication. The Paley Report's sales were considerably greater than the Government Printing Office expected them to be, but the 1947 Dewhurst edition still sold nearly twice as many copies.[37] *New York Times* coverage of the publication of each study was about the same.[38] In other words, public visibility cannot explain the Paley Report's remarkable success. Therefore, its success must have been due to its content, format, or sponsorship, rather than to the public relations effort that went into promoting it.

The first and most obvious explanation for the greater influence of the Paley Report is that Dewhurst was a noted scholar, while Paley was rich and famous. The fact that Paley's name adorned the report, and, more generally, that the report was the product of a blue ribbon presidential committee, not only provided an inherent attraction, but also clearly signaled the arrival of something important. Of course, Paley had little to do with the actual formulation of specific forecasts, but his direction of the project implied that he and other important men of affairs supported the basic policy message of the report—namely, that the nation was in danger of running out of a number of strategic materials (including petroleum) within the time frame of the forecasts, 1975.

The fact that *Resources for Freedom* contained a clear message was its second advantage. The Dewhurst study took the very sophisticated approach of converting future needs into the dollar equivalents required to fulfill these needs. As a consequence, however, it was regarded as highly technical and difficult to summarize in terms of *broad* policy implications. Considering that

33

forecasts generally are not stored in all their detail in the minds of policy-makers, but rather are incorporated into general expectations, a forecast with a clear and simple message has an obvious advantage over one that is seen as a collection of numerous technical facts and recommendations, regardless of how valid these may be.

The usefulness of specific *Resources for Freedom* forecasts was also enhanced by the fact that the individual projections could be used by policy-makers whether or not they accepted the policy recommendations of the report. Left in terms of the physical measurement of various resource requirements, the Paley Report forecasts were more adaptable to the specific preferences and policies of diverse policy-makers. *Resources for Freedom* noted what demands for materials were likely; *America's Needs and Resources* told policy-makers how much they would have to spend. To accept the forecasts of the Dewhurst study practically required acceptance of its very specific recommendations. In contrast, any forecast of the Paley Report, like any projection of the Census Bureau, could be used as a simple piece of information without dictating a particular policy.

The Dewhurst study lacked clear policy implications and additionally was too specific in presenting forecasts as policy recommendations. This double failure reflects the fact that there are two channels of impact for such a study: the promotion of its recommendations and the provision of information (i.e., future use of the study's forecasts). Paley's *Resources for Freedom* was promotionally prominent because it conveyed a clear message; it was influential in providing information because it left its forecasts in a neutral form. Dewhurst's *America's Needs and Resources* concentrated on specific, recommendation-linked forecasts, and thus obscured its basic message and limited its applicability.

The plight of the Dewhurst study is revealing in light of the suggestions by many forecasting authorities that projections should be made more meaningful by tying them to, or embedding them in, explicit policy recommendations or alternatives. If policy-makers really respected the importance of integrating forecasts into a systematic decision-making process, they might appreciate receiving a "package" of forecasts and policy recommendations. However, policy-makers generally guard their own initiative and autonomy in making policy, and are more receptive to modest projections that allow them, rather than the forecasters, to make the decisions.

The Limits to Growth MODEL

The most recent example of a general-audience forecasting effort of unquestionably great impact is the work directed by Jay Forrester and Donald Meadows under the sponsorship of the Club of Rome. The 1972 book *The Limits to Growth*[39] raised a storm of controversy, received a vast amount of publicity, and gave respectability to what many had considered an unthinkable position: that *no growth* is optimal for maintaining the world's standard of living. The Forrester-Meadows computer models, which were based on theoretical rather than empirical relationships among highly aggregated measures of industrial expansion, pollution, population, and food supplies, projected famine and depression by the end of this century unless industrialization is dramatically curtailed.

From descriptions of the content and context of the *Limits to Growth* controversy given in Greenberger, Crenson, and Crissey's *Models in the Policy Process* and in Clark and Cole's *Global Simulation Models,* [40] it is clear that the more obvious explanations for the study's impact must be dismissed. Its impact cannot be attributed to the originality of its argument, which has been a standard environmentalist position. It cannot be explained by the plausibility of the argument or the scientific validity of the method, judging by the severe criticisms leveled against it; nor can it be attributed to the prominence of individuals directly responsible for producing forecasts. The explanation of the powerful appeal of *The Limits to Growth* is found in other contextual factors.

The clearest source of the impact of *The Limits to Growth* was ths use of computer simulation modeling to generate the forecasts. Even if the argument was not original, it was for the first time "demonstrated" by what appeared to be explicit, objective, scientific methods. The aura of science, technology, and mathematics provided the plausibility that the core assumptions underlying the models lacked. Critics have pointed out that models, whether run on computers or not, express only the implications of the assumptions manifested in their equations; hence, they are only as valid as their assumptions. Therefore, the use of modeling can enhance the accuracy of a forecast only by guaranteeing internal consistency, and is not a remedy for faulty assumptions. Yet modeling can enhance the *promotion* of the forecast by giving it the appearance of technical sophistication.

Another source of the prominence of *The Limits to Growth* was the nature of its sponsorship. The Club of Rome's endorsement was important not only because of the prominence of the Club itself, but also because, as a group identified with "business types," its support of a "no-growth" conclusion attracted attention and provided additional plausibility that a group perceived as die-hard environmentalist never could have achieved. A good part of the shock occasioned by *The Limits to Growth* was due to the fact that it was issued under the auspices of a group that would be expected by most to oppose the no-growth position. Thus, it appeared that *The Limits to Growth* model had been so persuasive that it had convinced former advocates of the high-growth school. In reality, as Greenberger et al. point out, the Club of Rome intentionally sought out a team of researchers that could best justify the no-growth position.[41] Aurelio Peccei, an Italian businessman who headed the Club of Rome, had published his own book in 1969 with the revealing title *The Chasm Ahead.*[42] If it had been broadly known that many Club of Rome members were predisposed to the no-growth position prior to the "demonstration" of catastrophic consequences of growth provided by *The Limits to Growth,* the club's imprimatur may have done less in providing a large audience for the study.

This ironic situation suggests that forecasts can be promoted by exploiting the common perception that the support for, or opposition to, forecasts or other technical information *is* political; that groups normally support forecasts that serve their interests; and that, on the rare occasions when groups seem to support a forecast *despite* their apparent interests, this forecast is worthy of special attention. The fact that the Club of Rome members were not perceived as previously committed to the no-growth position created the impression that they were "objective"; and hence their support for the report indicated its high quality.

It should be noted that, although *The Limits to Growth* was undoubtedly successful in focusing attention on the potential drawbacks of industrial expansion, there is little evidence that it fully persuaded policy-makers, or even its sponsors. The Club of Rome subsequently sponsored a more elaborate world modeling effort headed by club members Mihajlo Mesarovic and Eduard Pestel, who claimed that their model was "fundamentally different from any previously developed."[43] This model is much more disaggregated than the Forrester-Meadows model (which had been criticized for ignoring regional differences), but it, too, ignores the crucial questions of validation and verification. In a sense, the study's prominence ultimately undid its plausibility, since its prominence elicited scathing attacks on its methodology, assumptions, and interpretation. This underscores an obvious but important point: the capacity to attract attention and the ability to persuade are quite different, and in fact may not occur together. While visibility may be a prerequisite of persuasion, it does not guarantee that the audience will be convinced.

SOME GENERALIZATIONS ON IMPACT

From this admittedly selective set of examples, a number of tentative propositions on the factors influencing the impact of specific forecasting efforts and institutions can be formulated.

1. The prominence and acceptability of a forecast (or other technical information) depend in large part on the prominence and acceptability of the programs, procedures, and institutions that serve as their "vehicles." That is, the medium strongly influences the impact of the message.

2. Therefore, regard for forecasts is strongly influenced by regard for the

institutions creating *or* sponsoring them, even if the sponsors really have little to do with producing the forecasts.

3. Support by sponsors who are *perceived* to be impartial can be a great asset to forecasts presented in a highly partisan atmosphere.

4. Acceptability of the forecast (or other technical information) is enhanced to the extent that a forecast can be portrayed as "firm" information. The straight projections in *Resources for Freedom* had greater impact than the more elaborate Dewhurst recommendations. Census Bureau forecasts, presented as mechanical extensions of various sets of explicit assumptions, come very close to monopolizing population projections.

5. Forecast use generally stops short of explicitly calculating policy recommendations on the basis of forecasts (and other technical input) plugged into algorithms. Policy-makers are naturally loathe to jeopardize their power by relying on such explicit mechanisms. Hence, forecasts with clear policy *implications,* which, however, do not force policy choice, are most likely to be accepted.

6. The qualities that enhance a forecast's impact—clear connections between what the forecast implies and optimal policy choices—may reduce its acceptability on the part of policy-makers. Both the Census Bureau's success and the relative obscurity of the Dewhurst studies are consistent with this inverse relationship between the forecasts' "boldness" and their acceptability. However, there is no consistently inverse relationship between acceptability and ultimate impact, because forecasts (such as those of the Paley Report) can be influential by focusing attention or by molding the climate of opinion, even though they are not seen as closely linked to specific policy alternatives.

7. Apparent methodological sophistication can enhance the acceptability of a forecast (as in the case of *The Limits to Growth*), but only as long as the methodology produces plausible results and does not usurp the policy-maker's final decision-making prerogative.

8. The acceptability of a given forecast is enhanced to the extent that the organization(s) in which it is formulated and used enjoys a high level of perceived goal consensus. The greater use of forecasts in private corporations and the greater success of PPBS in the Defense Department's salad days seem to support this proposition.

CHAPTER 3

POPULATION FORECASTING

In several respects, population forecasting is the most basic projection task. Compared to any other forecasting task, population forecasting has a longer history, a more central role in the development of forecasting techniques, and a greater importance in forecasting other trends.

The long history of population forecasting in the United States (Benjamin Franklin, among others, engaged in the pastime) is itself responsible for the fact that many forecasting techniques were developed first in population forecasting and later applied to other areas. By the time forecasting in energy, transportation, and economics had become widespread (for the most part, after World War II), demographic forecasting already had gone through many developments in technique. Population forecasting is, therefore, a good starting point for the examination of forecasting methods and the assumptions underlying them.

A more practical reason for paying attention first to demographic forecasting is that population forecasts are very often the most crucial element in forecasting trends that are directly or indirectly based on the number of people engaged in relevant activities. Ironically, this is because many forecasters focus on the level of *individual* behavior in specifying the dynamic element of future patterns. When a projection is based on assumptions of the average individual's propensities to act, *per capita* trend assumptions emerge and must then be coupled with population growth to yield the aggregate results. Aviation forecasts provide a clear example of dependence on the individual-level focus. In theory, the growth in the number of private aircraft can be explained completely in terms of production trends in the aircraft industry, or strictly in terms of the availability of hangar space, or even in terms of the aggregate growth pattern alone. Usually, however, aviation forecasts are generated by isolating the per capita demand for air travel (to project the size of the airline fleet) and the per capita demand for private aircraft. For problems such as "How many aircraft will the airports of 1980 have to accommodate?" the per capita projections, generally based on assumptions of economic and

This chapter is based on the author's article "Techniques and Accuracy of Demographic Forecasting," in Political Development and Change: A Policy Approach, *ed. Garry Brewer and Ronald Brunner (New York: Free Press, 1975).*

social trends, must be "multiplied through" by the most likely total population level for each time period. While this is certainly a plausible approach to forecasting trends that aggregate many individual decisions or actions, it does make the forecast dependent on the accuracy of the population projections.

The importance of population projections in energy demand forecasting is clearly indicated by the fact that more variation has been found in population assumptions than in per capita consumption assumptions underlying total energy forecasts. A 1965 study of sixteen energy forecasts by the U.S. Energy Study Group showed that the forecasts' variation in population projections for 1975, 1980, and 2000 were roughly 8.5 percent, 2.5 percent, and 8.0 percent of respective means. The per capita consumption forecasts varied by 4.0 percent, 2.0 percent, and 7.0 percent.[1] Thus, the differences in total energy consumption forecasts come more from differences in population projections than from different views on individual energy use. If the per capita approach is used to determine the total consumption of energy, a given error in the population projection (say, 10 percent) will be translated into the same magnitude of error for the energy consumption, unless, of course, other errors happen to compensate for it. Therefore, population projections are important because they introduce variation (which reflects uncertainty) into the forecasts of population-dependent trends, and ensuing errors in population projections will show up as equally grave errors in these forecasts.

TECHNIQUES OF POPULATION FORECASTING

The methods that have been applied to population forecasting reflect a developmental pattern that can be described basically as increasing sophistication and refinement in the formal accounting procedures that weld together the implications of core assumptions on the dynamics of population change (births, deaths, and migration). These refinements have been accomplished primarily through *disaggregation:* the separation of broad, summary statistics into narrower categories. What has not been developed in the methodological maturation of population forecasting is any theory or explicit approach for addressing the core assumptions upon which these forecasts are based. Some of the earlier forecasts had a stronger theoretical foundation (whether correct or not is another question) than the most recent efforts at demographic forecasting.

Philosophical approaches to population forecasting have varied primarily in the relative importance given to *theories* of population growth. At one extreme, a forecaster may maintain that a particular theory of population growth dictates a specific growth pattern; the only significance of the historical pattern is to establish how far the theoretical pattern has advanced. At the other extreme, a forecaster may rely totally on the historical growth pattern to

39

project further growth, while ignoring the insights of theory. Either of these approaches can be applied to the extension of the unitary trend of total population, as the early forecasters did, or to narrower, multiply disaggregated trends that comprise the total population.

ATHEORETICAL CURVE-FITTERS: THE ULTIMATE IN EXTRAPOLATION

When the first methodologically explicit forecasts of U.S. population began to appear at the turn of the century, forecasters had at their disposal the long series of total population growth reports provided by the decennial census, and a very incomplete understanding of population dynamics. Population growth obviously had something to do with the preference for large families, the nation's still largely agrarian nature, which encouraged this preference, the advances in hygiene and medicine, and the flood of immigration. On the other hand, urbanization was advancing, family size was affected to some extent by economic depressions (which were highly variable and poorly understood), and America had become a melting pot of people of quite diverse childbearing tendencies. It would have taken an extraordinarily bold effort at that time to build up a projection of total U.S. population on the basis of separate projections of the fertility and mortality of each segment of the population. Such an effort would require the forecaster to predict the efficacy of medicine, the magnitude (and perhaps ethnic composition) of future immigration, and the complex interaction between urbanization and predispositions toward large or small families. In contrast to the complexities and difficulties of monitoring the mechanisms of population growth, the overall growth trend itself was a simple, smooth curve. In the choice between the simple curve and the morass of complicated underlying dynamics, the early forecasters understandably chose the curve.

From 1891 through the 1920s, a number of population forecasters sought to extend the unitary population trend according to the growth curve they saw in the overall historical pattern. This was extrapolation in its ultimate form. Instead of simply applying the growth rate of the immediately preceding period (e.g., five or ten years), these forecasters searched for the growth curve established by the entire historical trend. They observed that, although the population level had been increasing, the rate of increase was gradually diminishing. All of the efforts of Pritchett, Gannet, and Sloane were devoted to finding a curve that fit this pattern, and to calculating future population levels with this "well-fitting" curve.[2]

At first glance, extrapolation might seem to be a rather devil-may-care approach predicated on the assumption that "things will continue as they are." While it is true that extrapolation can be used in an off-the-cuff fashion by forecasters with little familiarity with the dynamics of the trends under study, extrapolation can also be justified on a much more profound and

40

sophisticated basis. Extrapolation really signifies complete dependence on existing trends, without any additional input from the forecaster's theoretical understanding or intuitive judgments of the underlying processes. These processes are responsible for existing trends, whether or not they are understood by the forecaster. The rationale of extrapolation is that, when these processes are not well understood, their past behavior (i.e., the existing trend) is a more reliable indication of future patterns than are the potentially false signals indicated by the forecaster's incomplete understanding. It is a position of intellectual modesty rather than blasé confidence. These early forecasters saw a pattern in the historical growth of population and were content to follow this pattern into the future. Whether their approach was cast in mathematical terms (for example, Pritchett found that the equation $P = A + Bt + Ct^2 + Dt^3$, where P is the population, t is time, and the other terms are constants, fit the past pattern of population growth when the constants were estimated with old data), or verbally, they still relied on the simple population curve, which seemed to unfold with elegant simplicity, despite the complexity of demographic dynamics.

CURVES FROM THEORY

Other forecasters have also assumed that the entire (past, present, and future) pattern of population growth can be described and predicted with a particular curve. The specific dimensions of the curve would be those that make it fit most closely with the existing data. The crucial question is how to decide what *type* of curve is appropriate. The early forecasters discussed above used existing data alone, and invariably they chose an uncomplicated type of curve without "inflection points" (i.e., changes from convexity to concavity or vice versa). In contrast to this reliance on past data, the biologist Raymond Pearl introduced the practice of deriving the type of curve from theoretical assumptions of the nature of population growth.[3]

Pearl advocated the "logistic law" of population growth, which was developed from observations of population dynamics of animals (such as fruit flies) in controlled experimental conditions. Based on experiments in which populations bred in the context of constant supplies of food and space, the logistic law calls for an initial acceleration in population increase, followed by a symmetrical deceleration of the increase, ultimately resulting in a stable population level. Thus, the S-shaped logistic curve implies a leveling off of population.

Although the analogy between human being and fruit fly would seem to break down on the point of fixed space and food, other justifications beyond resource exhaustion would lead one to expect a human logistic population growth pattern. For example, the increasing urban proportion that usually accompanies population growth, coupled with the fact that urban fertility is generally lower than rural fertility, could result in a lower overall birthrate and therefore a slackening of population growth. Numerous theories calling for an automatically lowered fertility rate in large populations attribute it to factors as diverse as social complexity, rational calculus, or alienation. Therefore, Pearl could have justified a logistic curve for human population growth without invoking fruit fly behavior.

But there is another problem—beyond the question of whether or not logistic curves are appropriate—in using a logistic curve as a description of population growth. Logistic curves come in all sizes. If the midpoint (i.e., inflection point) of a particular logistic curve comes late, the entire curve will be very long, and the ultimate population level will be higher than that for smaller logistic curves with earlier inflection points. In other words, the date at which accelerating growth becomes decelerating growth is crucial for establishing the magnitude of population growth. Small and temporary fluctuations in the rate of growth may easily be mistaken for the inflection point.

Pearl cannot yet be criticized for falsely predicting that U.S. population growth is logistic, because this may yet prove to be the case. So far, U.S. population growth has been roughly exponential, and an exponential curve is similar to the portion of the logistic curve preceding the inflection point. However, Pearl concluded that the decreasing growth period had commenced in the 1910–20 decade. His mistake was in overestimating the significance of the relatively small 1910–20 population increase. It was the first ten-year increase that was lower than the increase of the previous decade, but had he not been so rigidly committed to assuming that population growth would necessarily be strictly logistic, he might have discounted this fluctuation, attributing it to the absence of 2.5 million military personnel serving overseas and thus separated from their wives, and to the death of 100,000 of these men in the prime of life. The yearly growth chart for the 1910–20 period does indicate that the decline in the growth rate occurred within the 1917–19 period. Nevertheless, Pearl interpreted this growth rate decline as the inflection point of the U.S. population growth. By expecting the overall growth rate to be a single phenomenon characterized by great (and almost mystical) regularity, Pearl assumed that the 1910–20 drop signaled a continual long-term decline in the growth rate. On this basis he projected the population would very gradually level off at 197 million, reaching approximately 157 million by 1960.

The great irony of population forecasting is that Pearl's totally incorrect choice of that particular logistic curve had an enormously misleading influence on later forecasters, but his own five-, ten-, and twenty-year forecasts were quite accurate. The low birth rate of the Depression years saved Pearl's short-term projections, but by the time of the so-called postwar baby boom in the late 1940s his error had become obvious.

42

Other demographers—even those who used completely different methods—came to assume that birth rates would steadily decrease and that overall growth also would decrease. Pearl went even further by assuming that: (1) the growth rate decline was an inevitable event rather than the reflection of specific, and perhaps temporary, conditions; (2) the decline in birth rate would necessarily cause a decline in successive annual numerical increases; and (3) small changes in the growth rate were inevitably indications of major trends to come. The first assumption was disproved when the birth rate began to increase again in 1937, yet the demographers still assumed that future rates would decrease. The second assumption ignored the fact that a decreasing birth rate *per unit* of population may still produce an increase in numerical growth, since the population base to which the rate applies is steadily increasing. The third assumption reduced the capacity of Pearl's approach to pick out the major changes from among the confusing array of minor fluctuations, such as the 1910–20 decrease in the growth rate. In short, dealing with population growth as a unitary trend concealed some of the dynamics that might have been able to sensitize a forecaster to the existence and significance of deviations from his theory.

TECHNICAL ADVANCES IN ACCOUNTING

The Component Approach. Developments leading to the sophistication of projecting population forecasts immediately followed the introduction of Pearl's simple method, perhaps in reaction to it. When later combined, these developments would form the projection technique in use today.

The first advance was made in 1928 by P. K. Whelpton and W. S. Thompson, well-known demographers employed by the Scripps Foundation.[4] Both served on the National Resources Planning Board, one of the most prominent sources of forecasts during the 1920s and 1930s. They separated the formerly undivided growth rate into its obvious components of birth rate, death rate, and migration rate. Earlier forecasters had of course realized the composition of the growth rate, but Whelpton and Thompson were the first to generate separate and explicit projections of these rates, and then combine them to reconstruct the overall growth rate. Breaking down the growth rate into its components allowed for a finer analysis of lower-level trends; Whelpton and Thompson isolated the past birth and death rate trends of the urban, rural, native white, foreign white, and nonwhite sectors, and extended the past numerical trend of each sector to a near-future time. Then, reweighing the sectors on the basis of their newly projected proportions, they repeated the extension process to the next time period. Their iterative model enabled them not only to project fine details of population composition, but also to view the numerous potentially important trends that had been balanced out or otherwise hidden within the overall growth rate.

43

Of course, Whelpton and Thompson's choice of component breakdown represented only one of the many reasonable ways to "decompose" the pattern of population growth. The forecaster's need to choose the most useful component breakdown—the best way to separate the problem of understanding population into manageable subtasks—is a challenge facing any problem-solver confronted with complex dynamics.[5] It is therefore quite expectable that Whelpton and Thompson's introduction of component breakdowns did not constitute *the* definitive component breakdown for succeeding generations of demographers. Instead, post–Whelpton-Thompson population forecasting can be viewed as further elaboration on the component idea.

The component approach also led Whelpton and Thompson to a much less deterministic conception of population growth. Seen only as the outcome of many different trends, population growth admits of more variability and uncertainty in its future levels, which depend on the many unpredictable social and economic background variables affecting the component rates for the various sectors. Whereas Pearl was convinced that his projections had to be right, Whelpton and Thompson's projections were "merely statements of what the size . . . of the population would be at specified future times if birth rates, death rates and immigration were to follow [a] certain specified trend."[6] In their 1933 projections, Whelpton and Thompson proved they were serious about the indeterminancy of future population growth by publishing several different series of projections to accommodate different assumptions about these rates.

Although the most prominent feature of the Whelpton-Thompson approach was disaggregation, simple extrapolation was still required to extend the various component trends. For this reason the component approach is essentially an accounting method; disaggregation into components provides the *framework* for projecting specific component trends, but does not tell the forecaster how to forecast these components. The forecaster still must choose from among extrapolation, theory, intuitive judgment, or some other basic means for extending each trend.

The Cohort Approach. In 1930 another advance through disaggregation was introduced: the explicit breakdown of the population by age. It is not surprising that this innovation was introduced by two actuarial statisticians of the Metropolitan Life Insurance Company, L. I. Dublin and A. J. Lotka.[7] The method takes full advantage of the actuarial breakdown of the age-specific mortality rates that are the heart of insurance-risk calculation.

Earlier forecasters, including Whelpton and Thompson, had considered age distribution less formally in forecasting birth rate and death rate trends. But the explicit age breakdown enabled forecasters to follow each cohort through its life stages, applying the appropriate birth rates and death rates for each generation. Thus, an important implication of the age group refinement is that it substitutes age-specific *fertility* and *mortality* rates for the birth rates and death rates used by earlier forecasters. Dublin and Lotka demonstrated that the observed birth rate and death rate, like the overall growth rate, were compound measures that could be misleading when considered as indivisible units. The women in a population with a currently high birth rate are not necessarily more fertile than other women; there simply may be relatively more women in the childbearing age group within that population. Similarly, a high death rate may be explained by a large proportion of elderly people rather than by a high "natural" mortality rate. By making the cohort breakdown, Dublin and Lotka were able to take into account the future fertility and mortality rates of cohorts that had not reached the age at which their potential had been reflected by prevailing birth rates and death rates.

Dublin and Lotka put their technically unobjectionable method to very unorthodox use, however, which resulted in large forecast errors. They assumed that the American people had acquired an inherent level of "true reproductive activity." Within each age group, fertility and mortality rates were constant over time. They believed that in 1930 the population's true "fecundity" was actually in balance with its "mortality." This meant that, if the age distribution had been regular (i.e., if the smooth pyramidal age distribution, produced by the prolonged operations of a constant birth rate and death rate, prevailed), the birth rate would have canceled out the death rate. But because the population was "overloaded" with people in midlife, due to immigration and a recently declining birth rate, more births were occuring than deaths. By assigning constant age-specific birth rates and death rates to each cohort for successive generations, Dublin and Lotka generated declining overall birth rates and increasing death rates that would smooth out the bulge in the age distribution pyramid. In this way the crude rate of increase would eventually (in 1970) reach the "true" rate of increase, namely, zero.

Dublin and Lotka never justified their assumption that for any given age cohort the fertility and mortality rates will be constant; indeed, they quoted a change in the true rate of increase from 5.2 per 1,000 in 1920 to 0 per 1,000 in 1930. Perhaps they believed that, once the bulk of disruptive immigration was over, the rhythm of population regeneration would return to its natural course. It would seem, however, that their assumption of constant age-specific birth rates and death rates showed a blatant disregard for the social and economic factors influencing fertility and mortality, while their choice of zero as the true rate of increase was a strained and unsubstantiated justification of the stabilizing theory of growth.

The result of imposing this assumption of balanced fertility and mortality rates was a set of forecasts that seriously underestimated long-term future

45

population growth. This error was not the outcome of the use of the cohort approach, but rather the straightforward implication of inappropriate core assumptions on the behavior of the population.

THE CONTEMPORARY APPROACH: A SYNTHESIS OF TECHNIQUES

Contemporary population forecasting differs from other projection tasks in two related respects. First, population forecasting, more than any other forecasting field examined in this study, is dominated by a single institution, the Census Bureau. Census Bureau forecasts are almost invariably the projections used by policy-makers and by forecasters of other trends that rest on population growth.[8]

Second, the Census Bureau does not present a single forecast, but offers numerous "series" of projections based on different assumptions of fertility, mortality, and migration rates. Presumably, the user is to pick the projection or projections he regards as most plausible. Viewed from another angle, Census Bureau forecasts are simply the mechanical application of various sets of these rates within the following framework: Population = Previous Population + Births − Deaths + Net Immigration. The user can make the important predictions—the rates— and the Census Bureau simply traces out the implications of these rates. Perhaps the attraction of the Census Bureau projections is that they do not impose a forecast, and the whole series, as long as it encompasses a broad range of rate assumptions, is not likely to be proven "wrong."

However, the fact that Census Bureau forecasts do not explicitly indicate a single preference poses a problem for appraisal. Since appraisal requires a comparison between predicted and real levels, what is *the* prediction when the forecaster refuses to be pinned down to a specific forecast? But this is also a problem for forecast-users, and therein lies the solution to the appraisal problem. While publishing several projection series does serve the purpose of keeping policy-makers aware of the inherent indeterminacy of future population levels, the forecast-user, if he does not consider himself to be a population expert, is hardly in a good position to choose from among the alternative series provided by the Census Bureau. He is well advised (and more likely) to rely on the implicit cues of the Census Bureau presentation of forecasts to infer which series the Census Bureau demographers "really" believe to be most likely. Most policy-makers who use the Census Bureau population projections choose the *middle* series, presumably on the assumption that the Census Bureau demographers have evenly arrayed their alternative rates to be higher and lower than the most plausible, middle projection. Since this is the way multiseries forecasts are generally interpreted, this is the way they should be appraised: in terms of the accuracy of the middle one or two series.

The population projections of the 1940s did not adopt Dublin and Lotka's valid advance of the cohort method, perhaps because Dublin and Lotka's age-specific breakdown was hidden within such a large set of complicated methods and assumptions. Whelpton and Thompson's method of projecting birthrates and death rates for the six combinations of urban, rural, native white, foreign white, and nonwhite was simpler and could accommodate the grosser distortions in population age structure by incorporating their presumed effects in the projections of birth rate and death rate trends, without using formal mathematical methods to determine just how much difference age structure would make.

Census Bureau forecasters accepted Pearl's assumption of the inevitability of a decline in population increase, even though the decreasing birth rate, the main justification for predicting a logistic leveling, had reversed itself in 1937 to a small increase that even World War II would affect only slightly. Pearl's assumption of imminent growth rate decline, with its aura of scientific certainty, had been around for so long that it was accepted as fact long after its justification had disappeared. Thus, the Census Bureau's estimates were formed by combining projections of constant numerical migration (hence, a decreasing *rate* of migration), fairly constant death rates, and declining birth rates for all sectors. The bureau followed Whelpton's example of publishing several series of projections based on varying assumptions that, in their diversity, tended to obscure the fact that the median assumption, the one that would generate the projection series most likely to be used as "the" projection, called for a declining growth rate. Generally, the series of *highest* projections used the current birth rate as the birth rate for future years; the other two or three series assumed lower birth rates than were current.

Starting around 1953, Census Bureau forecasters, perhaps stung by professional articles criticizing the poor performance of prior projections,[9] developed a more elaborate projection method that combined Dublin and Lotka's cohort method with the population segment breakdown suggested by Whelpton and Thompson. They could use the different age-specific fertility and mortality schedules for the white and nonwhite, rural and urban populations to follow each cohort into future years to determine the number of its survivors and its contributions to the birth rate. Therefore, the age-specific fertility rate could be distinguished from the birth rate, which reflects temporary population age distribution rather than an inherent characteristic of fertility. They would abandon gross death rates in favor of age-specific mortality rates. Yet they would retain the distinctions between groups within the population that would be likely to have different fertility and mortality schedules. It appears, however, that the urban-rural distinction is not currently being used to define population segments, probably because of the frequently arbitrary reclassifications of rural areas to urban status on the basis of population growth.

In the mid-1950s, belief in the *inevitability* of birth rate reduction was

47

finally abandoned. However, a vestige of Pearl's thinking still remained in the bias toward lower birth rates. Of the various series representing different fertility rate assumptions, the one projecting the *highest* rate was based on the existing fertility level, thus making the bulk of future projections reflect declining fertility.[10]

One other methodological aspect is important. In the process of inferring future trends from existing data, the forecaster must attempt to distinguish between the beginnings of major changes and the fluctuations or temporary deviations that have no significance for future trends. Thus, one facet of "method" is the *sensitivity* of the population model: the extent of influence on future prediction brought to bear by current deviations from previously long-range trends. If real data are expected to adhere precisely to the theoretical values stipulated by the model, the projections will be very sensitive to minor changes in trends.

The logistic model is a risky choice (whether it is appropriate is another matter) because it depends on a small change in growth rate to cue the expectation of major change. Other curve-fitting models suffer from the same problem. The most recent data points are the most important in determining what direction the curve will follow in the future, but there is no way to determine to what extent these points reflect temporary fluctuations, nor is there any way to diffuse the effects of misleading fluctuations when they cause recent data points to deviate from the ultimately true curve of growth.

The component method provided the first means for determining the influence of temporary fluctuations. By breaking down the growth rate into birth rate, death rate and migration rate, a current deviation from a previous long-term trend could be attributed to change in fertility, mortality, or migration, which in turn could be attributed to a permanent or a temporary cause. For example, the decline in growth rate between 1917 and 1920 could have been explained by the unusually large decline in birth rate, which in turn was easily attributed to the temporary conditions of war time troop absence.

The cohort method has the capacity to diffuse the effects of temporary fluctuations. By determining which age cohort is experiencing a change in fertility or mortality rate responsible for an overall change in population growth, the forecaster can adjust his birth and death schedules for that cohort alone, thereby minimizing the overall effect of the fluctuation to the extent that it is specific to only a limited set of age cohorts.

When the component and cohort methods are combined, projections are much less susceptible to the exaggeration of temporary fluctuations, because a more precise focus of change can be identified and adjusted. For example, if the growth rate were to decline for two years, the curve-fitters would have no choice but to assume that the population was leveling off and would continue to do so. Using the component method, the projector could at least identify the cause of the growth rate decline as a decline in birth rate or migration rate, or an increase in death rate. By using the combined component and cohort methods, the projector could determine that, for example, the source of change was confined to a marked increase in the mortality rate of the sixty- to seventy-year-old white urban cohort. The public health records of the two years would indicate whether the increase in mortality was due to a temporary cause, such as an influenza epidemic, or to a fairly chronic one, e.g., emphysema. In the latter case, census data would reveal the sizes of the white urban cohorts entering into that age period, which could be relatively smaller or larger than the current cohort.

EVALUATING DEMOGRAPHIC FORECASTS

The various projection methods discussed above can be evaluated either in terms of the correctness of their underlying theoretical assumptions or in terms of how close the predicted population levels come to actual levels. Both are important. Inadequacies of theoretical assumptions, *if* recognized by potential forecast-users, can jeopardize the plausibility and hence the use of the forecasts. Inaccuracy detracts from the actual policy-making utility of the forecast. However, once the accuracy of a forecast has been determined (i.e., after the target date), it constitutes a more basic indication of the forecast's validity than does the prior plausibility. Therefore, the following analysis focuses on the accuracy of predictions rather than the plausibility or validity of their methods and assumptions. The validity can be gauged to some extent by the record of accuracy, as long as there are sufficiently many forecasts to balance out the occasional instances of predictions based on faulty methods or assumptions which turn out to be correct "by accident." The importance of the perceived plausibility of the forecasts is considered in a later section.

The inaccuracy of population forecasts can be expressed as the percentage of error of a prediction made in year X for the target year $X + t$:

$$\frac{\text{actual population in year } X + t - \text{predicted population in year } X + t}{\text{actual population in year } X + t} \times 100\%.$$

Allowing t to equal five, ten, or twenty years, a comparison of projections of different "lead times" can be made. Some projections do not provide estimates for precisely these spans, so, in order to avoid discarding these cases, predictions made in other than decade or half-decade years are treated as if they had been. For example, projections made in 1909, 1928, and 1941 are treated as if they had been made in 1910, 1930, and 1940 respectively.

The inaccuracy of population projections shown in table 3.1 and figure 3.1 contradicts the widespread impression that newer methods are necessarily

Table 3.1: Errors of Population Forecasts

Year	Source	5-yr. Error (%)	10-yr. Error (%)	20-yr. Error (%)	1960 Error (%)	1970 Error (%)	1975 Error (%)
1891	Pritchett	—	1.8	2.5	22.9	24.7	29.0
1900	Pritchett	—	2.5	7.6	22.9	24.7	29.0
1909	Sloane	—	3.9	6.2	14.3	18.7	—
1909	Gannet	—	2.3	3.3	6.9	11.0	—
1920	Pearl-Reed	—	0.4	3.4	11.9	18.7	19.3
1925	Pearl	0.6	0.2	3.2	11.9	18.7	19.3
1928	Whelpton	—	4.3	0.4	9.4	17.1	18.3
1930	Dublin-Lotka	—	3.4	5.8	18.1	27.4	—
1933	Whelpton-Thompson	0.4	1.5	11.5	17.1	25.5	27.6
1938	Whelpton-Thompson	1.0	6.8	17.0	17.0	25.0	26.5
1940	Census Bureau, P-3, #15	2.9	6.7	18.7	18.6	26.9	28.0
1943	Whelpton-Thompson	5.2	11.2	20.9	16.5	24.3	26.2
1947	Census Bureau, "Forecasts 1945–75"	—	9.7	19.5	—	—	24.3
1949	Census Bureau, P-25 #18	6.1	11.5	—	11.5	—	—
1950	Census Bureau, P-25, #43	2.8	5.8	—	5.8	—	—
1953	Census Bureau, P-25, #78	2.5	4.3	2.0	2.6	3.5	2.0
1955	Census Bureau, P-25, #123	1.6	1.7	1.7	1.6	1.4	1.7
1958	Census Bureau, P-25, #187	0.0	2.1	—	0.4	2.1	7.5
1962	Census Bureau, P-25, #241 & 251	—	2.4	—	—	2.4	7.6
1964	Census Bureau, P-25, #286	0.4	4.0	—	—	0.4	4.0
1966	Census Bureau, P-25, #329	0.2	2.9	—	—	0.2	2.9
1967	Census Bureau, P-25, #381	—	3.4	—	—	0.0	3.4
1970	Census Bureau, P-25, #448	1.0	—	—	—	—	1.0
1971	Census Bureau, P-25, #470	2.0	—	—	—	—	2.0
1972	Census Bureau, P-25, #476	—	—	—	—	—	2.0
1972D	Census Bureau, P-25, #493	—	—	—	—	—	0.4

more successful methods. Instead, the projections of the early curve-fitters, especially Pearl, were generally more accurate in their ten-year projections than were the forecasts derived by the more sophisticated component and cohort methods used later, even though, for twenty-year projections, the accuracy of the curve-fitters and the Whelpton-Thompson and Dublin-Lotka approaches was about the same. The five-year forecasts of the early forecasters were every bit as accurate as the forecasts made via the elaborate procedures of the 1960s.

The worst predictions came in the period between 1938 and 1949. The large errors were especially embarrassing in light of the prevailing faith in the progress and increasing sophistication of the methodology. How bad are these forecasts? Considering that the bulk (generally over 80 percent) of the population ten years hence is already alive when a ten-year forecast is made, a 10 percent discrepancy can only be regarded as a major error. While there are explanations for such disasters, the extenuating circumstances on which they are based do not stand up to close scrutiny.

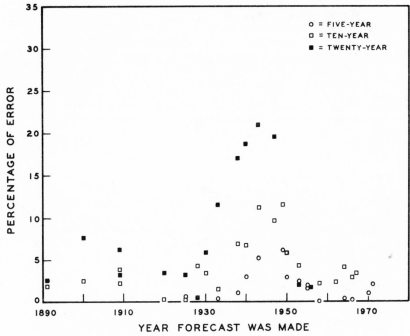

3.1. Errors of Five-, Ten-, and Twenty-Year U.S.
Population Forecasts

The first defense that comes to mind is that the accuracies of predictions made at different times are not really comparable, because the population growth of some periods is more volatile, erratic, and thus inherently more difficult to predict. According to this argument, the large errors of the forecasts of the late 1930s and the 1940s can be attributed to the *inherent* difficulty of predicting the population growth of the 1940s and 1950s.

One way to control for the volatility of population growth is to express the inaccuracy of ten-year predictions (not all sources provided five- or twenty-year predictions) as the percentage of error divided by a measure of the variation in growth rate during the ten-year period, namely, the mean absolute deviation of single-year rates from the period's overall annual rate:

$$\% \text{ of error of prediction}/(\sum_{i=1}^{10} [\mid \text{overall annual rate} - \text{rate in year } i \mid]/10).$$

As table 3.2 reveals, essentially the same *relative* magnitudes of error differences remain. Consequently, the underestimates of the 1938–49 period cannot be attributed to more volatile or erratic population growth. In fact, the variability in yearly growth rates during this period does not exceed that of earlier periods.

51

Table 3.2: Forecast Errors Standardized by Growth Rate Variability

Year	Source	Percentage of Error of 10-yr. Prediction	Mean Deviation from Decade Growth Rate	Percentage of Error Divided by Mean Deviation
1900	Pritchett	2.5 (+)	0.076	32.9
1909	Sloane	3.9 (−)	0.353	11.0
1909	Gannet	2.3 (−)	0.353	6.5
1920	Pearl-Reed	0.4 (−)	0.253	1.6
1925	Pearl	0.2 (−)	0.310	0.6
1928	Whelpton	4.3 (+)	0.129	33.3
1930	Dublin-Lotka	3.4 (−)	0.129	26.4
1933	Whelpton-Thompson	1.5 (−)	0.435	3.5
1938	Whelpton-Thompson	6.8 (−)	0.291	23.4
1940	Census Bureau	6.7 (−)	0.291	23.0
1943	Whelpton-Thompson	11.2 (−)	0.131	85.6
1947	Census Bureau	9.7 (−)	0.131	74.0
1949	Census Bureau	11.5 (−)	0.054	213.0
1950	Census Bureau	5.8 (−)	0.054	107.4
1953	Census Bureau	4.3 (−)	0.134	32.1
1955	Census Bureau	1.7 (−)	0.134	12.7
1958	Census Bureau	2.1 (−)	0.204	10.3
1962	Census Bureau	2.4 (+)	0.204	11.8
1964	Census Bureau	4.0 (+)	0.146	27.4

A more subtle claim of extenuating circumstances maintains that projections can be expected to forecast only those future conditions which remain undisturbed by unforeseeable and unpredictable nondemographic events, such as wars, economic depressions, and other catastrophies. Efforts to classify and evaluate projective techniques would be useless if it were true that future population growth is inherently unpredictable. After reviewing the disastrous projections made prior to 1954, John Hajnal maintained that

these factors whose effects on future growth we can calculate are likely to be frequently outweighed by the unpredictable. It is this which accounts for the failure of more complex techniques to yield more accurate results than simple techniques and which casts doubt on the value of forecasting. We cannot hope to develop better methods which yield forecasts clustering more and more closely around the true future population. New and more complex techniques which may yet be invented are, I think, just as liable as past techniques to be fairly often upset by the unpredictability of history. They will probably just as often—and that means rather frequently—give results which are very wide of the mark and less accurate than crude guessing.[11]

Deciding whether population is predictable is equivalent to judging the magnitudes of variation caused by demographically unpredictable events, e.g., wars or depressions. The population growth data for the periods directly before and after the world wars contradict Hajnal's impression that such major events render future population levels hopelessly unpredictable. Both wars had little *net* effect on population growth. The initial lulls in growth were followed by compensating increases, as would be expected of returning servicemen restoring life plans interrupted by the wars. Since the predictions made during the 1938–49 period were all too low, the post war "baby boom" has been blamed as the occurrence responsible for the unexpected increase in birth rate and hence in population. The argument is this: The boom resulted from the occurrence of World War II, a phenomenon which demographers could not have been expected to predict from demographic data. Hence, the boom itself was inherently unpredictable through demographic forecasting.

In fact, the statistics of postwar population growth betray this reasoning. Figure 3.2 shows that population growth during and after the war had the net effect of rather smooth growth as predicted linearly from the yearly growth rate from 1937 to 1942. The same pattern can be seen for the period surrounding World War I. The high birth rates and overall growth rates during the postwar periods only compensated for the births postponed because of the wars. The perception that growth during the post-1945 period was a "boom" resulted from the unfulfilled expectation of a radical *decrease* in the pace of population growth that never materialized. By this time, however, there were no data that could justify this assumption of decreasing growth. Because the assumptions underlying the forecasts of the 1938–49 period were so isolated from the existing facts of the population growth rate, the forecasts deviated sharply from the actual growth pattern, resulting in extremely large prediction errors.

The fundamental error of these forecasts seems to be that fertility rate assumptions were formulated and then maintained despite contradictory empirical facts. Initially, these assumptions were derived from abstract theory (*à la* Pearl and Dublin and Lotka) and a certain degree of wishful thinking:

The pre-eminent American student of future population during the 1930's and 1940's, P. K. Whelpton was persuaded of the desirability of an imminent stabilization of population size. In his 1947 report, Whelpton adduced arguments tending to show that the U.S. was not below its long run economic optimum population. He observed, moreover, that the slackening of growth would be favorable to the interests of conservationists and that it might lead to improvement in the quality of the population.[12]

Once this assumption became embedded in the conventional wisdom of American demography, it lingered on beyond the point where any reasonable argument on stabilization of the population level could be made. This phenomenon of "assumption drag," the continued use of assumptions long after their validity has been contradicted by the data, has several sources. First, it is understandable in terms of the socialization of experts. The received wisdom of any field is questioned only rarely. Second, there is often great skepticism that the empirical data that *seem* to contradict a longstanding assumption amount to more than the misleading temporary fluctuations discussed previously. Third, there often seems to be an inordinate delay before reliable *real* data are recorded, gathered, and disseminated. Fourth, many forecasting ef-

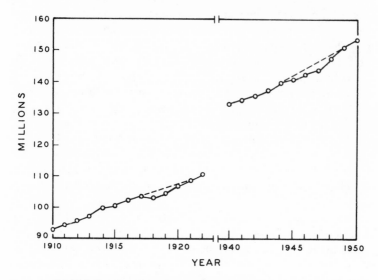

3.2 U.S. Population: 1910–1922 and 1940–1950

forts that involve long preparation retain the empirical assumptions that prevailed initially but that may have become obsolete by the time of publication. Since the retention of obsolete assumptions can affect the crucial core assumptions that largely determine the accuracy of the forecasts, and since the sources of this problem are multiple and chronic, "assumption drag" is one of the most serious problems of practical forecasting. The forecast-user should carefully examine the behavioral assumptions underlying any forecast (unfortunately they are often buried under layers of methodological trappings) at least to determine whether or not they are based on antiquated data and theory.

The forecasts of the mid-1950s and 1960s regained some of the accuracy lost in previous decades. Even so, the accuracy of these forecasts is no better than the accuracy of the earliest forecasts. For the 1960s forecasts, a similar (though less damaging) case of "assumption drag" is evident. Whereas during the 1930s and 1940s the obsolete assumption was that the declining birth rate would continue indefinitely, during the 1960s forecasters overcompensated for the population spurt of the previous decade and were very slow to acknowledge the reduced birth rate that led to an unexpectedly low population level in 1975. Thus, the 1962 forecast for 1975 population was in error by slightly more than 7.5 percent.

The magnitudes of error shown in figure 3.1 reveal that, as would be expected, short-term predictions are in general more accurate than long-term predictions. To express this tendency more plainly, figure 3.3 shows the magnitudes of error of predictions of 1960, 1970, and 1975 population levels

54

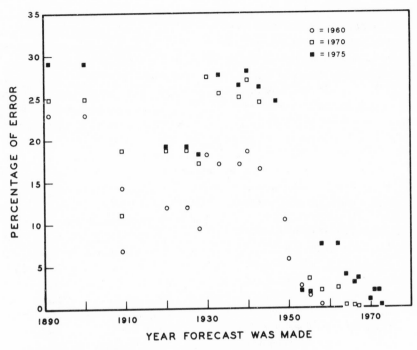

3.3. Errors of 1960, 1970, and 1975 U.S. Population
Forecasts

in order of the date of prediction. For all three target years there is an eventual convergence of later projections to the correct population level. The later projections, produced closer to the target date, would be expected to improve as more recent data became available. There is less room for error in making a short-term forecast than in making a long-term one. Yet the convergence is neither smooth nor monotonic. For the 1960 population level, Gannet's fifty-year-old forecast was more accurate than the Census Bureau forecast made in 1949. And, again, the 1938–49 projections, despite the availability of newer data, were worse than the older predictions. Since the projections are for a fixed year, this comparison of prediction accuracy cannot be attacked on the grounds that differing accuracy is due to different degrees of inherent difficulty in predicting the population trends of the period. In comparing the accuracy of all predictions of 1960, 1970, and 1975 population levels, it is clear that the relative success of each approach is the same as that manifested in the comparison of five-, ten-, and twenty-year projections.

The utility of figure 3.3 lies in the fact that it provides a better graphic display of the relevance of lead time (or, to put it another way, recency) to the accuracy of population forecasts. Predictions of the 1960 population level did not come consistently close to the actual level until 1950, and predictions of the 1970 level did not come close until about 1955. For 1975, fairly accurate forecasts were made in the mid-1950s, but immediately thereafter serious overestimates checked the convergence toward the actual level. Not until 1966 were the forecasts for 1975 consistently accurate. Thus, predictions more than fifteen years old were unreliable for projecting the population levels for these three target dates. For 1970 and 1975, projections more than ten years old were not consistently accurate.

Once the maximum time span of reliable forecasts is established, the important question becomes whether to produce forecasts of even greater length, on the grounds that some idea of the distant future, no matter how uncertain, is better than none. This question must be posed in terms of the usefulness of very long-range forecasts, as well as in terms of accuracy.

The catch is that the presentation of very long-range forecasts affects the plausibility of the whole set of forecasts. The overall correctness of a given projection series is often evaluated in terms of the plausibility of its longest forecasts. For population forecasting, the short term is simply more predictable. It is clear that the accuracy of short- and medium-term forecasts is not necessarily associated with the accuracy of long-range forecasts. Both Pritchett and Pearl produced remarkably accurate five-, ten-, and even twenty-year forecasts, but their forecasts for 1960 and 1970 were highly inaccurate. Either of these methods could be rejected in terms of their long-range results; Pearl predicted that U.S. population would never exceed 197 million, and Pritchett predicted for the 2900 a population level of 40 *billion* Americans. It is ironic that Pearl himself debunked Pritchett's approach by pointing out how ludicrous the *ultimate* implications of Pritchett's method were.[13] The lesson seems to be that, since projections *will* be judged and accepted according to their overall plausibility, the forecaster is well advised to confine his projections to only that period for which he believes projections are useful. It will always be tempting to allow a promising method to churn out its projections indefinitely into the future, but these most distant forecasts could well jeopardize the credibility of the entire endeavor. By foregoing the very distant projections, the forecaster's short-term and medium-term projections will stand untainted by what may be seen as absurd long-range guesses.

PROSPECTS FOR POPULATION
FORECASTING

Compared to the bold, if sometimes incorrect, assumptions of earlier forecasters, today's projection methods seem somehow sterile. Indeed, the multicategory method currently in use is more of an accounting system than a means of selecting population growth assumptions. The current method is certainly indisputable as far as it goes, since the disaggregation of population into cohorts, and of population growth into components, "costs" nothing in terms of adding potentially unwarranted assumptions to the analysis.

From the technical point of view, demographic projection methodology has continually improved. The most significant improvement has been the progressive refinement in the choice of basic behavior upon which trend assumptions must be made. Accounting methods that can convert basic information (such as age-specific fertility rates) into total population growth patterns for a given population structure allow forecasters to focus their assumptions on the most basic behavioral indicators—namely, age-specific fertility and mortality rates—rather than on cruder indicators such as total fertility rates, general birth rates, or even general growth rates.

Nevertheless, accounting methods have not eliminated the necessity of assuming a future trend in *some* factor. Even perfect accounting devices cannot fully correct the errors in the core of any projection—the assumptions of the future trends in basic behavior. Given age-specific fertility and mortality rates, accurate population projections can be generated to any point in the future. But where are these fertility and mortality rates coming from? Too often they are derived from the most primitive assumption, that "all trends will continue as they are now," and are then hidden by elaborate methods.

The cohort-component method permits a careful accounting of trends, but the modern forecaster still must wrestle with the same demographic assumptions that his predecessors faced. He must generate "mini-projections" for each of his many cohort-components. If he simply takes current fertility and mortality schedules and applies them iteratively, he will make Dublin and Lotka's very strong assumption of a constant, inherent capacity for fertility; if the forecaster does not assume constant fertility, he must decide which trends manifested in existing data for each cohort-component will continue in the future. Thus, even though the modern methods are more sophisticated in their disaggregation of population growth, the forecaster still faces the dilemma of whether current trends are "noise" or significant changes.

Consequently, the real progress in population forecasting will come not in the further elaboration of technique, which is even now adequate to accurately and consistently trace out the implications of given fertility and mortality assumptions. It will come via studies of the social, economic, and technological determinants of fertility and mortality.

The social and economic factors that affect family size and longevity have been examined in great detail through the decennial censuses and the special studies and surveys of the Census Bureau. Urbanization, economic prosperity, and the like have had easily discernable effects. However, to capitalize on these indicators of demographic change in the prediction of future population patterns, it is also necessary to forecast the trends of these social and economic conditions. Thus, demographic forecasting, though the most basic forecasting task, is heavily dependent on the ability to forecast these other trends.

The importance of technological forecasting to demographic projection rests on two potentials: effective birth control and dramatic medical advances. So far, the problematic aspect of population forecasting has been the fertility rate, since mortality and migration have changed only very gradually. The alteration of fertility rates involves not only strictly technical developments in prophylaxis, but also changing social mores concerning contraception and abortion. It is a telling commentary on the difficulty in predicting the technical side of contraception that a multiexpert Rand Corporation study of future technological innovation, conducted in 1963 and published in 1964, produced a median prediction of 1970 as the date of the advent of "effective fertility control by oral contraceptive or other simple and inexpensive means."[14] In fact, Ovulin was introduced in 1964, the very year in which the survey was conducted.

Mortality factors, though of modest importance to date, may become extremely important for population predictions if major causes of death are eliminated or dramatically reduced through medical advances. Several forecasting efforts on the future of medicine have predicted the eradication of such major diseases as cancer, diabetes, hepatitis, and thrombosis by the 1980s.[15] These life-prolonging breakthroughs, as well as the devices, laws, and customs governing birth control, are largely discrete events, however. Therefore, population projections that must hinge ultimately on these predictions are particularly perilous. One combination of events—e.g., the inability to overcome any of the major diseases and the perfection of even more effective birth control—would yield a very different population picture than would other plausible combinations. When one considers that this relatively new technological dimension of population growth contributes its own uncertainty to the continuing uncertainties of social, economic, and cultural change, the outlook for more impressive population forecasting is not promising.

CHAPTER 4

ECONOMIC FORECASTING

Economic forecasting has acquired importance and even a certain mystique over the years through its connection with high finance, fortunes won or lost, and the cruciality of economic trends for the social and political life of the nation. Economic forecasting is by far the most institutionalized projection task. Not only are numerous public and private organizations devoted to the routinized production of economic forecasts, but there are also routinized compilations of these forecasts.[1] Heavily funded research projects are engaged in the search for more reliable techniques. Economic forecasting has become a distinct subfield to a much greater extent than demographic or energy forecasting; its technical literature is on a par with that of the technological forecasting discipline. But economic forecasting has also acquired a mixed reputation for reliability. In terms of conveying the implications of different approaches and the confidence limits appropriate for each type of forecast, a gap is growing between the forecaster and the policy-maker.

Intellectually, the pursuit of economic forecasting has been fascinating because of two tensions in the way economists over the years have attacked the forecasting problem. Tension exists between the approaches that attempt to capture the complexity of the economic system, and those that search for simple and immutable economic relationships or rhythms that would permit forecasters to cut through the complexity. Tension also exists between the approaches directed at the systematic improvement of methodology through the "scientific method" of testing the results of explicit procedures, and the approaches employing judgment to capitalize on experts' experience and intuition.

The policy-maker may appreciate the intellectual diversity of economic forecasting in the abstract, but may find this a hindrance in the practical search for forecasts that best suit his purposes. Such intellectual tensions create corresponding problems for policy-makers trying to gauge the general reliability of economic forecasting and the comparative advantages of specific methods. The assumptions and reasoning involved in a specific application of judgmental forecasting are inaccessible to the policy-maker, but this also holds for very complicated procedures such as econometric models, which modelers themselves often find difficult to analyze. The simplest procedures, which include theories of unvarying cycles and fixed sequences of trends, rest on arguable assumptions about the nature and regularity of economic phenomena. A policy-maker who is not an economic theorist cannot be expected to resolve issues that have kept prominent theorists arguing for generations. It is difficult enough—though very important—for the policy-maker simply to keep track of the key assumptions that are embedded in the techniques employed by economic forecasters. Thus, policy-makers are not in a position to evaluate different approaches on theoretical grounds.

Difficulties in appraising the theoretical underpinnings of forecasting procedures have long affected the credibility of economic predictions. Esoteric methods have been ridiculed, even though some have proved to be correct in their predictions. John Kenneth Galbraith relates an example of R. Babson's predictions of the Great Depression, which were ignored because of the unorthodox methods he used to derive them:

> The methods by which he reached his conclusions were a problem. They involved a hocus-pocus of lines and arcs on a chart. Intuition, and possibly even mysticism played a part. Those who employed rational, objective and scientific methods were naturally uneasy about Babson, although their methods failed to foretell the crash. In these matters, it is far, far better to be wrong in a respectable way than to be right for the wrong reasons.[2]

Appraisal on grounds of performance also can be problematic, particularly when only parts of the performance record are examined. While implausibility is one obstacle to credibility, methods are more often abandoned when they lead to dramatic errors, usually at the threshold of major changes in the structure of the economy—precisely when the forecasting task is most difficult. Thus the "Harvard ABC curve" approach, a forerunner of the leading-indicator approach used today, was abandoned when it failed to predict the 1929 crash.[3] The labor market analyses used during World War II to predict the postwar economy were discredited when the predicted depression did not materialize.[4] Most recently, signs of disillusionment with the econometric modeling approach can be detected among forecasters (though not yet among forecast-users) because of its failure to predict the economic downturns of the 1970s.[5]

However, prominent failures are not typical failures. Therefore, to abandon a particular method, or to downgrade forecasting in general, because of highly publicized shortcomings in periods of radical change, is to respond to the exceptional case rather than to the routine situation, for which the bulk of forecasts are made. A forecasting procedure can be valued for its ability to operate in the generally short (but important) periods of crisis, or in the longer periods of noncrisis, depending on the specific purposes for which the forecasts are used. In any event, the general record of forecasting performance, rather than the unrepresentative instances of notable failures (or successes), provides a more balanced appraisal of the value of forecasting.

The uses and methods of economic forecasting vary considerably according to the length of the forecast. Short-term forecasting, which is usually defined as forecasting with a time horizon of less than two years, is used extensively in making immediate business and economic policy decisions. Long-term forecasting, which in practice usually implies time horizons of five years or more, enters into long-range corporate and governmental planning, and also serves as a basis for the prediction of other trends. With the exception of econometric models, which recently have been applied to long-term as well as short-term forecasting, the approaches to long- and short-term forecasting are quite different. For this reason, the records of short-term and long-term economic forecasting are treated separately in this chapter. The performance of short-term forecasting is analyzed with particular attention to the relative contributions of different methods. In the case of long-term economic forecasting, for which the methods are much more mixed, and often unspecified, performance is evaluated with a greater emphasis on the overall levels of accuracy.

SHORT-TERM ECONOMIC FORECASTING

Short-term economic forecasting has become a very big business, despite the scanty and rather inaccessible evidence of its reliability. American corporations spend a great deal of money on economic forecasts. In March 1975, *Fortune* reported that three of the most prominent econometric modeling operations—the Wharton Economic Forecasting Unit (headed by Lawrence Klein), Data Resources, Inc. (led by Otto Eckstein), and Chase Econometrics (headed by Michael Evans)—have corporate clients who pay more than $10 million annually to receive quarterly forecasts and participate in seminars on the economic outlook.[6] Considering that this is a conservative figure derived from the basic rates for clients (excluding extra charges for specialized forecasts), and does not include the revenues of other private forecasting services such as General Electric's MAPCAST and the University of Michigan's annual economic outlook seminars, the total easily exceeds $20 million annually.

Moreover, most large corporations and many governmental units also have their own forecasting staffs, which develop specialized projections relevant to each organization's activities and resource needs. The federal government supports the economic forecasting efforts of the Commerce Department's Bureau of Economic Analysis (formerly the Office of Business Economics), the attempts at judgmental and econometric-model forecasting by the Federal Reserve Board, and the projections of the Council of Economic Advisors. The forecasting operations of such agencies as the Federal Aviation Administration, the Federal Highway Administration, and the Federal Energy Administration require short-term economic forecasts in projecting trends that depend on the economic context.

61

Considering the profusion of economic forecasts and the money spent in preparing and purchasing them, it is not surprising that short-term economic forecasts have become a standard tool for many policy-makers—or at least an available tool. The problem for most policy-makers is not a shortage of economic forecasts, but rather a lack of guidelines as to what magnitudes of errors the available forecasts are likely to have. The logic behind an economic forecast, particularly if it is generated by a complex model, is usually too inaccessible to the policy-maker for him to be in a position to evaluate its *a priori* plausibility. Different methods or models that make the same core assumptions about the social and political context (including governmental policy) can produce different forecasts. Consequently, policy-makers can easily obtain forecasts, but cannot easily determine to what extent they should accept them.

The faith of policy-makers and the general public in the reliability of short-term economic forecasting has been influenced by the difficulties encountered in predicting the onset and economic aftermath of the 1973 energy crisis. Economic forecasts since 1973 have been relatively inaccurate. Stephen McNees, who has monitored the record of prominent economic forecasting efforts, reports that "economic forecasters have come under a barrage of criticism for their performance for the 1974–75 recession. Their record over the early 1970s shows that those errors were unprecedented in magnitude. . . ."[7] However, the significance of this failure is difficult to determine. Have sufficient modifications been made in the forecasters' theories (both explicit and implicit) to avoid such failures in the future? Was the "economic structure" altered significantly, such that accurate forecasting for this period was too much to ask? To what extent can the policy-maker trust the forecasts he has to deal with today, now that the change in economic structure (if, indeed, there has been one) is apparently accomplished?

Important questions can also be raised with respect to the methodology of the forecasts. Although the typical policy-maker has neither the time nor the specialized expertise to check each forecast step-by-step in great detail, he can easily determine the broad methodology employed in making the forecast. If a particular approach proves to be consistently superior to others, as demonstrated by its record in previous forecasts, even a policy-maker without specialized expertise in economic forecasting can choose it from among the large number of methods available. This is not to say that the past record of a particular approach will necessarily be duplicated in the future, but, without evidence to the contrary, a relatively successful approach is obviously a good bet for continued relative success.

Just as important is the need for the policy-maker to have sufficient mastery over the techniques employed by the forecasters to be able to discover the basic assumptions implicit in, and sometimes masked by, the overlay of methodology. The importance of the validity of key assumptions in determining the accuracy of forecasts—which is the most important lesson to be drawn form this examination of many fields of forecasting—means that the policy-maker's consideration of these assumptions is the best "plausibility check" he has for establishing his confidence in the forecast.

Finally, the policy-maker must balance the gains in short-term forecast accuracy with the financial costs of the forecasts, the time required to prepare them, and the limitations in the policy-maker's flexibility to get answers for specific questions he has about the future.

TECHNIQUES OF SHORT-TERM ECONOMIC FORECASTING

Economic forecasting for the "short term"—usually less than two years—has special significance in the debate over the methodology of forecasting. The shortness of "short-term" highlights the time constraints involved in preparing a forecast, and thereby emphasizes the question of how much "theoretical content" ought to be part of the forecasting effort. Must a fundamental, systematic, theoretical approach to understanding the dynamics of economic change be abandoned because of the sheer impossibility of accomplishing "fundamental" analysis in the time allotted? If so, the "quick-and-dirty" methods of extrapolation, quick judgment, and rules of thumb will emerge as the best that can be done. If not, some means of packaging fundamental understanding into a mechanism capable of producing forecasts rapidly will have to be found. Martin Shubik pointed out in 1966 that the "chartists"—those who forecast by extending curves and lines (the term is taken from stock market forecasting)—cannot be dismissed lightly simply because of their lack of attention to fundamental mechanisms underlying the phenomena they address. "Chartists" can make their forecasts quickly, whereas a "fundamentalist" might take far too long: "A chartist can come up with some sort of fairytale in ten or fifteen minutes. If you do not have more time, perhaps that is the best you can get. We have a simple fundamentalist approach for being dead right about the year 2000. We could spend the next thirty-four years studying the year 2000 and issue our report on January 1 of that year."[8]

The fundamentalists' answer is the econometric model: "Instead of throwing away yesterday's knowledge, we should try to build methods that utilize it in a more or less automated manner. . . . We gradually build an incremental systematic process that involves, among other things, linking large data-processing procedures with models or conceptual frameworks."[9] Thus, the challenge centers on the question of whether econometric models, which certainly can spew out forecasts rapidly, actually embody (or can embody) fundamental understanding of economic behavior.

At first glance it would appear that the forecasting performance of existing econometric models could answer this question. But, in fact, two problems are involved in relating the performance of econometric models to the question of whether they have the potential to combine fundamental understanding and the capability of "instant analysis." The first problem is simply that current models can always be regarded as preliminary; models are always under development. The second, and more serious, problem is that econometric models can be interpreted in two very different ways. They can be accepted at face value—as explicit theory of how the economy is believed to behave and therefore of how the forecasts are actually made. Alternatively, the models can be regarded as "black boxes" that permit their operators' own *ad hoc* judgments to appear as the output of awesome technological sophistication. The latter view reflects the fact that, in economic forecasting, as in other forecasting fields, practical approaches generally comprise some *mixture* of techniques. Nevertheless, bearing in mind that eclectic approaches are the rule rather than the exception, it is possible both to categorize these practical mixes in terms of which techniques predominate and to judge their performance.

The prevalent short-term economic forecasting techniques, in descending order of current use,[10] are the *judgmental* approach, which covers the whole gamut of nonexplicit inferences; the *econometric-modeling* approach, which employs formal econometric models; and the *indicators* approach, which employs preselected economic trends as leading signals of economic expansions and contractions. The time spans covered by "short-term" economic forecasting are too short for extrapolation and other simple trend-extending techniques to be very attractive. Although extrapolations are often used as benchmarks in evaluating the performance of other short-term forecasting techniques, and sometimes do the job better,[11] practicing forecasters generally rely on more complex techniques that incorporate more information, theory, or intuition.

The Judgmental Approach. As with all judgmental approaches to forecasting, the rationale behind the use of judgment in economic forecasting is that the human mind is the most sensitive and comprehensive evaluator of the diverse evidence on what the future holds. The fact that all of the logic behind judgmental conclusions cannot be stated explicitly is, according to this rationale, an inevitable result of the intricacy and subtlety of human thought and intuition, rather than a limitation of the method.

Critics of the judgmental approach point out that judgment unaided by explicit procedures has no way of systematically determining why forecasts go wrong. Consequently, there is little reason to expect that judgmental forecasting will improve much in the future, because of the inherent limitations on intuitive understanding of the complicated processes that comprise the economic system. Judgmental economic forecasting, which does not entail high operating costs, will continue to be a favorite standby, unless more explicit methods prove to be more accurate and reliable. This is not to say, however, that mistakes produced through judgmental economic forecasting are any less costly to the policy-maker than mistakes produced through other techniques.

Econometric Modeling. In the 1950s a dramatically new approach to economic forecasting emerged from earlier attempts to describe the entire economy as a set of mathematical equations. In 1939 the Dutch economist Jan Tinbergen developed a tentative model of the U.S. economy which demonstrated that a plausible description of the important aspects of macroeconomic behavior can be encompassed by a fairly small set of equations.[12] Like all the models following it, Tinbergen's model was produced by specifying, on the basis of theory or observation, plausible relationships among economic variables such as prices, wages, investment levels, and so on. The equations that relate time-specific levels of these variables with one another involve a number of constants (or parameters) set statistically at values that enable the model to reproduce *past* patterns of the economic process most accurately.

Tinbergen's model was presented in almost narrative form, with the introduction of each equation (or family of equations) sandwiched between explanatory prose. Thus, it was a heuristic and theoretical exercise, and did not yield a complete, well-specified model that could actually convert initial-condition inputs into outputs describing how the economy would behave. Since that time, however, better historical data, technical advances in mathematical economics and statistics (econometrics), and the advent of computers have made the operation of elaborate explicit models feasible, though expensive.

Econometric models consist of equations that determine the values of important economic variables for a given point in time by relating them to current or previous values of other variables. Thus, the value of each variable calculated within the model (endogenous variable) is updated by each complete sequence of the model, on the basis of some combination of its previous value, other endogenous variables, and given values for variables not calculated in the model (exogenous variables). There are two sorts of equations: *identities,* which express relations that are true by definition (e.g., "total spending equals governmental spending plus nongovernmental spending"); and *behavioral equations,* which express empirical propositions on how the economy behaves (e.g., "consumption equals some constant multiplied by disposable income"). Obviously the behavioral equations are the heart of any econometric model. The number of behavioral equations establishes the intricacy of the model, and the kinds of variables involved in the behavioral equations convey the theoretical orientation of the modelers (e.g., monetarists' models give greater emphasis to monetary factors).

Each behavioral equation has three aspects: the nature of the variables, the form (or structure) of the equation, and, in order to operate the model, the values for the constants (parameters) involved in the equation. For example, consumption may be predicted from disposable income, but how? One of the many means of relating consumption to disposable income is the simple form "consumption equals a constant (i.e., parameter) multiplied by disposable income." But what is this constant? While in theory parameters can be chosen theoretically or even arbitrarily, in practice they are estimated by determining statistically which values for the model's parameters allow the model to conform most closely to some set of actual historical data. Therefore, the model's performance in "predicting" the pattern of this parameter-estimation period can be very misleading, since the parameters are deliberately chosen to force the model to fit that period. With enough parameters to manipulate, any model can be made to fit a given historical sequence, regardless of how well that model works for other time periods. The accuracy of a model in reproducing the results of the parameter-estimation period is likely to be considerably greater than its accuracy in forecasting future trends, for which the parameters already estimated for the model may not fit as well.

An unlimited number of models, differing in the nature of their variables and the relationships among variables, can account for any given pattern of past economic trends. At the option of the model-builder, factors such as inventories, specific industry patterns, or money supply can be emphasized or completely ignored. The selection of parameters to mold the model's output most closely to historical data makes this flexibility possible.

In view of this potential diversity in models adequate for explaining past patterns, the similarity of most econometric models is quite striking. The reason for this similarity is not to be found in the scarcity of other plausible possibilities. Rather, it stems from the fact that the models grew out of a common tradition best characterized by the work of Klein and Goldberger, who, along with a host of other economists, integrated Keynesian economics and sophisticated technique into the basic approach of Tinbergen.[13] Subsequent models have been elaborated and (presumably) refined, primarily through the more extensive disaggregation of variables for which finer historical data have become available. Nonetheless, the approach and the choice of variables have been so similar that it is appropriate to speak of most econometric models as comprising a single "family" of models. In fact, development of the prominent econometric models has been a nearly communal enterprise by a limited number of economists, whose names frequently overlap in the "authorship" of the various models. This overlap of modelers does not detract from the quality of the models; indeed, it is a rare opportunity for experimentation with variants of the same basic theme. What it does mean is that the forecasts emanating from the majority of prominent econometric models are not strictly distinct or independent judgments.

Nevertheless, the developers of econometric models do disagree on some important points. A vew models reflect another theoretical orientation: the so-called monetarist position, as opposed to the Keynesian structuralist orientation of the bulk of the models of the Klein-Goldberger tradition. Monetarist models place the rate of expansion of the money supply at the heart of their behavioral equations. Keynesian models emphasize fiscal policy (i.e., governmental expenditures) in establishing demand, production, employment, and so on, and relegate monetary expansion to a secondary or superficial position in the causal network of economic forces.

The appropriate size of econometric models also is a major point of contention. The size of a model represents its elaborateness and intricacy, and therefore engages the debate over the comparative advantages of parsimony versus complication. Larger models, with more variables and more equations, are more complete descriptions of the entire economic system.[14] A majority of the prominent models have been enlarged in an effort to refine and elaborate the earliest models, which were basically experimental efforts designed to demonstrate that "it could be done." Thus, the early (1960) Duesenberry-Eckstein-Fromm model, with only twenty-eight equations, gave way to Eckstein's DRI model of 368 equations, as well as the 226-equation Brookings model developed by Duesenberry, Fromm, and others. The OBE, Michigan, and Wharton models also were enlarged over time, as were the Liu model (transformed into the Liu-Hwa monthly model) and the 1963 Evans model (elaborated for Chase Econometrics).[15]

On the other hand, some fairly recent models have been formulated on the principle that simplicity is superior because it excludes the extraneous factors that cloud the effects of important factors. Simplicity, it has been argued, keeps a model manageable and permits the modeler to evaluate the plausibility of the interactions among variables that the model specifies. This has been the rationale of the small model of Friend and Taubman and the more recent model of Ray Fair.[16] Understandably, simpler models are preferred by economists who advocate simpler economic theories. Thus, the monetarists Leonall Anderson and Keith Carlson have developed an extremely "small" model of only eight equations, known as the St. Louis Federal Reserve Bank "reduced" model.[17] An earlier model by Gallaway and Smith, published in 1961, was able to make do with only five explanatory variables because of its heavy reliance on the money supply variable.[18]

Finally, there is some disagreement among modelers on whether the forecaster's "judgment" should play a part even in the operation—as distinct from the creation—of the econometric model. Econometric models are not different from other methods merely because a computer is generally used in their operation; given enough manpower and time, these models *could* be operated by hand. All the computer provides is the capacity to do many calculations quickly. What really distinguishes the econometric models is their explicitness of procedure.

The forecasting model, particularly if it is to employ a computer for its calculations, must be absolutely explicit in the operations involved; the computer can do only precisely what it is asked to do. Therefore, the computer model cuts off intuition, which is involved in the creation of the model itself (i.e., in the selection of variables and relationships), at the point of actually running the model. This means that the outcomes of the forecasting efforts are not necessarily known in advance by the forecaster or the programmer, since very surprising results can emerge from the intricate interactions of the equations included in the model. Once the model's output is determined, however, intuition may re-enter in the forecaster's interpretation of the results and in his decision to accept or reject the model's projections.

Thus, in the actual formulation of *most* econometric-model forecasts, judgment and intuition play an important role. The modelers' reliance on judgment is strikingly illustrated by the paradox of the superiority of *ex ante* forecasts. Numerous studies have shown that, contrary to expectations, short-term economic forecasts that require the forecaster to project the values for exogenous variables often are much more accurate than parallel forecasts that incorporate the *actual* values for these exogenous variables.[19] Since the former, *ex ante* forecasts are subject to errors in projecting the exogenous variables, one would expect them to be less accurate than the *ex post* forecasts, which by definition are free of these errors.

The resolution of this paradox lies in how the exogenous variables' values are determined by forecasters making *ex ante* forecasts with econometric models. While the need to make such projections puts an extra burden on the forecaster, it also gives him great flexibility to bring his model's forecasts into line with his own judgment. As Bert Hickman notes, greater accuracy emerges from

changing the preliminary assumptions on exogenous variables and constants until the resulting forecast falls within the range thought to be reasonable—which is principally responsible for the improvement in ex ante forecasts. From this point of view, the model serves primarily to assess judgmentally the general implications of the forecaster's assumptions on future exogenous developments, including his ad hoc adjustments for anticipated changes in structure since the sample period, and for the correction of apparent specification errors."[20]

When the forecaster does not have the opportunity to pick exogenous values that make the model's results reasonable, econometric models generally do worse than either judgmental forecasts made without econometric models or simple extrapolation mechanisms, as indicated by the poor performance of *ex post* forecasts. However, this does not mean that forecasting with econometric models is inferior, or that this effort is somehow fraudulent because judgment enters into it. Rather, it means that econometric forecasting is really a "package" consisting of the model and the forecaster interacting in a fairly complicated fashion. Most econometric models are not fully automated machines producing forecasts without the aid of a human operator.

A few modelers, of whom the most articulate is Ray Fair, take the position that, unless econometric models *are* fully automated, they are little more than window dressing for the judgment of their operators.[21] These modelers might argue that the poorer performance of *ex post* forecasts demonstrates not the need for judgment, but rather the need to improve the specifications of models that produce poor results without the aid of judgmental adjustments.

The actual performance of judgment-free econometric models can be evaluated from the records of independent efforts at forecasting with "pure" models, for which exogenous variables are provided mechanically rather than by the forecaster's judgment of "what will work." The Fair model was specifically designed to test how well the explicit econometric model *per se* can predict future economic trends. It is a rather simple model (though in the Keynesian, structuralist tradition) that provides its own estimates of exogenous values. The Bureau of Economic Analysis (BEA, formerly OBE) operates two versions of a larger model: one with the usual input of judgment in the choice of exogenous values, but another with a mechanical procedure for choosing exogenous values.

The Indicators Approach. The indicators approach is based on the premise that interactions among different aspects of economic activity are consistent enough to establish regular sequences of economic "events" (i.e., changes in the direction or rates of various trends).[22] If these sequences are regular, some events—such as increases or decreases in inventories, the number of new businesses formed, or the money supply—will consistently signal *subsequent* changes in trends worth predicting: GNP, employment, inflation, and so on. Changes in leading indicators must also precede these shifts in other trends by *uniform* intervals from one business cycle to another; otherwise, the indicators may signal a major economic change but fail to predict *when* the change is to occur. Therefore, the success of forecasting with leading indicators depends on the uniformity of the dynamics of business cycles from one point in time to another.

The search for consistent leading indicators can be conducted either theoretically or empirically. Economic *theories* of the business cycle dynamic can yield propositions as to which events will regularly precede others. Empirically, the time-series patterns of all recorded trends can be examined to identify those which qualify as leading indicators. The most prominent lists of business cycle indicators, those produced periodically by the National Bureau of Economic Research, basically have been developed through the empirical approach. The first NBER list, compiled by Wesley Mitchell and Arthur Burns in 1938, was based on a study of about 500 series; later lists were compiled from 800 series.[23] According to NBER procedure, the most consistent indicators are chosen through this empirical examination of time series, but are then scored not only in terms of their consistency level, but also according to their theoretical importance, their ready availability, and the length of lead time in advance of the changes predicted.[24]

The validity of the indicators approach in making predictions for a given future period depends on whether the historical sequences still pertain. The mere fact that 20 or 30 indicators, out of a total pool of more than 800, turn out to be highly correlated with historical fluctuations in GNP does not necessarily mean that they are fundamental or predictive of future cycles, especially when fundamental changes in economic structure—and therefore in economic dynamics—are or will be occurring.

PROBLEMS IN APPRAISING SHORT-TERM ECONOMIC FORECASTS

The appraisal of short-term economic forecasts is complicated by the vastness of the economic forecasting effort, the multiplicity of forecasting tasks and appraisal criteria, and the different degrees of predictability of different historical periods and time spans. These complications require some standardization and reduction in the forecasting tasks appraised and in the accuracy measures used to evaluate them.

Economic forecasting often involves predicting many economic trends—gross national product, industrial production, investment, inflation, and so on—all of which are important for governmental and private policy-makers. However, to limit the appraisal task to manageable dimensions, this study focuses on gross national product forecasting. In its current-dollar (nominal) and constant-dollar (real) forms, GNP is the most inclusive economic trend. Not only is it the most frequently and prominently forecasted economic trend, but its forecast errors generally correspond to and reflect forecasting errors on other, less aggregated levels. Although the errors of individual components of GNP logically need not correspond to errors in total GNP (since separate component errors could offset one another when aggregated to the level of GNP), in fact the accuracy of forecasts of other economic trends (such as industrial production) has been found to be roughly the same as that of GNP forecasts.[25]

GNP forecasts may project either the level of GNP or the change in GNP. The record of forecasting GNP *change* is more meaningful, however, because any error in forecasting GNP change is due exclusively to mistakes in anticipating future economic trends, while an error in predicting levels of GNP may also result from mistakes in estimating the GNP level at the time the forecast is made. Moreover, the change in GNP, rather than its absolute level, expresses how the economy is performing. The advances and declines in gross national product are more relevant than the magnitude of GNP *per se*.

GNP forecasts are made for a multiplicity of time spans. Some cover spans of from one to six quarters; some are strictly annual (often made at the end of the previous calendar year); one econometric model (by Ta-Chung Liu and

70

Erh-Cheng Hwa of Cornell) even forecasts by monthly intervals. The present study is confined to quarterly and annual forecasts because they are the most commonly used intervals and because they represent the "very short" and the "fairly long" short-term forecasts.

Since the GNP level at any point in time is a specific quantity (revisions notwithstanding), quantitative measurement of the errors in GNP forecasts is of obvious applicability. However, unlike the trends in population and technological progress, GNP has not been a continually increasing quantity, because of business cycle patterns. Therefore, correctness in predicting the *direction* of change in GNP also can serve as a basis for evaluating economic forecasts, and indeed is the only alternative when forecasts are expressed only in terms of the direction of change.

Quantitative errors in economic forecasts have been expressed in two ways. The most straightforward error measure is the average of absolute differences between the forecast and the actual value. Underestimates and overestimates are treated equally by adding the magnitude of the error, regardless of sign, to the total absolute error, which is then divided by the number of forecasts to obtain the *average absolute error*.

The other, slightly more complicated error measure is the *root-mean-square error*, which is the square root of the average squared error. This measure, which is used mainly because of its tractability for statistical analysis (e.g., it can be "decomposed" neatly into the errors caused by bias, random error, and inefficiency),[26] has less intuitive appeal. It is calculated by summing the squared errors produced by the discrepancies between actual and forecasted values, dividing this total by the number of forecasts to get the average, and finally taking the square root of this average to offset the previous squaring operation. The resulting measure is always at least as great as the average absolute error for the same set of forecasts. It also gives extra weight to the largest errors of a set of forecasts, so that a set with more extreme errors (even though offset by greater accuracy in its other forecasts) will have a higher root-mean-square error than another set of forecasts with the same average absolute error.[27]

Either of these measures used alone would be an adequate indication of inaccuracy. In almost all cases, the greater the average absolute error of a set of forecasts, the greater the root-mean-square error. However, some important error analyses have been carried out with each of these measures, and, unfortunately, conversion from one measure to the other (without raw data) is impossible. Consequently, both error measures are employed in the following appraisal, thereby permitting a larger number of studies to be included.[28]

Ironically, evidence on the forecasting accuracy of econometric models has been inaccessible to policy-makers primarily because relevant tests are often buried among a slew of other tests. Economists have subjected econometric models to a large battery of tests that are not relevant to evaluating the practical utility of econometric models as forecasting instruments. For example, all of the well-known models have been applied to the time period from which their parameters were estimated. They have also been run with the *correct* values for the exogenous factors (*ex post*) after these values become historical fact. Both tests help to evaluate the theoretical validity of the models, but are *not* equivalent to running the models for the time periods *outside* the parameter-estimation period and predicting the values of exogenous variables (*ex ante*).[29] Applying the model to the parameter-estimation period determines how well the model fits the historical data upon which it is based, but does not gauge the model's effectiveness in forecasting economic trends for other periods, for which those particular parameters *may* not be correct. The *ex post* forecasts can isolate errors due strictly to the equations of the model, but by the same token they disregard the errors arising from the failure to correctly project the exogenous variables. In light of these considerations, the "true" test of an econometric model's actual utility in forecasting (though not necessarily its theoretical validity) is its accuracy in predicting *ex ante* for periods outside the parameter-estimation period.

Often the indicator approach is not used to make quantitative forecasts. Since the approach relies on some—but not all—of the factors affecting economic activity, indicator forecasters usually do not attempt to make precise estimates of future GNP, industrial activity, and the like; the left-out factors are likely to have some impact that cannot be captured by the indicators used by the approach.[30] Instead, the indicator approach is devoted primarily to predicting the *direction* of economic change. Leading indicators are used to forecast whether and when economic downturns will occur or recoveries will ensue. Lagging indicators are used to confirm the continuation or turning points of aggregate trends (like GNP) after the fact, but before reliable data on the aggregate trends themselves become available. Consequently, the primary challenge of the indicator approach is to predict the occurrence (or absence) of turning points, a task also accomplished by the other economic forecasting approaches incidentally as they are applied to the prediction of quantitative levels. While the prediction of direction of economic trends obviously conveys less information than the prediction of specific levels, the direction of change is obviously of greater relevance than the magnitude of the change.

Precisely when an economic turning point is reached is a matter of some debate. The National Bureau of Economic Research, which provides more-or-less official datings for business cycle turning points, admits to the uncertainty of dating these reversals and to the arbitrariness of some of the dates ultimately chosen as peaks or troughs.[31] Therefore, the ability to predict the exact month in which the turning point will occur is not as meaningful as the ability to predict a turning point within a span of several months.

One reasonable test of the ability to anticipate future turning points is the probability that, three months prior to an actual turning point, the forecaster can predict that a turning point will occur within six months after the prediction is made. This test is useful because (a) it does not require the forecaster to predict exactly which month will mark the turning point; (b) it incorporates a time horizon—six months—which is reasonable from the policy-maker's point of view and (c) some data are available for this test.

A less stringent test is the ability to predict a turning point at any time within the coming year. This test can be applied to forecasting efforts that project monthly, quarterly, or semiannual figures at least a year into the future.[32] The ability to predict a turnabout in economic trends within the coming year obviously would be useful for policy-makers in charge of economic policy, as well as for those who plan activities or facilities whose usefulness depends on the level of economic activity (such as expansions of energy facilities). Some data on this test also are available.

ACCURACY OF SHORT-TERM ECONOMIC FORECASTS

Since 1968 the forecasting records of about fifty separate forecasting operations have been compiled by the American Statistical Association and the National Bureau of Economic Research. The accuracy of the median forecasts has been analyzed in several studies and represents the median forecast errors of a broad sample of prominent forecasters using various methods.[33] According to Su and Su, the root-mean-square errors in 1958 dollars for the period from late 1968 to mid-1973 were $3.0 billion and $6.1 billion for quarterly and annual nominal-GNP forecasts, and $3.4 billion and $7.0 billion for quarterly and annual real-GNP predictions. The average absolute errors for the ASA-NBER median forecasts for the somewhat later (but overlapping) period from mid-1970 to mid-1975 were $3.4 billion and $9.5 billion for the quarterly and annual nominal-GNP forecasts and $4.3 and $11.8 billion for the real-GNP forecasts. Since average absolute errors are never greater than the corresponding root-mean-square errors, the most recent period must have been more difficult to forecast, particularly for the annual predictions.

The seriousness of these errors can be evaluated in terms of the magnitude of typical quarter-to-quarter or year-to-year changes in the levels of real and nominal GNP. In the last half of the 1960s (i.e., 1965–69), the average change in nominal GNP was $12.8 billion in 1958 dollars quarterly and $50.1 billion annually. For real GNP, which does not reflect inflationary expansion, the changes were $6.8 billion and $27.0 billion. During the first half of the

73

1970s (i.e., 1970–74), the nominal-GNP changes were somewhat higher; $16.1 billion and $62.3 billion. The real-GNP changes were $8.1 billion and 24.3 billion for this recent period.[34]

The errors generally encountered constitute about a quarter of the magnitude of change for nominal quarterly forecasts, and about an eighth of the change for nominal annual forecasts. The inflationary trend apparently provides some assured predictability for the annual forecasts of current-dollar GNP. However, for real-GNP predictions, the relative errors are much more serious because the actual changes have been considerably lower. The quarterly errors are nearly half as great as the quarterly changes, and the annual errors are about a third as great as the annual changes.

The generally greater proportional accuracy of annual forecasts over quarterly forecasts illustrates the limits of the general rule that recency increases accuracy. The reason for this "paradox" lies in the nature of the reality rather than the nature of the forecasting task. Even when seasonally adjusted, the quarterly pattern of GNP is very unstable. It reflects the short-lived effects of inventory shifts, temporary bottlenecks, strikes, and so on. Within a year's time many of these effects are compensated for or balanced out, which leaves the annual change in GNP to reflect the longer, smoother patterns of growth or decline. Long-term business cycles, depending on selection criteria and historical interpretation, have run from ten to thirty years, with fairly smooth annual patterns predominating between the turnaround periods. Thus, while the quarterly trends show a "saw-tooth" pattern, the annual trends smooth out these temporary fluctuations and are, therefore, more "predictable."

Even though the proportional errors of annual forecasts are smaller than those of quarterly forecasts, it is still true that the absolute discrepancies of the longer forecasts are greater. Therefore, recency is an important asset for relatively accurate forecasting. In other words, because the accuracy of forecasts deteriorates as the time span between making the forecast and the target date increases, the most recent forecasts for a given period are likely to be more accurate. This is clearly illustrated by the differences between the accuracy of econometric models for the 1970–75 period, as shown in figures 4.1 and 4.3. When McNees analyzed the record of econometric models, he noted that some of the forecasts were issued early in each quarter, some in midquarter, and others late in the quarter.[35] The later forecasts are generally more accurate than the others, and the midquarter forecasts are more accurate than the early-quarter predictions. Fels has demonstrated the same effect in the accuracy of turning-point forecasts: the shorter the time between the prediction and the target date, the greater the possibility of correct prediction.[36]

The overall record of turning-point forecasts has been quite disappointing, however. Rendigs Fels's 1968 study provides data relevant to the half-year test. Fels examined the record of two forecasters using the indicators approach. Of their forecasts made three months prior to the economic peaks of 1957 and 1960 and the troughs of 1958 and 1961, only two out of eight predicted that a reversal would occur within the six months following the prediction.[37] Upon examining the success of eight other forecasters using an "eclectic" approach, Fels concluded that their record was about the same as for those using the indicators approach.[38]

Victor Zarnowitz reports that, on the one-year test, quarterly and semiannual judgmental forecasts covering the period 1948–63 correctly anticipated only three out of nineteen turning points that occurred within the year following the forecasts. Even if the set of forecasts with the worst record in anticipating turning points is excluded, Zarnowitz's sample still scores only three out of eight. Zarnowitz concluded that "the record, whichever way one looks at it, simply does *not* indicate any significant ability to predict a turning point several months ahead."[39]

EFFECTS OF METHODOLOGY

The fairest comparison of different forecasting methods lies in the record of forecasts actually made by practicing forecasters for the same period. The forecasting records compiled by the American Statistical Association and the National Bureau of Economic Research can indicate the relative success of each approach, since each forecaster was asked to indicate his methodology. However, only rarely was a single method used exclusively; in most cases the forecasters indicated that other methods were employed along with their primary method.

The ASA-NBER forecasts for the period from late 1968 to mid-1973 have been analyzed in terms of primary method.[40] About 20 percent of the forecasters used econometric models as their primary method, compared to the 60 percent who classified their approach as the "informal GNP model," defined as "a judgmental forecasting device which predicts each major component of GNP based on the forecaster's judgment and other exogenous variables." About 10 percent of the sample classified their dominant methodology as the "leading indicators" approach.

There are modest differences between the econometric and judgmental records, with the judgmental forecasts usually reflecting greater accuracy. Root-mean-square errors of quarterly econometric forecasts ($3.6 billion for nominal GNP and $4.4 billion for real GNP, both in 1958 dollars) are slightly worse than the corresponding errors of the judgmental forecasts ($3.1 billion and $3.7 billion). Annual (i.e.. the average for four quarters) econometric forecasts for real GNP also are less accurate ($8.3 billion versus $7.9 billion), but nominal-GNP forecasts have been more accurate with the econometric method than with judgment ($6.2 billion versus $6.5 billion).

This compilation also provides a glimpse at the *quantitative* record of the indicators approach. For both quarterly and annual forecasts of nominal GNP during this period, the indicators approach was considerably less accurate than the "informal GNP" approach. In 1958 dollars, the root-mean-square error for quarterly forecasts was $3.9 billion for the indicators approach, compared to $3.1 billion for the judgmental approach. Parallel errors for annual forecasts were $8.3 billion compared to $6.5 billion. The indicators-approach errors in forecasting real GNP were slightly worse than the judgmental errors: $3.9 billion versus $3.7 billion for quarterly errors; $8.2 billion versus $7.9 billion for annual errors.

TRENDS AND PROSPECTS OF SHORT-TERM FORECAST METHODS

The comparative accuracy of current econometric forecasts is important in itself, but reflects only the state of the art at one point in time. Since econometric models are continually undergoing development, a more important question is whether the econometric forecasting efforts are themselves showing any improvement over time.

There are many indications that econometric models are the "wave of the future" for short-term economic forecasting. The model-builders have been prospering in terms of research grants and professional recognition. Naturally, the research support for the development of econometric models is not simply for their use in forecasting, since the models are essentially developments of explicit economic theory. Nevertheless, every effort at improving econometric models makes them more attractive as forecasting devices. During the period from 1968 to 1975, the proportion of forecasters included in the ASA-NBER survey using econometric models as their primary forecasting method increased from about one-eighth to one-third. In the March 1976 survey nearly 60 percent of the forecasters reported using the results of either their own or outside econometric models (though not necessarily as their primary method).[41]

On the other hand, a skeptic might argue that the modifications and elaborations in econometric models are in effect only replacing one set of equations of mediocre validity with another. He might maintain that econometricians are forced to change their models as reality reveals their limitations, and that a fixed model (even allowing for changes in parameters) cannot hope to keep up with the changes in the structures of a real economy. Furthermore, he might argue that *no* model can capture the nuances of the intricate interactions that occur in a real economy, nuances that can be appreciated only through human judgment and intuition. Consequently, the skeptic's position would be that, although models are continually being created and modified, and may appear to be *theoretically* more sophisticated, the performance of newer models will not be appreciably better than the performance of older ones.

This proposition can be tested by comparing the accuracy of older and newer models. However, economists have shown little interest in examining changes in the accuracy of econometric models over time. They have been much more interested in examining the "here and now" of the most recent models. Consequently, there are no treatments of model accuracy covering the performance of the full range of models over many years. This analysis can be accomplished, however, by combining the results of studies that focus on the various time periods.

Linking the results of different time periods presents two problems. Some periods may be intrinsically more difficult to predict, thereby obscuring the extent of improvement in the models themselves. The record of each period's judgmental forecasts provides one direct indication of predictive difficulty. Unfortunately, the record for judgmental forecasts is not available for all periods for both error measures, nor do the summaries of judgmental forecast accuracy always cover precisely the same time periods. Therefore, this comparison cannot be absolutely conclusive, though there are adequate rough indications of each period's difficulty.

The other problem of comparability is simply that, because of inflation, errors of the same current-dollar magnitude produced at different times are not equivalent. To improve comparability, all *errors* are expressed here in terms of 1958 dollars, even for predictions of the change in nominal (i.e., current-dollar) GNP.

Thirteen prominent econometric models currently in operation have been subjected to extensive error analysis. However, for two of the newest models, results of valid tests of forecasting capability have not been published. Therefore, information on the forecasting capability of specific current econometric models is limited to eleven models, although the survey of forecasters conducted by the NBER provides some information on the general forecasting record of econometric models. The accuracy levels of the eleven well-tested models are given in figures 4.1–4.6, along with the records of earlier models.[42]

The figures express two kinds of results. First, some errors are reported for the actual forecasts generated by the individuals or institutions responsible for the model, usually for a period of several years. Since modelers are continually changing and refining their models, the "model date" for results such as these is the year in which the model is operating. Hence, for models actually run over long periods, there are many "model dates." We have designated such results by extending horizontal lines to cover the period actually forecast, thereby calculating the model's error as its average error for the period. However, since our interest is in determining whether accuracy changes over time, we have broken down the time periods into three-year segments

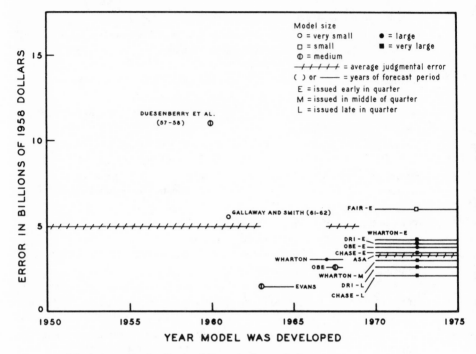

4.1. Average Absolute Errors of Quarterly Current-Dollar
GNP-Change Forecasts of Econometric Models

whenever the original period exceeded four years. In this way, anomalous
results of a single year are balanced out, and changes in accuracy over longer
time periods can be detected.

Second, some results represented in the figures were produced by
economists who took particular specifications of models (i.e., the models'
equations) and applied these to the task of forecasting for some time period *as
if* the models were actually being run to forecast future economic activity.
Since the models tested in this way were fixed versions, each is designated in
the figures by the year of the version adopted for testing. The periods covered
in the test are indicated in parentheses. It can be seen that they do not
necessarily correspond to the model year (the horizontal axis of each figure),
though in every case the forecast test period is later than the period used to
estimate the model's parameters.

Some of the earlier models are direct predecessors of currently operating
versions. Because of the communal nature of the development of econometric
models, and the fact that parts of the old models have been merged into the
newer ones, the genealogy of the models is very difficult to establish, and is

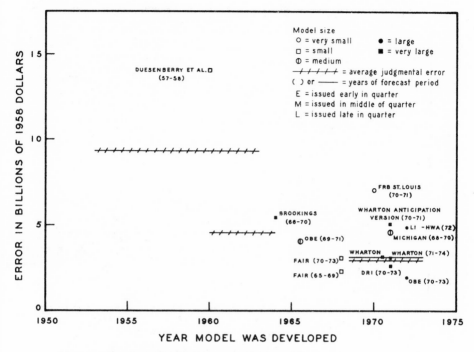

4.2. Root-Mean-Square Errors of Quarterly Current-Dollar
GNP-Change Forecasts of Econometric Models

not germane to the analysis of trends in accuracy. The important point is that
the more recent models are more elaborate than the earlier models, and represent considerable investments in model-building.

In addition, the figures include the accuracy levels of judgmental forecasts
for various periods.[43] These levels serve as standards, inasmuch as they reflect
the forecasting difficulty of the periods to which they pertain.

Figures 4.1–4.4 relate to quarterly forecasts: the first two are simply different error measures (average absolute and root-mean-square) of nominal-
GNP forecasts; figures 4.3 and 4.4 show the same for real-GNP predictions.

The bench marks of judgmental forecast accuracy for different periods
basically indicate that the trends in accuracy of econometric models cannot be
explained by the fact that some periods are significantly more difficult to
forecast. The accuracy of quarterly judgmental forecasts of nominal GNP is
quite stable in terms of average absolute errors. The parallel root-mean-square
error for the 1953–63 period is considerably higher than for later periods, but,
in terms of the judgmental forecast record since 1960, the level of accuracy
has been fairly steady. The accuracy of real-GNP quarterly forecasts has been

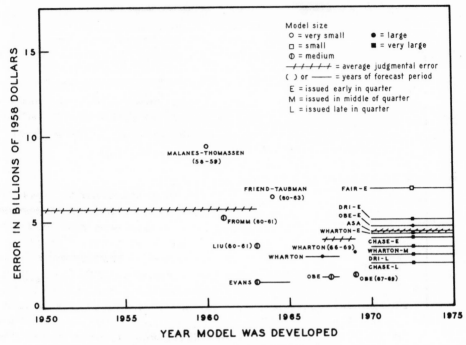

4.3. Average Absolute Errors of Quarterly Real-GNP-Change
Forecasts of Econometric Models

even more consistent, according to the average absolute errors displayed in figure 4.3. Although the record for root-mean-square errors extends only from 1970 to 1973, the consistency of the much longer span of average absolute errors implies that the root-mean-square errors have been consistent also, since both error measures are calculated from the same individual errors.

The discouraging message of these comparisons is that econometric forecasts have not become more accurate. The high percentage of errors of the earliest models (Duesenberry et al. and Malanes-Thomassen) is not typical of the record for the early and mid-1960s, which was consistently as good as, or better than, the record for the late 1960s and early 1970s. Even if the poor recent performance of the judgment-free Fair model and the simple monetarist FRB-St. Louis model are disregarded, the recent models show no advances over the earlier models. Figure 4.1 shows that, in terms of average absolute errors, models operated between 1970 and 1975 were in general less accurate than the earlier versions of the Evans, Wharton, and OBE models of the mid-1960s, even though the judgmental bench mark for the later period was somewhat better. Figure 4.2, which displays a somewhat different but partially overlapping set of models for which root-mean-square errors have been

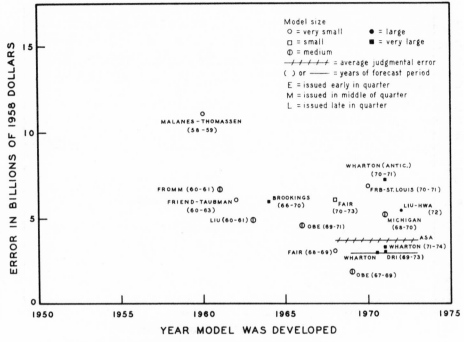

4.4. Root-Mean-Square Errors of Quarterly Real-GNP-Change
Forecasts of Econometric Models

reported, shows comparable error levels, centered on $5 billion in 1958 dollars, for the models developed since 1964. Again, the judgmental-record indication of the inherent difficulty of predicting each period does not permit the interpretation that more recent models are actually better but have faced a more difficult forecasting task. The same pattern is repeated for the quarterly forecasts of real GNP. The average absolute errors of the 1960s model are considerably lower than the errors for the 1970s, though the forecasting difficulty of the periods is about the same. The root-mean-square errors for the 1960s are about the same as for the 1970s, but they are more consistent than the later errors.

The record for annual GNP forecasts is much the same. Figures 4.5 and 4.6 display the errors of various models in predicting nominal and real GNP.[44] The longest record is that of the University of Michigan model, which has been forecasting real GNP since 1953. The three-year averages of absolute errors for this model vary greatly, showing no trend toward improvement. Moreover, the 1963 Evans model shows generally greater accuracy in forecasting for 1964–65 than the later Wharton and OBE models do in forecasting for the late 1960s, for both real and nominal GNP. In turn, these models are

81

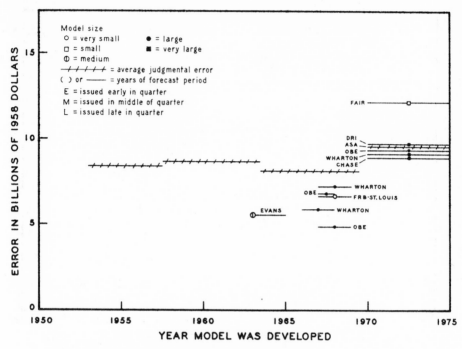

4.5. Average Absolute Errors of Annual Current-Dollar
GNP-Change Forecasts of Econometric Models

more accurate than their 1970s versions as they performed from 1970 to 1975.
While the judgmental bench mark does indicate greater forecasting difficulty
for the 1970–75 period than for earlier periods, the deterioration of the
models' performance exceeds the deterioration of the judgmental standard.
Moreover, while the earlier forecasts of econometric models were more accurate than the judgmental annual forecasts, the econometric forecasts of the
1970s were worse than comparable judgmental predictions.

Judgment-free econometric models are considerably less reliable than comparable models using some judgmental input. Although the Fair model per-
forms as well as other econometric models for some periods, its recent
(1970–75) performance in predicting both real-GNP and nominal-GNP quarterly changes is clearly worse; its absolute errors of about $6 billion for
current GNP and $7 billion for real GNP compare to errors of other economet-
ric models ranging from $2.5 billion to $5 billion (see figures 4.1 and 4.3).
The "mechanical" version of the OBE (BEA) model is even worse: the
1970–75 average absolute error for quarterly real-GNP forecasts is also $7
billion, and the error for current-GNP forecasts is over $6.5 billion. (These
results are not included in the figures because the BEA (OBE) itself seems to
put more credence in its judgmental-econometric forecasts, which are in-

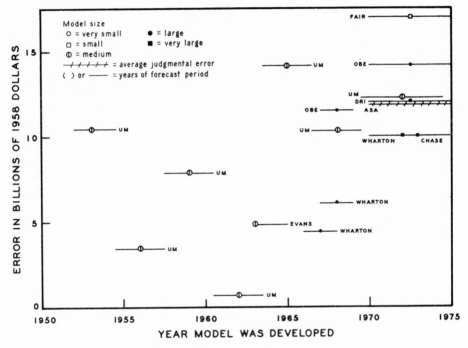

4.6. Average Absolute Errors of Annual Real-GNP-Change
Forecasts of Econometric Models

cluded). The annual forecast errors of the BEA mechanical model are over $9 billion in 1958 dollars for nominal GNP and $15.5 billion for real GNP. The Fair model errors are over $12 billion and $17 billion. These errors are higher than the annual errors of all the other models for the 1970–75 period.

The importance of model size is difficult to assess because recency and largeness occur together, and thus their effects are hard to separate.[45] The smaller, earlier models are less reliable, but whether this is due to their size or to their primitiveness is debatable. Moreover, the smallness of the Fair model may account for its poor record, but the fact that the Fair model uses no judgmental adjustments is a more likely explanation, since the larger, judgment-free BEA version is equally inaccurate. The few monetarist models (Gallaway and Smith, FRB-St. Louis), which by the nature of their theoretical orientation are very small, have fared poorly as well. Therefore, small models in general have performed poorly, but their unreliability is probably due to the concomitants of smallness rather than to smallness *per se*. There is to date no definitive evidence that for econometric models "bigger is better."

Before econometric models are discarded as an expensive luxury, it should be noted that the unconditional forecasting task examined here **83** is only one of the capabilities of econometric models. Even beyond the possible usefulness of econometric models in the development of economic theory, the models can accomplish certain policy-relevant tasks that judgment cannot accomplish as well. Most importantly, the ability to trace out the repercussions of changes in exogenous factors (e.g., government policy), or in the economic structure, gives econometric models a much greater potential for *conditional forecasting* than can be expected from expert judgment alone. The models can perform " policy simulations" to determine the intricate consequences of various policy alternatives.[46] Although an empirical comparison of the abilities of models and judgment to anticipate the consequences of policy change is precluded by the counterfactual nature of policy simulations, the enormity of the task of establishing and tracing the necessarily large number of interactions would seem on *a priori* grounds to virtually require an econometric model.

The same lack of improvement in practical forecasting shown by econometric models holds for the leading-indicators approach. Like the models, the indicators approach is undergoing "research and development," with the usual hopes for future improvement. In the 1960s the leading-indicators approach generated forecasts that were passable, if not quite as accurate as the judgmental predictions. The ASA-NBER record shows that more recent leading-indicators forecasts have the worst record of accuracy of the three major methods. The same skepticism that has surrounded the econometric models may be leveled against the leading-indicators approach: perhaps the "progress" in selecting new indicators is in effect replacing one mediocre set of indicators (that happened to fit past patterns) with another (that happened to fit a somewhat more recent past pattern). The inaccuracy of the leading-indicators approach could probably be dismissed if the approach were new and "experimental"; in fact, its antecedents predate the 1935 work of Mitchell and Burns, and extend back to the search for business cycle omens in the 1920s and even earlier.

The lack of improvement in leading-indicators forecasts supports the position that the method's inadequacies are not due to a failure to develop the method's potential, but rather stem from inherent limitations in the assumptions and conditions required for the validity of the approach. If the crucial assumption of the regularity and uniformity of economic sequences is correct, it is surprising that more than fifty years of searching for these sequences has not produced results on a par with unstructured judgment.

LONG-TERM ECONOMIC FORECASTING

The demand for long-term economic forecasting results from its centrality to so many aspects of private and governmental planning. The use of any resource, from manpower to energy, depends either directly on the magnitude of economic activity, or on the quantity of spendable income which that economic activity provides. Thus, not only are private fortunes at stake in corporations' gambles in predicting economic trends, but the entire society's smooth functioning depends on policy-makers' abilities to predict economic trends as they impinge on the supply and demand of transportation, energy, education, manpower, housing, and so on. This is strikingly illustrated in a pioneering study by J. Frederick Dewhurst et al. for the Twentieth Century Fund, published in 1947 and updated in 1955, which vividly establishes the comprehensive importance of economic and financial trends.[47] After analyzing the *impact* of economic expansion on future life styles and resource uses, Dewhurst et al. express the resulting *requirements* in terms of the financial expenditures necessary to provide them. The level of economic output is regarded as both creating *and* fulfilling future needs.

Long-term economic forecasts are consequently fundamental to the projection of many other trends. GNP projections enter into most resource-demand forecasts, such as projections of energy use, either implicitly (as in the case of judgmental forecasts) or explicitly (through correlations or through models that directly express resource use as a function of GNP). They also provide a good portion of the context necessary to forecast social and political trends. Because long-range economic forecasts cover such an important aspect of the context for other trends, inaccuracies in economic forecasts induce serious inaccuracies in forecasting these trends.

TECHNIQUES OF LONG-TERM ECONOMIC FORECASTING

Long-range economic forecasting is very different from short-term forecasting. Prediction of short-term economic trends depends on the capacity to understand the intricacies of the existing economic structure—i.e., to use the linkages connecting factors such as money supply, inventories, and employment levels. In long-range economic forecasting, these short-term fluctuations need not be accounted for so carefully. What is most crucial for the long term is anticipation of *changes* (or lack of changes) in economic structure. Some of these changes may be gradual, such as improvements in productivity through technological advances, but others may be "discontinuous," such as an oil embargo, military conflict, important new laws, or material shortages.

Besides the occasional simple extrapolations of the unitary GNP trend, long-range economic forecasting in the post–World War II period has been dominated by two methods employing component breakdowns. The choice of component division depends on many factors, including the specific interests of the forecasters, the availability of data, and, most importantly, the forecaster's opinion of what trends can be projected reliably into the future. One approach, probably the most popular, is to focus on the capacity of the economic system to *supply* the goods and services that comprise the gross national product. Specifically, the task is to project productivity (i.e., output per worker per hour), which is assumed to increase at a predictable rate, reflecting technological advance. The other approach is to forecast GNP as consumption, by projecting the *demand* for goods and services.

Of course, the productivity approach is not as simple as it appears. To link productivity to GNP, forecasters must also project the size of the working force (a demographic and social forecast), the level of unemployment (an economic and political forecast), and the average number of hours worked (a social and economic forecast). Beyond these problems, there are no clear-cut guidelines for projecting productivity. Although it is obviously related to technological progress, productivity also depends on all the factors that determine whether there is sufficient demand for greater output. Most productivity projections do not explicitly balance out the complex relationship between capacity and demand; either the balance is accomplished judgmentally or it is assumed that demand will keep up with the prospects of high output.

The consumption approach may break down the demand components in a number of ways: by broad sectors (e.g., governmental, commercial, industrial, and residential; or agricultural and nonagricultural) or by specific product and service categories. To keep track of how demands in one sector create demands in another, these connections are often represented by an "input-output matrix," which represents the requirements of each sector for the outputs of the others. No matter what demand component breakdown is chosen, the forecaster still faces the task of projecting these components, which is a large and intricate undertaking normally accomplished through some usually unspecified combination of judgment and extrapolation.

Five sources have produced a large number of the long-term economic forecasts examined here: the National Planning Association, the Joint Economic Committee of the U.S. Congress, the Economics Department of McGraw Hill, the Committee for Economic Development, and the Organisation for Economic Cooperation and Development. The National Planning Association, which publishes such projections nearly every year, began with productivity projections in the 1950s, added an examination of the demand side in the late 1960s (although apparently the productivity trend was still considered definitive), and integrated the two methods in an econometric model by 1970.[48] The staff of the Joint Economic Committee of the U.S. Congress periodically has projected long-term GNP trends, using the productivity approach but with numerous caveats introducing other factors. The Economics Department of McGraw-Hill generates long-range GNP projections that are used as a basis for specialized forecasts of energy, transportation, and other trends published by the various McGraw-Hill trade journals. The McGraw-Hill methodology is not definitively described, nor are the methodologies of the Committee for Economic Development and the Organisation for Economic Cooperation and Development.

Although, in the past, cyclical theories aroused much excitement as a means of foretelling the economy's future, they have not been employed in serious and precise long-term GNP forecasts in the post–World War II period. The application of cyclical theories to the practical task of long-range forecasting has been limited for two reasons. First, although the notion that unvarying cycles determine broad economic trends has had a strong appeal, confidence in a particular characterization of the cycles (their timing and amplitude) for actual forecasting is another matter. The cycles that have been found by fitting different combinations of cycle lengths and amplitudes to historical patterns show only a rough correspondence to reality. Moreover, even if a perfect fit were achieved, this fact would not prove the invariance of the cyclical pattern, since even a randomly generated pattern will fit *some* combination of multiple cycles. Thus, the status of cycles that do fit the historical pattern is quite problematic. Without additional and independent support for the chosen combination of cycles (such as a strong theoretical rationale), projecting this combination of cycles into the future is a risk that most forecasters are unwilling to take.

Second, many economic policies in the United States, particulary those affecting money supply and governmental spending, are designed in this post–*laissez faire* era precisely to be *anticyclical*. Such policies have the potential to eliminate, and certainly to alter, prior patterns of business cycles. Therefore, even if a particular combination of cycles was basic for a previous period, its applicability to the future may be negated by anticyclical measures.

PROBLEMS IN APPRAISING LONG-TERM ECONOMIC FORECASTS

There are two obstacles to the complete appraisal of long-range economic forecasts. First, the mixture and ambiguity of methods preclude appraisal in terms of the relative accuracy of different methods. Second, minor changes in the definition and historical data of GNP make it difficult to calculate meaningfully the accuracy of forecasts in their original form, but this problem can be resolved by recalculating the forecasts on a consistent basis.

Although the productivity and consumption approaches are analytically distinct, two circumstances cloud the attribution of a specific method to practical applications. First, as with any approach employing judgment, there is no way of knowing whether some of the judgmental inputs in the use of one method implicitly convey the reasoning or intuitions of the other. Most forecasters using either the productivity or the consumption approach freely acknowledge their use of judgment. Second, most applications are either mixed or unspecified. In either case the predominance of one of the approaches is difficult to establish and additionally is not very meaningful. For example, if a forecaster's methodological description emphasizes productivity, but also includes a statement such as "the projections take into account the capacity to absorb the output" or "an attempt was made to reconcile these projections with the rate of growth of demand," attributing more importance to one method than to another would be arbitrary. The difficulty lies in the fact that output and consumption are by definition equal; therefore, if the forecaster is to consider both aspects at all, they must be equilibrated.

In evaluating long-range economic forecasts, periodic revisions in the "actual" levels of GNP present a minor problem. Forecasts applying the same growth rate to different bases will obviously produce different results, even though the relative changes will be about the same. The "revised actual levels" are not the "actuals" to which the forecast is addressed. Differences between the base levels assumed by the forecaster and the base levels ultimately established by later revisions should not cloud the accuracy of the forecasts themselves. The same holds for differences between target-year levels that are consistent with assumed base levels and the revisions later introduced. To surmount this problem in the present study, forecasts that were not already in the annual-percentage-change form were converted to this form. Then this annual growth rate was applied to the most recent estimate of the base-year GNP.[49] This procedure provided adjusted forecasts that presumably are what each forecaster would have made if he had been using the same values for base-year GNP levels as have now been established by the latest revision. These forecasts were then compared to the target-date levels of the same most recent series, in order to calculate the discrepancies between actual and predicted values.

ACCURACY OF LONG-TERM ECONOMIC FORECASTS

The errors of fixed-length GNP forecasts are displayed in figures 4.7–4.9.[50] The levels of accuracy of five-, ten-, and fifteen-year real GNP forecasts made since 1950 are remarkably similar. Errors for both five-and ten-year forecasts have a median of about $40 billion in 1958 dollars, but the ten-year forecasts have a greater mean error of about $63 billion (compared to $52 billion for the five-year forecasts) because of a few extremely large errors. Fifteen-year forecasts have a median error of $60 billion an a mean error of $65 billion. Thus, recency is of little value in long-range real-GNP forecasts of these spans. Apparently, business cycles and more short-lived economic fluctuations are hardly more predictable five years in advance than they are fifteen years in advance, and are no more predictable now than they were in the 1950s. The forecasts show no tendency toward greater accuracy over time.

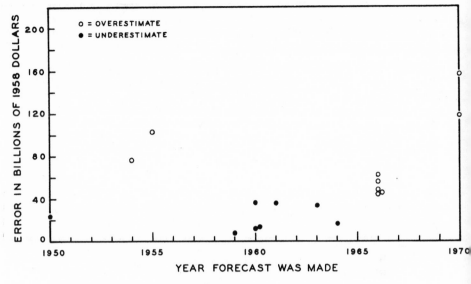

4.7. Errors of Five-Year Real-GNP Forecasts

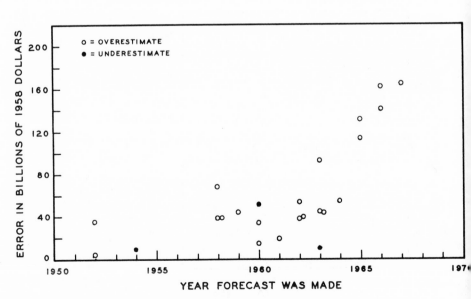

4.8. Errors of Ten-Year Real-GNP Forecasts

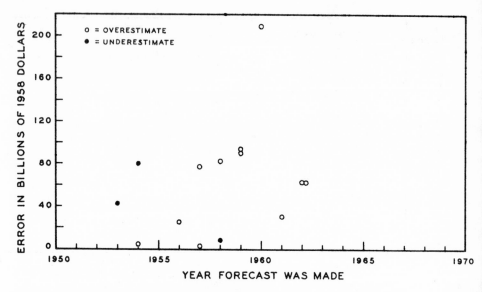

4.9. Errors of Fifteen-Year Real-GNP Forecasts

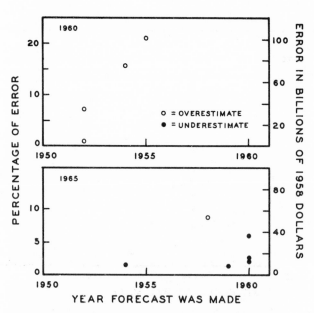

4.10. Errors of 1960 and 1965 Long-Term Real-GNP
Forecasts

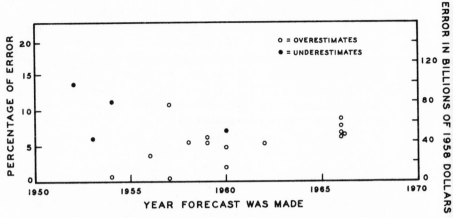

4.11. Errors of 1970 Long-Term Real-GNP Forecasts

The same conclusions can be drawn from the errors of forecasts approaching 1960, 1965, 1970, and 1975. None of the error patterns of figures 4.10–4.12 indicates that forecast accuracy improves as the target date nears. In fact, for 1975 forecasts, accuracy deteriorated through the 1960s. More recent periods appear to have been more difficult to forecast. Predictions for 1965 have an average error of less than 5 percent, whereas the errors of 1970 forecasts average between 5 and 10 percent, and most predictions for 1975 made since 1965 have errors of between 15 and 20 percent.

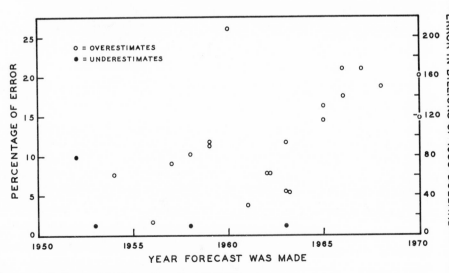

91   4.12. Errors of 1975 Long-Term Real-GNP Forecasts

Almost invariably, the long-range judgmental projections of GNP reflect a growth rate that exceeds the historical rate. One reason for this is the forecasters' focus on the *potential* of the economy. Since productivity is associated with what appears to be the accelerating march of technological progress, the focus on productivity practically forces the forecasts to assume high rates of growth. Balancing off the effects of increasing productivity are the trend toward a shorter workweek and the possibility of higher unemployment. However, changes in the workweek have been very gradual, and high levels of unemployment are very difficult to predict in the long run, particularly when antiunemployment policies are available to policy-makers. The combination of assumptions of increasing productivity, only very modest declines in the workweek, and historical rates of unemployment yields GNP estimates that do not capture the retarding effects of cyclical downturns, and instead projects GNP at a higher rate than has yet been experienced for very long periods. Of course, it is conceivable that a technologically more sophisticated economy somehow freed of recessions would produce such growth, but the past use of the productivity approach has resulted in significant overestimation.

CHAPTER 5

ENERGY FORECASTING

Policy-makers involved with America's energy issues have learned a great deal about the importance of forecasting in the formulation of energy policy. The electricity shortages beginning in the mid-1960s, the recent oil and gas shortages, and the chronic problem of energy-related pollution all point to both the necessity and the difficulty of energy forecasting.

Energy problems caused by unforseen demand have occurred fairly often, even though many such problems have not achieved the public status of "crisis." A true crisis can exist even if there are no actual shortfalls in supply. The costs involved when unforeseen energy demands occur are usually manifested not in actual shortages that paralyze day-to-day economic activities, but rather in the makeshift measures of very low efficiency which must be adopted to provide adequate energy. This has been the case, for example, in the supply of electricity for the Northeast since the mid-1960s. To meet the unexpected demand, electric utilities have had to resort to inefficient, low-power gas-turbine units to make up for the lack of more efficient conventional fossil-fuel or nuclear plants. Utilities turned to gas turbines because they could be installed rapidly to avert the immediate crisis, while the more efficient plants would have required much longer periods of planning, litigation, and construction.[1] Similarly, petroleum shortages usually can be met, but only through highly inefficient means. Oil can be extracted from domestic wells more rapidly than is optimal for total supply. Alternatively, oil imports can make up the shortage, but at the cost of generally higher prices and, often, political liabilities.

Thus, energy forecasting is required to prevent actual shortages of energy supplies and, more broadly, to avoid situations in which policy-makers are forced to provide energy very inefficiently. In fact, energy forecasting is a crucial step in the policy process for any aspect of energy use that requires substantial "lead times" for development or involves physical limits imposed by resource availability. In addition to the lead times required to arrange for the discovery, extraction, and transport of the basic energy fuels, long lead times are needed to plan and construct facilities for the conversion of fuels into power. On the fuel-gathering side, the mammoth tasks of building dams, pipelines, and offshore drilling platforms obviously require lengthy construction periods. In fact, for petroleum supply, the time period from initial exploration to actual production has been increasing as more remote oil reservoirs are tapped. On the conversion side, refineries and power plants require official approval, design study, and, of course, construction. Electric power plants currently require from three to seven years for construction alone.[2]

Because of these needs, more organizations are currently engaged in fore-casting energy demand and supply than ever before. However, the reception of their forecasts has been marked by skepticism on two counts: first, that the forecasters are competent; and, second, that they are free from biases serving the interests of the institutions they represent.

The onset of the "energy crisis" had much to do with the public's skeptical attitude toward the competence of energy forecasting. The abruptness of the oil embargo, and the fact that it was a political as well as an economic act, fostered the deceptive impression that energy problems are temporary emergencies of an unpredictable nature. This perspective naturally encour-aged a short-term outlook that focused on short-range trends and the im-mediate balance of energy supply and demand. Today, however, there is a growing recognition that energy problems are not temporary—in fact, a re-view of the energy literature shows that this was by no means our first energy crisis.[3] But, as we shall see, there is no question that forecasting energy demands in the face of volatile economic and energy supply conditions is a much more difficult task than forecasting for stable periods. Thus, the energy problems of the past five years, like many circumstances involving a high degree of uncertainty, pose an important dilemma: the more uncertain the future, the more imperative the need to anticipate it. The need for accurate forecasts is greatest when forecasting is likely to be at its worst.

An equally strong impression left by the oil embargo and its aftermath was that information provided by oil companies and other energy purveyors is deliberately inaccurate. A major thrust of the 1974 congressional hearings on energy matters was to force the oil companies and other energy suppliers to disclose their actual reserves, supplies, and exploration prospects.[4] During the same period, utility companies apparently benefitted from higher rates granted, in part, on the basis of their own testimony on supply shortages and the prospect of much higher future demands. In this atmosphere of powerless-ness and recrimination, it is easy to understand the suspicions raised against the energy suppliers and the distrust felt toward their analyses, including their forecasts.

In situations like the energy debate, in which "technical information" is a very important promotional tool, it is crucial to have *alternative* sources of information. But, even when these are available, their reliability is open to question, as in the case of the CIA estimates of world petroleum supplies invoked by President Carter in April 1977 to support his own energy program. Is the CIA technically competent to forecast energy supplies? Are their figures biased—deliberately or not—in favor of the policy?

If, indeed, there are biases in the forecasts of private and governmental sources, it is important to identify them. If not, it is equally important to clear the air so that information provided by "interested" parties can aid in policy-making instead of being dismissed as biased.

In this chapter we will examine energy demand forecasts in three important areas: electricity, petroleum, and total energy. Petroleum and electricity are obvious targets of forecasting, since oil and electricity shortages have been at the center of our energy problems. The importance of total energy forecasts is less obvious, however, since total energy is such a highly aggregated concept.

The accuracy of total energy forecasts is significant because it indicates how well forecasters can anticipate the broad context in which specific energy projections are located. Often, the future demand for specific fuels or energy forms is derived from its share of the total demand. The rationale for this "top-down" view is that the demand for different sources and forms of energy is interrelated because of substitutability among fuels and energy forms. For many uses, natural gas can replace electricity; coal fueled electricity can replace petroleum; fuels can be converted into energy via electricity or through direct combustion. The total energy demand can be met through many "mixes" of these fuels and forms, with the proportions varying according to the relative prices and supplies of each type.

Total energy supply is also important *per se* because of the general *effects* of energy use. For example, pollution levels are sensitive to almost all sources of energy (with the exception of the relatively unimportant contributions of solar and wind energy). Finally, there are no easy remedies for mistakes in anticipating total energy demand. Shortages obviously cannot be compensated for by seeking substitutes, since total energy encompasses all sources and uses. In the following pages we will appraise the accuracy and biases of energy demand forecasts, determine what impact (if any) the source and methodology of the forecast have had on its outcome, and explore the possibility that energy forecasting is improving. Finally, we will review the attempts to estimate petroleum reserves, a crucial aspect of future energy supply and one of the most controversial aspects of the energy debate.

ENERGY DEMAND FORECASTING

GENERAL FORECASTING METHODS

The methods applied to forecasting energy demands differ in three respects. First, there is the perennial question of whether to separate out components to be projected independently, and, if so, which component breakdown to use. Energy consumption may be broken down in terms of sources, uses, geographical regions, and so on. The component breakdown is usually clear from the text or the presentation of the forecast.

Second, there are various alternatives for extending the existing trend or trends. While there are numerous plausible ways of classifying these alternatives, one classification has been adopted here, not only because it captures the distinctions considered important in the literature on forecasting, but also because the distinctions generally can be inferred from the texts containing the original forecasts. Nevertheless, the methodology of a forecast is not always explicitly stated, and occasionally several methods are applied in the same forecasting effort. In such cases, the forecast has been dropped from the analysis of the effects of methods, unless the authors indicate which method was most important in their final conclusions on future trends. These methods are: *trend extrapolation,* where future growth rates are assumed to be the same as past or current rates; *correlation,* where energy consumption is explicitly calculated from projections of other trends (such as GNP or population) that are assumed to correlate with energy consumption; *judgment,* where future growth rates are determined primarily through the judgment of the forecasters without being *explicitly* tied to given trends or projections, although such factors may have been taken into account *subjectively* by the forecasters in arriving at a judgment; *multiple opinion,* where growth rates are determined by averaging several existing or solicited forecasts by other experts; and *modeling,* where growth rates are outcomes of fairly elaborate, explicit, quantitative models linking energy consumption to numerous social and economic variables.

Finally, the scope of the overall forecasting effort in which a particular energy trend is included is the third methodological aspect. It is plausible that a broad forecasting effort which places each trend within the context of competing energy sources and uses would better anticipate future patterns, since the availability or cost of one fuel affects the use of another, and the use by one sector limits the availability of energy for another. Many of the electricity and petroleum projections presented here were taken from comprehensive studies of future energy use. Just as embedding overall energy projections in a broader study of energy-related forecasting would have theoretical advantages, placing forecasts of specific energy trends within the total energy context should enhance the consistency and plausibility of the projections. The two ways of achieving this sort of integration are, first, to forecast all energy sources rather than just one, and second, to treat such energy use or supply as a subdivision of the total, as opposed to considering the total simply as the sum of the parts. Once a total level is established, it may be divided according to source or use or both. Comprehensive forecasting provides at least the opportunity for awareness of the constraints imposed by overall supply, while the subdivision approach (as opposed to simply adding up the demands of each energy sector, which is termed the building-block approach) ensures that these considerations will be taken into account explicitly.[5] However, in practice the effort to be comprehensive may not be cost-free. The accuracy of each element of a comprehensive forecasting effort may suffer if less time and care are invested in forecasting each element in order to forecast them all. Therefore, the superiority of the subdivision construction over the building-block construction cannot be taken for granted, as some analysts do.[6]

ELECTRICITY DEMAND FORECASTING METHODS

The two dominant methods used for electricity forecasts have been correlation and judgment, accompanied by a respectable number of trend extrapolations. Multiple-opinion forecasts rarely are produced. Forecast models have been made only since 1970, and consequently very few are appraisable at this time.

The correlational and judgmental methods dominate because they are employed by McGraw-Hill's *Electrical World* and the Federal Power Commission, the two most active producers of electricity forecasts since the early 1950s. *Electrical World* forecasts, produced by the McGraw-Hill Economics Department, are published annually, and the FPC staff produces forecasts almost as often. These two sources also have very high visibility and credibility; they are cited more than any other forecasts of electricity consumption, and are frequently used as the base projections for other forecasting efforts. Because of the prominence of FPC and *Electrical World* forecasts, and the fact that roughly half of the projections examined here are taken from these sources, a detailed examination of their methodology is in order.

During the 1950s and early 1960s the FPC electricity forecasts were based on judgmental estimates of each *region's* future growth. Trends in population and GNP were examined, but the forecasts were not explicitly correlated with projections of these trends; nor were they extrapolated from the electricity growth trend itself. The contribution of "judgment" in this case was to posit that past growth rates in electricity use would gradually taper off.[7] By the mid-1960s, FPC forecasters began to rely much more on simple trend extrapolation. This shift reflected a growing belief that the post–World War II industrial and economic expansion was likely to continue indefinitely. These later forecasts thus abandoned the implicit assumption of the earlier FPC forecasts that electricity use was approaching some sort of ceiling.

In contrast, *Electrical World* forecasts were straightforward correlations between electricity consumption and projections of other important trends in the residential, industrial, and commercial use-sectors. For residential electricity consumption, for example, electricity use per customer (i.e., family) was multiplied by the number of future customers as determined by population forecasts. Similarly, industrial use was linked with forecasts of the Federal Reserve Board index of industrial activity and GNP. Like the FPC forecasts, *Electrical World* projections are not nested in a more comprehensive effort to forecast overall energy use, although the McGraw-Hill Economics Department forecasters may have been involved in forecasting other energy trends for their many publications.[8] *Electrical World* forecasts therefore exemplify the correlational method, while the FPC projections are judgmental at first, and later become extrapolational. However, the *EW* procedure obviously is not completely lacking in judgmental elements. For example, the figures for electricity use per residential customer are not derived from correlations, but rather are supplied either through the judgments of the McGraw-Hill forecasters or through extrapolation; the variability in these figures indicates that judgment rather than extrapolation was the method chosen. Furthermore, the selection of other trends to correlate with energy consumption also is a matter of judgment. By the same token, the FPC forecasters were very much aware of population and GNP trends, even if they did not use them explicitly. Some judgment certainly played a part in the later FPC "extrapolations."[9]

Other institutions have provided electricity forecasts, using judgmental, correlational, and trend extrapolation methods. However, except for the Edison Electric Institute, which annually produces only short-term forecasts,[10] no other source has produced a large number of original electricity forecasts. Consequently, in evaluating the importance of forecast methodology to the accuracy of the forecasts, the source of the forecast is not an important complicating factor, except for the *EW* and FPC series.

PETROLEUM DEMAND FORECASTING METHODS

Petroleum forecasting also has been dominated by the correlational, judgmental, and extrapolational methods. However, the correlational method, which was used in very sophisticated applications prior to 1950,[11] has been used only rarely since then as the dominant method, although judgmental forecasts are often implicitly based on relationships between oil consumption and various other trends (e.g., population and GNP). Since 1950 most petroleum forecasters have used extrapolation or judgment as their dominant approaches, rather than the more complex method of correlation, which is based on projections of other trends. This rather unusual abandonment of a presumably more technically sophisticated method, which was brought on by early failures to produce accurate forecasts, left the petroleum demand forecasting field wide open to "amateurs" and "experts" alike, since simple extrapolation and the invocation of "seasoned judgment" provide no special advantage for the technical expert over other forecasters.

The correlational method is complicated to the extent that the correlates of petroleum use are both multiple and complex in themselves. Demand for petroleum depends not only on the number of petroleum-consuming units, and therefore indirectly on population and economic growth, but also on technology, because greater efficiency of petroleum use reduces the consumption needed to accomplish the same tasks. Some correlational petroleum demand forecasts have explicitly isolated the efficiency factor by considering miles per gallon or unit of work per gallon as separate components. One of the earliest correlational forecasts, the American Petroleum Council's 1935 projection, calculated motor fuel demand by first forecasting the number of vehicles and the miles-per-gallon rate for the average car, then combining these components to produce the gasoline consumption forecast, and finally multiplying by a projected refining ratio to determine how much crude oil would be required to produce that volume of gasoline.[12] In other words, two technological forecasts were necessary, one for the efficiency of auto engines and the other for the efficiency of gasoline refining.

In contrast, more recent forecasts either have recognized the complexity of factors influencing petroleum consumption by accommodating such factors implicitly through judgment (a convenient refuge when systematic, explicit analysis of all factors is too difficult), or have chosen to disregard the complications completely by focusing solely on the existing trend. Both approaches provide shortcuts in comparison to an explicit, analytical method like correlations—extrapolation through simplicity, judgment through implicitness. The abandonment of explicit correlation may have been triggered by the inaccuracies of the early forecasts, which, as will be seen, underestimated future petroleum consumption by about the same magnitude of error as did the contemporaneous motor vehicle forecasts. Since gasoline and diesel oil for cars, trucks, and buses constitute such a large proportion of total petroleum use, the number of operable motor vehicles was a primary correlate for these early petroleum forecasts, and the unpredictability of the motor vehicle population was a convincing justification for dropping the correlational method *at that time*. However, by the time this method had been abandoned (i.e., after 1950), the future motor vehicle population actually had become sufficiently predictable to warrant the correlational method. Thus, the rejection of correlation stands as a clear-cut example of a method discredited through premature application.

Most of the petroleum forecasts made prior to 1950 and about half of those made after 1950 used the component approach, generally breaking down total petroleum consumption by major use (e.g., automotive, heating fuel, petrochemical). The component approach was used in both extrapolational and judgmental forecasts, demonstrating the independence of the use of components from the method chosen to extend the trends. For example, *National Petroleum News,* another trade journal that reports McGraw-Hill forecasts, has long used a straightforward extrapolation for each petroleum product, summing across products to determine total petroleum consumption.[13] In the 1952 Paley Report petroleum projections, Arnold Harberger used the judgmental approach to forecast use of specific fuels (motor fuel, kerosene, residual oil, lubricants, and a large category of "other"), and then added them to arrive at total petroleum-use levels.[14]

Extrapolational and judgmental forecasts were almost evenly divided in terms of whether they constituted parts of comprehensive energy forecasting efforts or were independent efforts. Several of the former were the results of the subdivision of total-energy projections into specific fuel sources.

A crucial difference between petroleum forecasting and electricity forecasting is the far greater feasibility of augmenting domestic petroleum supply should it be exceeded by demand. Therefore, unlike the electricity forecasters, petroleum forecasters can assume that, under normal circumstances, imports will easily reinforce domestic supply (though the level of importation could affect the price of oil); therefore, supply constraints usually do not figure prominently in petroleum projections.[15] Naturally, this has made the accuracy of petroleum forecasts vulnerable to cutoffs of foreign petroleum sources, such as the 1973 Arab oil embargo.

TOTAL ENERGY DEMAND FORECASTING METHODS

The approaches to forecasting total energy demand are quite similar to those used to forecast specific energy uses. Except for the recent efforts to use econometric models to simulate all energy growth trends, the methods of total energy forecasting have been the standard techniques of extrapolation, judgment, and correlation (sometimes based on components and sometimes not).

Total energy consumption may be considered as a unitary, comprehensive measure which can be understood and predicted through its own past trends or through other overall aspects of the social system, such as the sum total of economic activity, the total population linked with an estimation of per capita energy use, or a comprehensive measure of industrial output. Thus, total energy, though recognized as a highly aggregated measure, can be extrapolated, correlated, or otherwise projected as a singular entity. The forecaster may then break down this total-energy quantity into particular energy sources or uses, which obviously are constrained to sum up to the projected total.

Alternatively, total energy may be regarded as a summary *emerging from* separate forecasts of specific, narrower energy uses or sources. Separate forecasts of these narrower trends, projected on the basis of different factors relevant to each, culminate in the total level of energy consumption, but without engaging the overall trend directly. This method is analogous to the population forecasting technique of breaking down the entire population into racial or regional groups, and then finding the total by summing the projected populations of the components.

When total energy is projected as a unitary trend, it can be correlated with measures of economic activity, such as GNP. The underlying theory, supported by many empirical studies, is that the amount of energy required to accomplish a "unit" of economic activity is consistent over time, gradually decreasing as improved technology provides more efficient utilization of energy.[16] Therefore, increasing GNP leads to increasing energy use, but at a declining rate over time. Total energy consumption can thus be projected by first forecasting GNP, and then calculating energy use through a measure of **100** "energy use per dollar of GNP," which usually is simply extrapolated from the existing trend for this measure. However, the unitary trend of total energy also has been extrapolated straightforwardly, or extended through the forecaster's judgment that total energy will increase at an implicitly calculated declining rate.

When total-energy projections are built up from separately formulated forecasts of specific energy uses or sources, the methods used to project the components are often eclectic or unspecified. Part of the rationale of this building-block approach is to be able to use specific methods for each component. Nevertheless, in some instances one method is sufficiently dominant for the forecast to be designated as judgmental, extrapolational, correlational, or multiple-opinion.

ACCURACY OF ENERGY FORECASTS

The energy context in 1975 was sufficiently different from preceding periods to produce very different patterns of forecast errors. The shortages of petroleum and electricity, and the much higher prices of fuels in general, were major deviations from the "business-as-usual" patterns prior to 1970. There-

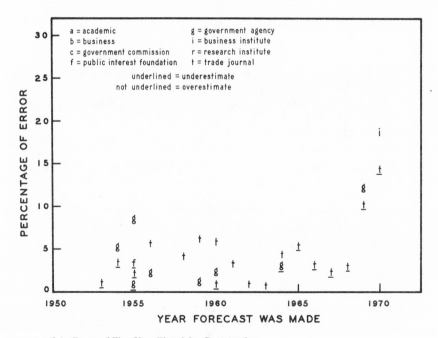

5.1. Errors of Five-Year Electricity Consumption Forecasts, by Source

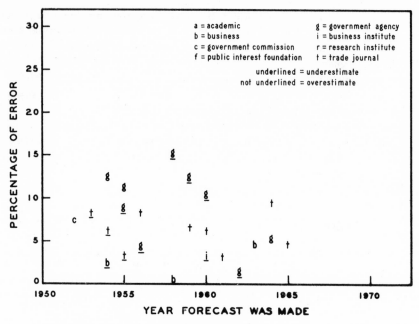

5.2. Errors of Ten-Year Electricity Consumption
Forecasts, by Source

fore, the following analysis distinguishes between forecasts with target dates
up to 1970 and those for 1975.

The typical accuracy of electricity forecasts with pre-1975 target dates is
strongly affected by the forecast length. Figures 5.1–5.7 reveal that the median error of fifteen-year forecasts is about 13 percent, compared to 6 percent
for ten-year forecasts and only 3.5 percent for five-year forecasts. In fact,
within five or six years of the target dates, almost all electricity forecasts are
within 6 percent of the real level. The approach curves of electricity forecasts
indicate that forecasts made more than five or six years prior to the target date
benefit from increasing recency as the target date nears, but that within that
five- or six-year period the accuracy level is fairly stable. The levels of
accuracy over time also appear to be stable. Even if the forecasts for 1975 are
disregarded, there is no evidence that five-, ten-, or fifteen-year electricity
forecasts have been improving over time.

Evaluating the significance of these electricity forecast errors is itself problematic, because of the possibility that the forecasts themselves (or the climate
of opinion they reflect) have affected the demand for electricity by influencing
the provision of available capacity. The pattern of electricity forecasts is one
of the few true examples of self-fulfilling predictions we have encountered.
Since potential external sources of electricity are very limited (in contrast to

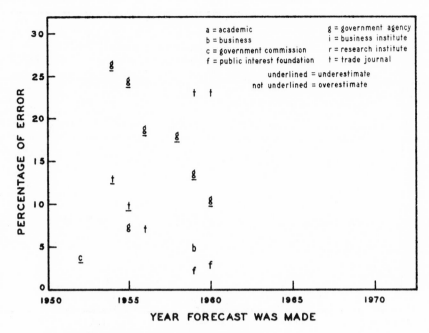

5.3. Errors of Fifteen-Year Electricity Consumption
Forecasts, by Source

petroleum supply, for example), there is an obvious balance of consumption
and supply whenever potential demand cannot be met. Consequently, if electricity forecasts that underestimate potential demand also discourage adequate
electric power expansion, the forecasts will "correctly" predict lower actual
consumption, regardless of potential demand. This appears to have happened
in the period of the middle and late 1960s with respect to forecasts for the
1965–75 period. In response to low expectations of growth, electric capacity
was not expanded rapidly, and the consequent fears of shortage led to various
policies designed to reduce demand (including higher prices, brownouts,
penalties for high consumption, and advertising campaigns encouraging
energy conservation), which had the desired impact of reducing electricity
use. In light of this effect, it is reasonable to consider the discrepancy between
forecasts and actual electricity demand as only a fraction of the discrepancy
between the forecast and the *potential* demand. Thus, we know that the
pessimistic forecasts of the mid-1960s, which ultimately showed five-year
forecast errors of only 4 percent, were still serious underestimates of potential
demand.[17]

Petroleum forecasts have been less accurate than electricity forecasts. As
figures 5.8–5.13 indicate, the median errors of fifteen-year petroleum forecasts made after 1950 are about the same as those for electricity forecasts—

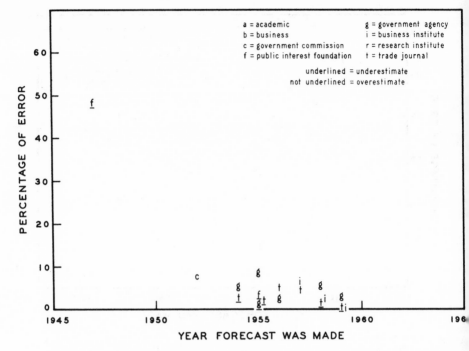

5.4. Errors of 1960 Electricity Consumption Forecasts,
by Source

about 13 percent—but the median errors of ten- and five-year petroleum forecasts are greater, about 10 percent and 6 percent respectively. The approach curves of petroleum forecasts do not converge to a high level of accuracy as consistently or as rapidly as do those of electricity forecasts. Although the forecasts of 1965 petroleum consumption were all within 10 percent of the actual level by 1958 and within 5 percent by 1960, the forecasts for 1970 exceeded a 10 percent error as late as 1969. Consequently, the recency of petroleum forecasts does not gain the policy-maker very much in terms of the accuracy of the forecast.

The marked improvement in petroleum forecasts starting around 1950 can be explained in part by the parallel improvement in motor vehicle forecasts (see chapter 6). Even though the future volume of automobiles and trucks is an explicit factor only in the early correlational projections of petroleum use, it enters implicitly into judgmental forecasts, insofar as judgments of petroleum demand recognize that much of this demand is automotive, and into extrapolations insofar as increasing numbers of motor vehicles have already established an upward petroleum-use trend. Motor vehicles account for more than a third of all U.S. petroleum consumption, so a more accurate estimate of

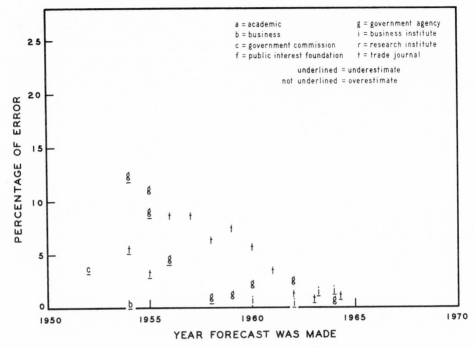

5.5. Errors of 1965 Electricity Consumption Forecasts,
by Source

the motor vehicle population ensures a more accurate forecast of petroleum use. More broadly, the improvement in petroleum forecasts after the immediate post–World War II period reflected the general improvement in forecasting U.S. trends which came about once the overall pattern of U.S. prosperity and expansion had been accepted as a permanent phenomenon. However, the improvements in accuracy that occurred right after 1950 were not followed by further improvements in the 1960s.

Forecasts of total energy are more recent, and therefore less easily evaluated, than electricity or petroleum forecasts. Although they began to appear in the 1950s, most total-energy projections do not have target dates earlier than 1975 (an unusual year for forecasts of all kinds), and in fact have 1980 as their first target date. Therefore, total-energy forecasts can be appraised through hindsight only to a limited extent (see Figures 5.14 and 5.15). There is little point in asking whether newer methodologies bring more accurate forecasts, since early forecasts are so sparse. There are too few forecasts targeted before 1970 to make approach curves for earlier dates meaningful. Even so, meaningful appraisals of general accuracy levels can be made. Except for the 1975 energy consumption forecasts made around 1960, which

105

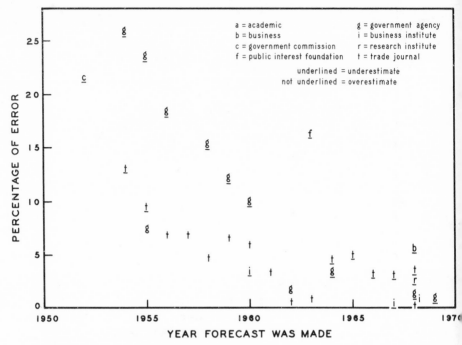

5.6. Errors of 1970 Electricity Consumption Forecasts,
by Source

were, in a sense, "right for the wrong reasons" (they projected moderately high, smooth growth instead of the actual pattern of very high growth followed by an abrupt dip), the fifteen-year total-energy forecasts have had an average error of approximately 10 percent. The ten-year total-energy forecasts have had a median error of 7 percent, and the five-year forecasts have been in error by about 3 percent, except for those with the 1975 target date. Therefore, the total-energy forecasts are slightly more accurate than the electricity projections and considerably more accurate than the petroleum forecasts. Greater accuracy in forecasting the broader trend is understandable in light of the fact that the total energy level cannot be affected by substitutive shifts from one fuel or energy form to another. The approach curve for 1970 total-energy forecasts, shown in figure 5.16, is rather flat, indicating that the total energy level for a "normal" year can be anticipated fairly accurately far in advance. By 1968 the median errors were under 5 percent, with no errors exceeding 11 percent. The approach curve for 1975, shown in figure 5.17, is utterly different, with forecasts made between 1970 and 1973 resulting in enormous errors because of their failure to anticipate the drop in energy consumption in 1974 and 1975.

106

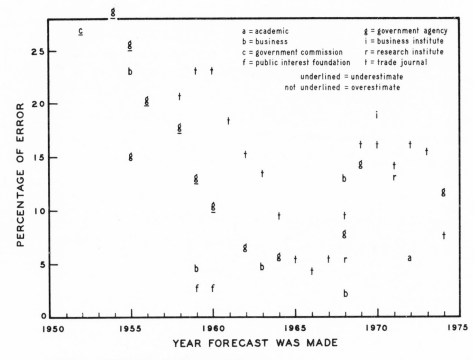

5.7. Errors of 1975 Electricity Consumption Forecasts, by Source

The pattern of errors and biases of all energy forecasts for 1975 is easy to explain. For all of the energy consumption trends examined here, forecasters were steadily adjusting their 1975 projections upward in light of continued energy-use increases. The forecasters learned to expect rapid future growth from the fact that rapid growth was occurring at that time. By 1960 (for total energy forecasts) and 1965 (for petroleum and electricity forecasts), these expectations had reached the level that ultimately proved to be correct, but, since energy consumption continued to increase rapidly, the forecasters continued to make upward adjustments, to levels beyond the actual 1975 level. In other words, *after* 1965 the business-as-usual extension of existing energy trends put the *expectation* for 1975 higher than the actuality of 1975, which was dampened by the unusual fuel-supply shortages. A simplified diagram of this pattern is shown in figure 5.18.

Thus, the two crucial points of this explanation are, first, that forecasters "learn" most from current trends and adjust their expectations accordingly; and, second, that the structural change in the role of energy in the American economy (i.e., the cost, limitations, and importance of energy and energy considerations) was not anticipated either quantitatively or qualitatively. This

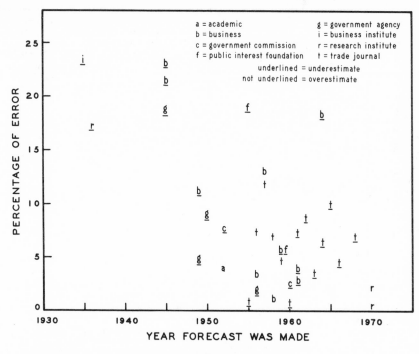

5.8. Errors of Five-Year Petroleum Consumption
Forecasts, by Source

same dynamic of adjustment provided increasingly accurate forecasts for the 1970 levels of energy consumption. But the 1973–74 shift in the energy balance was not (and could not be) anticipated or accommodated through adjustments based on "current experience" prior to 1973.

How far off are the 1975 forecasts in light of the volatility of the period preceding the target date? In other words, to what extent can the inaccuracies of the forecasts be excused by the fact that the period before 1975 was inherently less predictable than earlier periods? As we have seen with population projections, the volatility of a period can be expressed as the sum of annual growth rate variations from the mean growth rate for the period. Let us consider, then, the 1965–70 and 1970–75 periods in order to assess five-year electricity forecasts for the 1970 and 1975 target dates. During the earlier period, which had an annual electricity consumption growth rate of about 7.9 percent, the variation from this rate was on the average 1.1 percent for the five years of the period. For 1970–75, the annual growth rate averaged 4.6 percent, while the average variation from this mean was 2.9 percent. If these measures of volatility are divided into the five-year forecast errors (i.e., forecasts made from 1964 to 1966 for the 1970 target date, and those made

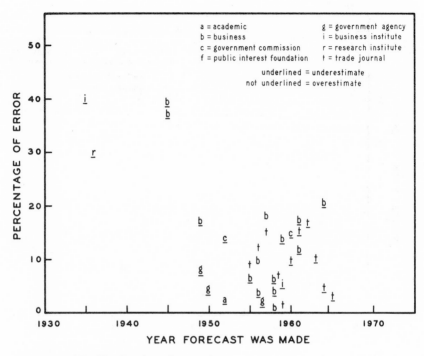

5.9. Errors of Ten-Year Petroleum Consumption
Forecasts, by Source

from 1969 to 1971 for 1975), the different levels of growth rate variability can be discounted. The 1964–66 five-year forecasts were, on the average, 4.2 percent off the true 1970 electricity consumption total. The 1969–71 forecasts were in error by 15.3 percent for the 1975 total. Therefore, even if differences in variability are controlled by dividing each mean error by the measure of volatility, the error for 1975 remains higher: 5.3 compared to 3.9 for the 1970 forecasts. While the later period was indeed more volatile, the later errors were worse than earlier errors by an even greater magnitude.

Although all major aspects of energy use are knit together in their connection with population, fuel supply, and economic activity (as measured, for example, by GNP or the industrial index), they are not all equally vulnerable to unexpected fluctuations in these basic trends. The unexpected downturn in energy supplies and economic activity just prior to 1975 had a greater impact on the electricity-use trend than on the petroleum-use trend, even though oil was the one commodity apparently most central to the crisis. While the 1975 petroleum-use forecasts made during the early 1970s certainly were worse than those made for earlier target years (e.g., 1965 or 1970), their typical error of 10 percent was better than the error of comparable 1975 electricity or

109

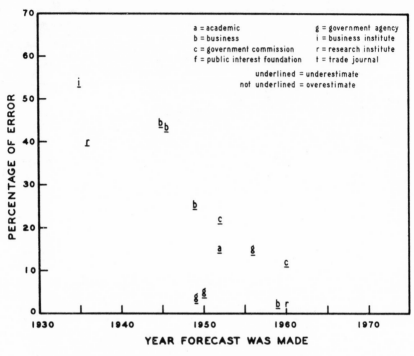

5.10. Errors of Fifteen-Year Petroleum Consumption
Forecasts, by Source

total energy forecasts, which averaged 15 percent. In other words, although electricity and total-energy forecasts are in general more accurate than petroleum forecasts (errors of 6 percent versus errors of 10 percent for ten-year forecasts), their accuracy declines more precipitously when an important structural change in the energy balance is encountered.

This means that policy-makers must evaluate the likely accuracy of the forecasts in terms of two very different scenarios: one involves the maintenance of the existing economic structure; the other involves structural changes. Of course, knowing this is of little help to the policy-maker unless he has some way of knowing whether structural changes are likely to occur. It is therefore useful for the forecast-user to know the probability of structural change, even if it is not the most likely outcome. "Lookout institutions," which are designed to monitor (without necessarily forecasting) the social and economic system in search of indications of problems, changes, or crises on the horizon, are particularly well suited for this purpose. The rationale of lookout institutions is "to conceive of possible futures," and to address these possibilities.[18] Anticipation of possible structural changes thus comes as a

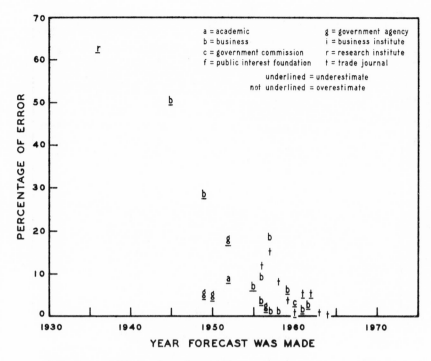

5.11. Errors of 1965 Petroleum Consumption
Forecasts, by Source

by-product of the lookout institution's scanning of potentialities, which is broader than the typical forecasting focus on *the* most likely outcome.

EFFECTS OF SOURCES

All institutional sites show approximately the same level of accuracy for each of the energy forecasting tasks examined here. This is not surprising, since forecast personnel often shuttle back and forth between government and industry, use basically the same methods, and share the same core assumptions. It does, however, contradict several widely held impressions.

First, apparently there is a rather widespread belief that forecasts produced by governmental agencies are not quite as good as those made by the private sector or by public commissions. Corporations and the government pay millions of dollars for the energy forecasts of firms like AD Little, Ebasco Services, Stanford Research Institute, and the Battelle Institute, yet governmental agencies forecast the same trends, often with as much diversity of methods as shown by the private forecasters. Prominent public commissions, such as the 1952 President's Materials Policy Commission (Paley Commis-

111

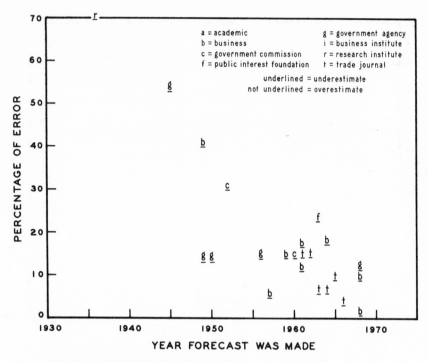

5.12. Errors of 1970 Petroleum Consumption
Forecasts, by Source

sion),[19] attract far more attention than do agency studies. When energy analysts use the forecasts of a single source as the basis for their analysis, they usually choose one of the more prominent private-sector studies, such as those of the Chase Manhattan Bank or the National Petroleum Council, rather than the equally elaborate governmental studies by the Bureau of Mines or the Office of Oil and Gas. This user's bias against governmental forecasts appears to be quite unjustified. If accuracy is the criterion for valuing forecasts, the governmental agencies have done just as well as the other sources. The Federal Power Commission's staff forecasts have shown a negative bias, but, even with this bias, they are as accurate as those of the private sector. If elaborateness and detail are valued,[20] the energy-balance models of Morrison of the Bureau of Mines[21] are on a par with the most elaborate research institute studies.

The comparable quality of governmental energy projections does not imply that policy-makers should withhold their financial support from non-governmental forecasters. The more opinions the policy-maker has at his disposal on the shape of the future, the more adequately he can prepare for

112

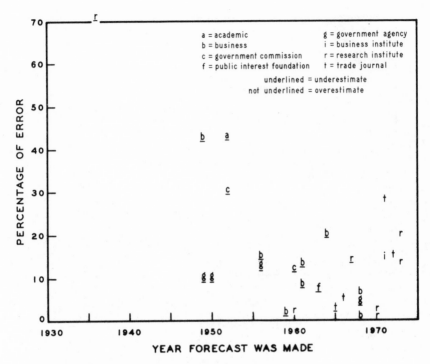

5.13. Errors of 1975 Petroleum Consumption
Forecasts, by Source

different contingencies. It does imply that governmental forecasts should not
be disregarded simply because more expensive, sometimes "flashier" private
studies are available.

The second widespread impression is that forecasts produced by private
businesses or business associations are deliberately inaccurate. Private energy
suppliers have come under attack each time energy problems pose the prospect of eventually higher profits for the companies. In such instances,
exemplified by the 1973–74 oil crisis, private forecasters are suspected of
biasing their projections.

The suspicions leveled against the private sector's energy information extend well beyond forecasts, into questions of the veracity of information
provided on *current* costs, inventories, known reserves, safety hazards, and
so on. The findings of this study do not touch on these questions, however.
Whether the oil companies have been deliberately misleading on the
availability of oil, or the electric utility companies have dissembled the costs
and hazards of their generating plants, are questions that cannot be answered
by examining forecast accuracy.

113

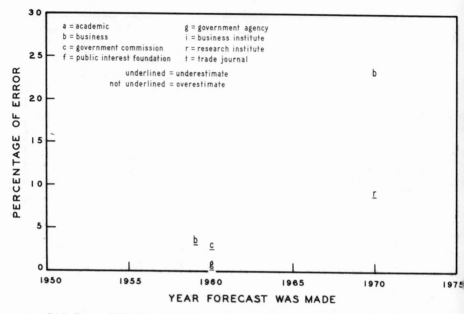

5.14. Errors of Five-Year Total Energy Consumption
Forecasts, by Source

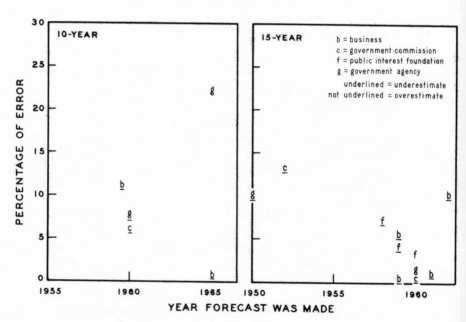

5.15. Errors of Ten- and Fifteen-Year Total Energy
Consumption Forecasts, by Source

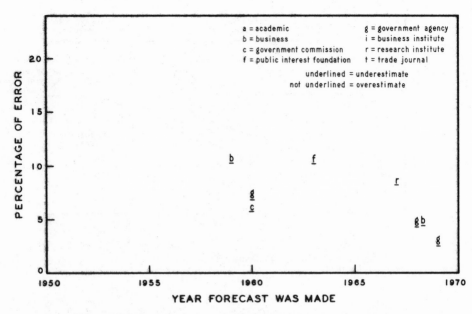

5.16. Errors of 1970 Total Energy Consumption
Forecasts, by Source

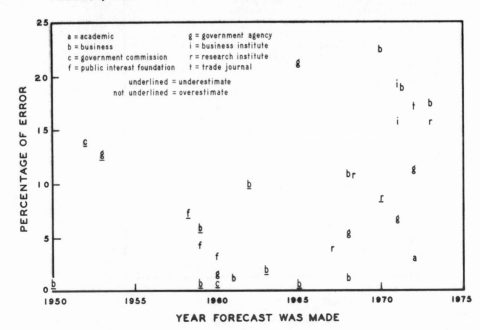

5.17. Errors of 1975 Total Energy Consumption
Forecasts, by Source

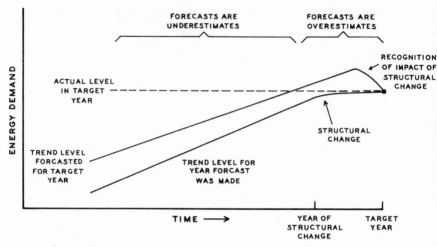

5.18. General Pattern of Energy Demand Trends and
Forecasts for 1975

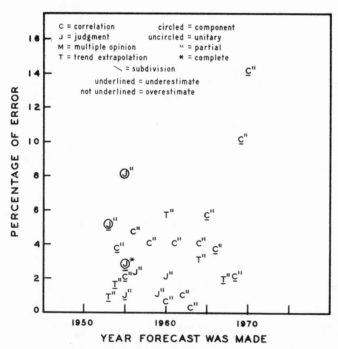

5.19. Errors of Five-Year Electricity Consumption
Forecasts, by Method

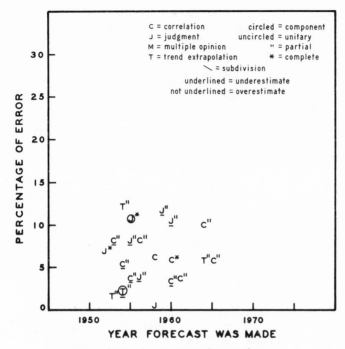

5.20. Errors of Ten-Year Electricity Consumption Forecasts, by Method

However, in terms of predicting long-term energy demand, for which mis-leadingly high projections *could* benefit energy suppliers (e.g., by promoting governmental incentives for oil companies' explorations or for electric utilities' expansions), private-sector forecasts do not show any bias. In general, common preconceptions of the future pervade all institutional sites at any point in time, yielding uniformly optimistic or pessimistic forecasts regardless of whether the forecasters sit in the private or public sector.

The one exception to this rule involves the government's electricity fore-casts, which, although as accurate as those of the private sector, do reflect a bias.

The long-range electricity forecasts made by governmental sources (primar-ily the FPC) have a pronounced pessimistic bias. Ten- and fifteen-year fore-casts by the government have produced twice as many negative errors as positive errors. The nearly even balance of optimistic and pessimistic private-sector forecasts indicates that the governmental bias is not simply a function of the *Zeitgeist* of the years in which the forecasts were made, nor is it the result of "unexpectedly dynamic" growth prior to the target years.

117

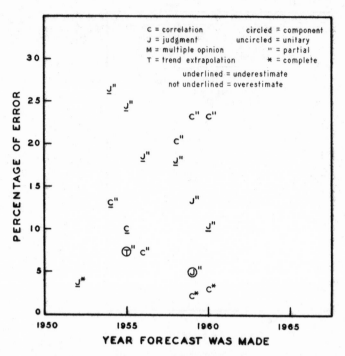

5.21. Errors of Fifteen-Year Electricity Consumption
Forecasts, by Method

On the most obvious and tautological level, the governmental forecasts are
pessimistic because the judgmental approach utilized by the FPC rejects the
plausibility of extrapolating high past growth into the future. Behind the
judgment, however, lies a built-in bias caused by the focus of the FPC's
preoccupations during the 1960s. In contrast to today's preoccupation with the
adequacy of energy supply, the main preoccupation of many energy policy-
makers during the 1960s was the inefficiency resulting from unused capacity.
The FPC's reports and its 1964 national power survey emphasized the gap
between capacity and demand, stressed the cost implications of excess capacity, and urged the promotion of greater electricity use (e.g., all-electric
homes) as a solution.[22] Apparently this concern with the problems of lower
demand colored the forecasters' expectations of future growth in the direction
of the perceived problem. It is revealing that *Electrical World,* written as
much for utility planners as for utility suppliers, seemed more concerned with
the problem of keeping up with demand, and forecasted higher demand trends
as well. The general lesson may be that the policy-maker should be aware of
the preoccupations of his forecaster, and expect the forecaster's worst fears to
color his results.

118

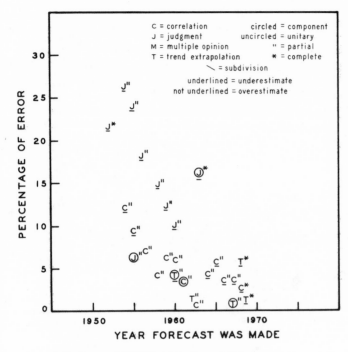

5.22. Errors of 1970 Electricity Consumption
Forecasts, by Method

EFFECTS OF METHODOLOGY

For each of the specific trends examined here, energy forecasting has been dominated by the same methods: trend extrapolation, judgment, and correlation, with an even mix of approaches representing the options for scope, division, and construction. While a few of these methodological combinations produce somewhat greater errors or some biases in forecasting one trend or another, methodology is of secondary importance for the accuracy of energy forecasts.

The overall evidence on the accuracy of electricity forecasts, shown in figures 5.19–5.23, suggests that no method is dramatically superior. However, for both the ten-year forecasts and the projections for 1970, the extrapolational and correlational methods produced more reliably accurate forecasts than did the judgmental method employed by the FPC and others. Since the correlational method is often akin to extrapolation (because the base projections to which the electricity trend is correlated are often themselves extrapolations), a plausible explanation for the superior performance of extrapolation and correlation is that these methods have in effect insulated the extensions of existing trends from the personal opinions of the forecasters, who in

119

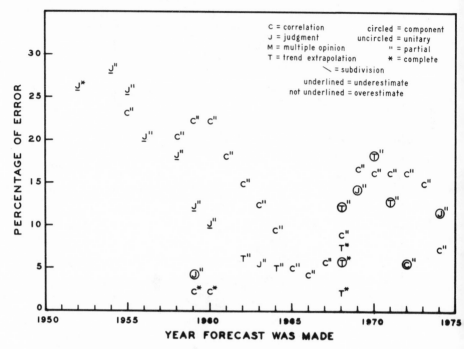

5.23. Errors of 1975 Electricity Consumption
Forecasts, by Method

general had doubts that the fantastic historical expansion in industrial capacity and energy use could continue. Most of the judgmental forecasts were pessimistic, reflecting obviously the "judgment" of the forecaster that the growth trend could not continue—when in fact it did until 1973. Nevertheless, the judgmental approach did not produce better forecasts of the 1975 electricity consumption level, despite the change in actual trend line.

The performance of petroleum forecasts employing different methods indicates that the choice of method is effectively irrelevant to the accuracy of these forecasts. Figures 5.24–5.29 indicate that correlation, extrapolation, and judgment produce forecasts of almost identical medians and ranges of accuracy. Trend extrapolations using very recent data do no better or worse than extrapolations using more historical data. The few multiple-opinion forecasts are of ordinary accuracy. The strategy of embedding petroleum demand forecasts within broader projections of total energy use does not help or harm the accuracy of the results; nor does using the subdivision approach. Furthermore, the approach of breaking down the overall oil demand trend into components of specific products (e.g., gasoline, fuel oil, etc.) or uses (resi-

120

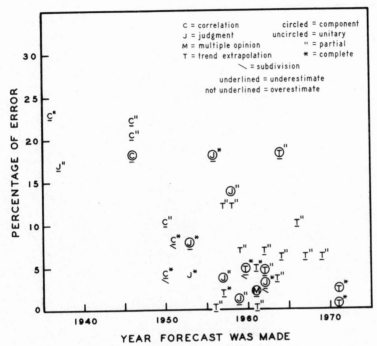

5.24. Errors of Five-Year Petroleum Consumption Forecasts, by Method

dential, automotive, etc.) does not provide greater accuracy than forecasts of the entire petroleum demand trend.

Only one bias consistently shows through the welter of methods and results. The subdivision approach, which calculates petroleum consumption as a proportion of previously projected *total* energy, has produced errors of only average magnitude, but these errors show a consistently pessimistic bias. This bias of underestimation is not surprising, since the rationale behind the subdivision approach is to introduce the total energy limit "to constrain the magnitude of the separate components."[23] Policy-makers should be aware that this method, which has the laudable purpose of sensitizing the projections of individual components to the constraints of the whole, has a built-in conservative bias. However, it is interesting to note that a bias, once recognized, is actually very promising, since upward adjustments to remove the bias would probably result in improved accuracy—a gain that cannot be achieved with procedures that already are unbiased.

Comparisons of total-energy forecasts of fixed lengths (i.e., five, ten, or fifteen years) reveal very little about the comparative advantages of different

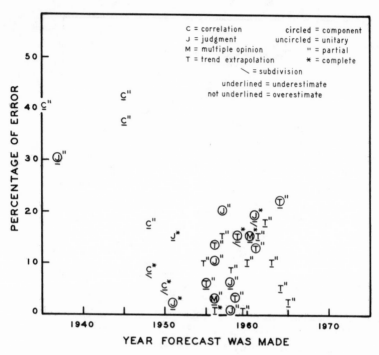

5.25. Errors of Ten-Year Petroleum Consumption
Forecasts, by Method

methodologies, because, as figure 5.30 demonstrates, the magnitude of error
is overwhelmingly a function of the year in which a forecast was made and the
year for which it was targeted. However, the patterns of errors for 1970 and
1975 forecasts (figures 5.31 and 5.32) show that, even when some control is
exercised over the differences resulting from different formulation and target
dates, different methods produce approximately the same levels of inaccuracy. Correlation, judgment, and extrapolation have produced both highly
accurate and highly inaccurate forecasts. The distinction between the
building-block and subdivision approaches also does not make much difference in terms of forecast accuracy or forecast bias. The lack of correspondence between the building-block approach and overestimation contradicts the widely held opinion that the building-block method has an inherent optimistic bias.[24] In fact, building-block forecasts are generally pessimistic when subdivision forecasts are pessimistic, and optimistic when subdivision forecasts are optimistic. Biases of optimism or pessimism are creatures of
the general outlook at specific points in time, rather than the shortcomings of
particular methods.

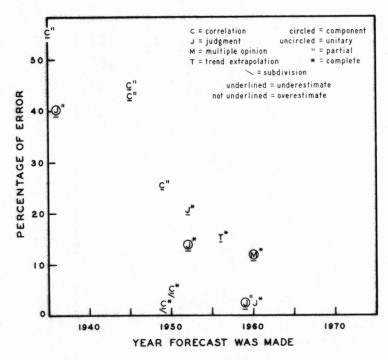

5.26. Errors of Fifteen-Year Petroleum Consumption
Forecasts, by Method

Ordinarily, it is conceivable that a failure to find performance differences between "types" of methods or approaches may be due to incorrect choices in categorizing types. For example, the correlation-extrapolation-judgment distinction may not be the one that reveals whatever is important for producing good forecasts. One can always argue that some other categorization will neatly separate the good forecasts from the bad. There are two reasons why this problem is not relevant to our energy demand analysis. First, we have examined all of the applicable differentiae—not only the rationale of the projection, but also the differences between complete and partial forecasting, subdivision and building-block composition, and unitary and component projection. If there is a hidden methodological distinction capable of isolating the accurate forecasts, it has escaped the awareness of the forecasters (as indicated in their own descriptions of their methods) and the theoretical literature on forecasting. Second, the same method, often employed by the same forecaster, has produced different results for different years and time horizons, but in no discernable pattern. For example, the straightforward extrapolation method of McGraw-Hill's *National Petroleum News* has produced both

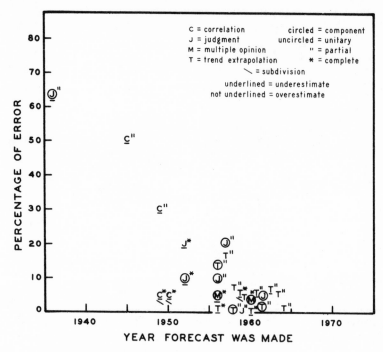

5.27. Errors of 1965 Petroleum Consumption
Forecasts, by Method

excellent and mediocre results for all time lengths. No matter how these forecasts are characterized in terms of methodology, the appraisal will necessarily be mixed.

Another explanation for the lack of significant differences in the accuracy of different methods cannot be dismissed so easily. It is possible—indeed, there is strong evidence in some cases—that forecasters often employ a mixture of methods even when one method is specified as the primary technique. Therefore, what appears to be a forecast using one method may be influenced by the implications of the other methods—and may share the improvements or liabilities that these methods impart to the ultimate accuracy of the forecast. Without an intensive study of each forecaster's procedures and the atmosphere of opinion in which he worked, it is impossible to say for sure how much influence other methods had on the outcomes. It is not known whether the forecaster's "judgment" was molded by his scratch-pad extrapolations, or (in some cases) whether his extrapolations or correlations were acceptable to him *because* they conformed to his personal judgment.

124

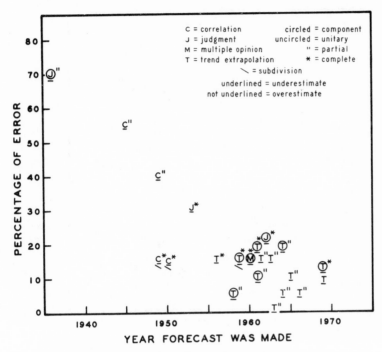

5.28. Errors of 1970 Petroleum Consumption
Forecasts, by Method

This is essentially an appraisal problem, but it also indicates something about the nature of the forecasting process that makes the analysis of "methodological effects" less important than the performance of the whole set of forecasts. Most forecasters do in fact use mixed methods. Therefore, the quality of a single method not only is difficult to determine, but is of little relevance to the bulk of forecasting efforts, for which particular methods are not used singly, but rather in consort with other methods.

IMPROVEMENTS IN ENERGY FORECASTING

There is no indication yet of improved methodology in forecasting energy demand. Although petroleum demand forecasts improved after 1950, this improvement came about not as a result of new forecasting techniques, but rather from a better understanding of the shape of the post–World War II world. The majority of energy forecasts produced during the last ten years are very similar in methodology to those of the previous decade. In fact, some of the 1940s efforts, particularly the correlational methods used by the Bureau of

125

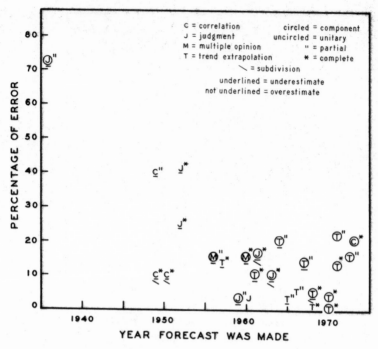

5.29. Errors of 1975 Petroleum Consumption
Forecasts, by Method

Mines forecaster Barnett in 1949–50[25] and by the oil companies in 1945,[26] are every bit as sophisticated as the correlational methods employed today, although today's data base may be better.

The only glimmer of hope for better forecasts in the future is the performance of the very few econometric energy models whose predictions for 1975 make them partially appraisable. Most full-scale energy models have been developed over the past five years, and therefore have not been applied to target dates before 1980. However, the two models applied to forecasting energy for 1975, the Belzer-Almon model for petroleum demand and the Tyrell-Mount model[27] for electricity and total energy, performed very well in forecasting for an obviously very difficult year. The Tyrell-Mount prediction for 1975 electricity use, which was optimistic by 5 percent, was the only forecast produced between 1969 and 1973 that was less than 13 percent in error. Their total-energy forecast (with a 3 percent error) was also the best for that period. The 1975 Belzer-Almon forecast of petroleum demand is the best post-1970 petroleum forecast. The success of these models may be coincidental; it may reflect a normally pessimistic bias that was proved right *this time* by the unusual events that affected the energy balance from 1973 to 1975. On

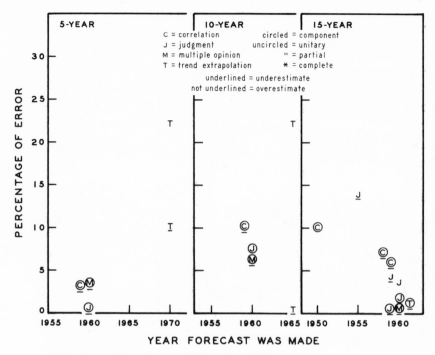

5.30. Errors of Five-, Ten-, and Fifteen-Year Total
Energy Consumption Forecasts, by Method

the other hand, it may signal that the modeling approach, which can incorporate the intricate interactions of supply, demand, substitution, and policy, is a
significant improvement over more limited methods. At this point, our only
consolation is that by 1980 it will be possible to take a harder look at how well
these models have performed.

Looking ahead to what is still "future," how much confidence should we
have in existing forecasts? What can we say about the shape of 1985, on the
basis of forecasts already on hand? By examining the post–energy crisis
projections, we can at least get an idea of the uncertainty in predicting energy
patterns in an era recognized as full of potential surprises.

The most recent energy forecasts—those made after 1973—are different in
form from earlier projections. They are more frequently based on econometric
models that weave energy into the fabric of economic interactions, and they
often take advantage of the flexibility of such models to spin out multiple
projections reflecting different contextual assumptions of "scenarios."

The use of interactive energy models obviously has been facilitated by the
parallel growth in econometric modeling undertaken by economic forecasters
127 (see chapter 4). Some of the elaborate econometric models produce energy

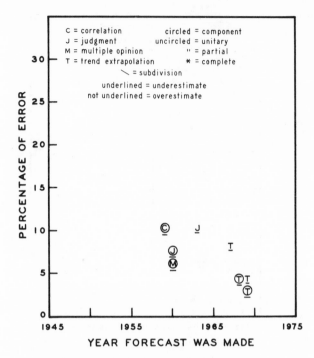

C = correlation   circled = component
J = judgment   uncircled = unitary
M = multiple opinion   " = partial
T = trend extrapolation   ∗ = complete
              ╲ = subdivision
        underlined = underestimate
      not underlined = overestimate

5.31. Errors of 1970 Total Energy Consumption
Forecasts, by Method

forecasts along with their projections of GNP, inflation rates, and the like.[28] But an additional push in the direction of modeling has been the recognition that, in times of changing structures and trends, many previously ignorable factors must be taken into account to explain energy growth. For example, the sensitivity of energy use to the price of fuels could be overlooked when cost was not a limiting factor, but now fuel costs—and the multiple factors that influence costs—cannot be ignored. Both extrapolation and correlation, which are premised on the stability of underlying relationships among energy and economic factors, lose their *prima facie* validity when these relationships are known to be changing. Intuitive judgments become unreliable when emerging patterns of energy use involve too many considerations for implicit calculations to handle. More than ever before, energy supplies, fuel prices, energy demand, and the level of economic activity are *mutually* constraining.

These are precisely the circumstances for which models that simulate period-to-period changes in supply, demand, and price factors were designed. These models can express mutual (and intricate) causation by calculating a time-specific value for each variable as a function of the others for each

128

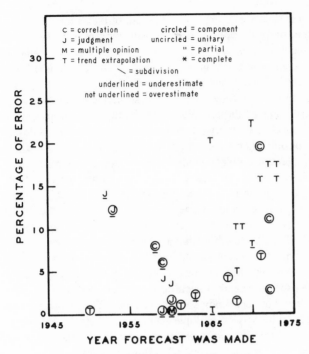

5.32. Errors of 1975 Total Energy Consumption
Forecasts, by Method

successive time period.[29] Thus, for example, electricity demand can be calculated from the average price of electricity at the time and the average price of
gas in the previous time period.[30] Demand for gas for that period can be
determined from the previous price of gas, the demand for electricity, and the
price of electricity. Unlike the more traditional econometric approach of
simultaneous equations, the simulation modeler does not "solve" a large set
of equations (i.e., determine consistent values for the variables involved in
the equations so that they can all hold at the same time) in order to determine
the values of energy variables. Instead, he updates these values by running the
set of equations for each time period.

The scenarios presented by the recent forecasts are usually differentiated in
terms of governmental policy options, various price levels of oil, or the
efficacy of conservation efforts. The rather sudden appearance of multiple
scanarios as the norm for energy forecasts signifies that the future of energy is
regarded as manipulable—that discrete decisions (such as OPEC's) have a
profound effect on energy use, and that manipulation has become a pressing
need for many governmental and private policy-makers.

The use of multiple scenarios complicates the task of presenting and comparing different sets of projections. There are no conventions as to how extreme the extreme scenarios are to be. Some forecasts cover scenarios ranging from "maximum conservation efforts" to "*no* conservation";[31] others may cover only the likely outcomes of the conservation efforts. Hence, the range of trends within a single forecaster's set of scanarios may reflect very different things—the range of the conceivable or the range of the probable.

Because of the noncomparability of entire forecast sets, the multiple-scenario forecasts considered here are represented only by that scenario which yields the median projections, unless another scenario is deemed most probable. The median forecast is a reasonable choice for several reasons: first, because forecasters attempting to cover all reasonable possibilities are likely to include the full range of scenarios, some above and some below the "most likely;" second, because forecast-users are likely to focus on the median forecast as the "middle-of-the-road" estimate. Therefore, by comparing median forecasts, our analysis can examine the range of what are meant to be, or presumed to be, the most likely projections. However, it should be noted that our focus on median scenarios and projections is not designed to convey the diversity and complexity of each study's set of scenarios. The fact that recent energy forecasts rely so heavily on multiple scenarios reflects the opinion of the forecasters that different outcomes are quite possible, depending on the actions of the government, the public, and other relevant actors. Our analysis is designed simply to determine whether the midpoints of various forecasts converge or diverge.

Table 5.1 represents the median results of a number of forecasting efforts conducted between 1974 and 1976. This compilation is representative rather than exhaustive.

Table 5.1: Recent Energy Demand Forecasts

Source	Year	Total Energy Demand (10^{15} BTU/yr.)		Electricity Generated by Utilities (billion kwhr./yr.)		Petroleum Consumption (million barrels/yr.)	
		1980	1985	1980	1985	1980	1985
Shell Oil	1974	83	98	—	—	8,300	8,030
FEA[a]	1976	—	99	2,574	3,348	—	7,556
FEA[b]	1974	87	102	—	3,990	6,077	7,423
Bureau of Mines	1975	87	104	2,769	3,960	7,433	8,375
Data Resources, Inc.	1975	90	106	2,589	3,383	7,099	8,158
Ford Foundation Energy Policy Proj.	1974	92	107	—	—	6,789	5,475
John Gray/NUS, Inc.[a]	1975	—	113	—	3,604	—	—
OECD[b]	1974	97	114	3,042	4,207	6,855	7,556

Continued

Table 5.1: Recent Energy Demand Forecasts *(Continued)*

Source	Year	Total Energy Demand (10^{15} BTU/yr.)		Electricity Generated by Utilities (billion kwhr./yr.)		Petroleum Consumption (million barrels/yr.)	
		1980	1985	1980	1985	1980	1985
AEC	1974	—	118	—	—	—	—
John McKetta/U. of Texas	1975	107	138	—	—	—	—
Westinghouse	1975	—	—	2,516	3,211	—	—
Joskow and Baughman/MIT[a]	1976	—	—	2,514	3,217	—	—
Oak Ridge National Laboratory	1975	—	—	2,530	3,245	—	—
Livermore Laboratory	1974	—	—	2,603	3,419	—	—
FPC Technical Adv. Comm.	1974	—	—	2,663	3,564	—	—
A. D. Little, Inc.	1974	—	—	2,724	3,715	—	—
ERDA[b]	1975	—	—	3,071	3,890	—	7,478
Young/U. of California[a]	1975	—	—	—	—	6,130	6,480
Bradshaw/ARCO	1974	—	—	—	—	—	6,680
Bureau of Mines	1974	—	—	—	—	—	6,989
Independent Petrol. Assoc.	1976	—	—	—	—	—	8,942

Sources: *The Petroleum Economist*, April 1974, p. 133; U.S., Federal Energy Administration, *National Energy Outlook, 1976* (Washington, D.C.: Government Printing Office, 1976), pp. 16–18, 239 (for electricity, figures recalculated from the 1974–1985 growth rate on the 1974 base of electricity *generation* of 1,877BK); idem, *Project Independence Report* (Washington, D.C.: Government Printing Office, 1974); U.S., Department of the Interior, Bureau of Mines, *United States Energy through the Year 2000, rev. ed.*, prepared by Walter G. Dupree, Jr., and John S. Corsentino (Washington, D.C.: Government Printing Office, 1975), p. 10 for total energy, p. 36 for electricity, and p. 63 for petroleum; Edward A. Hudson and Dale W. Jorgenson, "Tax Policy and Energy Conservation," Harvard Institute of Economic Research, Discussion Paper no. 395 (Cambridge, Mass., 1975); Joseph A. Yager et al., *Energy and U.S. Foreign Policy: A Report to the Energy Policy Project of the Ford Foundation* (Cambridge, Mass.: Ballinger, 1974), p. 247; John E. Gray, "Accelerating Supply and Use of Electricity: A Keystone for United States Energy Policy," *Public Utilities Fortnightly*, 27 March 1975, p. 18; Organisation for Economic Cooperation and Development, *Energy Prospects to 1985*, Report of the Secretary General (Paris, 1974), 1: 47; U.S., Atomic Energy Commission, *Nuclear Power Growth, 1974-2000* (Washington, D.C.: Government Printing Office, 1974), p. 11; John J. McKetta, "Today's Energy Sources—Their Projected Life," *Energy Communications* 1, no. 1 (1975): 16; J. H. Chiles and R. E. Reardon, *Projection of Trends in Economics, Loads, and Generation* (Pittsburgh, Pa.: Westinghouse Electric Corporation, 1975); Paul L. Joskow and Martin L. Baughman, "The Future of the U.S. Nuclear Energy Industry," *The Bell Journal of Economics* 20 (1976): 20; U.S., Energy Research and Development Administration, *A National Plan for Energy Research, Development, and Demonstration* (Washington, D.C.: Government Printing Office, 1975), 1: V-3; Jeffrey W. Young et al., "Land Use, Energy Flow, and Policy Making in Society," final report prepared for the University of California at Davis, Institute of Ecology, Interdisciplinary Systems Group, 1 September 1975 (mimeographed), pp. 407-49; *The Petroleum Economist*, November 1974, p. 406; U.S., Congress, Senate, Committee on Finance, *Hearings on the Energy Conservation and Conversion Act of 1975, July 10-18, 1975*, statement of C. John Miller, president of the Independent Petroleum Association (Washington, D.C.: Government Printing Office, 1975), p. 581.

[a]Median projection or scenario.

[b]Average of median projections or scenarios.

These recent forecasts reflect sharp reactions to the energy crisis. The future levels of energy consumption are seen as far lower than before. Compared to forecasts created between 1971 and 1973,[32] the more recent forecasts' median "intermediate" projections for 1985 are lower by about 15 percent for total energy, 20 percent for electricity generation, and more than 30 percent for petroleum consumption.

The range of estimates clearly reveals the uncertainty of our energy future. The range of the middle half of the forecasts (i.e., excluding the highest 25 percent and the lowest 25 percent of the 1974–76 forecasts) is a useful measure of the diversity of these most recent forecasts because it excludes the extreme cases that *may* have come about because some sets of scenarios were skewed toward high or low estimates. This range of middle projections runs from about 102 quadrillion to 113 quadrillion (10^{15}) BTUs for 1985's total energy consumption. This spread of about 11 quadrillion BTUs is more than twice as great as the comparable spread for the 1971–73 projections. The range of 1985 electricity generation forecasts is from 3,300 billion to 3,900 billion kilowatt hours, a spread which is one and a half times as great as that for 1971–73 forecasts. The range of petroleum consumption forecasts of recent vintage is about the same as that of the 1971–73 forecasts, but this is because the range for recent 1985 projections (from 7,000 million barrels per year to 8,000 million barrels) mirrors the much lower magnitude of oil consumption envisioned by the newer forecasts. In short, the post–oil embargo forecasts reveal a greater uncertainty about the future than do earlier forecasts. Of course, actual energy use in 1985 cannot really be less certain in 1975 than in 1971, but the magnitude of uncertainty is more evident in the variation shown by the most recent forecasts.

There is, of course, no precise way to determine now how great the errors of these forecasts will be. However, the spread of the middle range of forecasts is an indication of the minimum degree of error that may be expected from these forecasts, since different results in forecasting the same trend at the same point in time mean that some of the forecasts must be in error. As explained in detail in the chapter 7, one-half of this middle range, which represents the differences between the median and each of the upper and lower quartile values, reflects the *minimum* error that a "typical" forecast can have. For the 1974–76 forecasts, these minimum errors are about 5 percent of the median value for the total energy projections, 8.5 percent for the electricity forecasts, and 7.0 percent for the petroleum forecasts. Actual typical errors may turn out to be greater, to the extent that actual values diverge from the entire set of forecasts for each trend. It is notable that these *minimum* errors are nearly as great as the actual errors of ten-year projections for earlier target dates. It follows that recent forecasts can at best be only slightly better than their predecessors, and may in fact turn out to be worse.

ESTIMATING ULTIMATE PETROLEUM
RESOURCES

Projections of resource needs are meaningful to policy-makers only when they are linked with estimates of future supply. For some energy forms, such as electricity, future supply depends mainly on the effort and expense devoted to producing them; nature does not impose any practical finite limits. For primary natural fuels, such as coal, petroleum, and natural gas, however, the ultimate volume is fixed, since only insignificant deposits of each develop in fifty or a hundred years.

While geologists regard the estimation of coal resources as relatively simple (and the abundance of coal in the United States makes precise estimation less compelling), estimating oil or gas is quite difficult. There are no cut-and-dried surface indications for most oil and gas deposits, so estimates of ultimate oil and gas supplies are necessarily problematic inferences from geological or past-discovery experience.

Oil and natural gas form together; consequently, the problems of estimating the supply of both fuels are the same. Since the problem of petroleum reserves has received somewhat more attention, this study is limited to an examination of the estimation efforts for petroleum. Because of the co-occurrence of oil and gas, and the parallelism of approaches used to estimate them, the analysis of petroleum estimation can be extended directly to the estimation of natural gas resources as well.

Estimating petroleum supply appears at first blush to be a straightforward task of determining how much oil lies in the earth. It does not appear to involve a projection at all. In the recent energy debates, it has been portrayed as a matter of detective work to infer, from geological information on un-drilled areas and from past experience, the magnitude of this fixed quantity.

However, though the total amount of petroleum (produced or in-ground) is fixed, and therefore independent of future events, estimation of how much oil actually will be recovered (i.e., ultimate supply) must involve technological and economic forecasting, explicitly or implicitly. Technology is a major factor in determining the amount of oil ultimately to be retrieved because the total volume of oil extracted from identified fields depends on the efficiency of recovery. This efficiency has increased from about 15 percent before 1930 to around 35 percent today.[33] Ultimate production therefore depends significantly on the degree to which future technology can improve the recovery factor in petroleum extraction. Technological advances in the methods of discovering oil deposits also are obviously important in determining how much petroleum ultimately will be recovered.

Economic conditions affect ultimate supply in several ways. The higher the price of oil, the greater the number of potential oil fields for which exploration and production become profitable. Offshore and deep-sea drilling, expensive secondary recovery efforts, and exploration in hostile environments (such as northern Alaska) are profitable in some economic circumstances but not in others. Moreover, the volume of oil retrievable from a given site depends on the rapidity of pumping; rapid extraction leaves more oil behind, and is therefore less efficient in terms of the proportion recovered. Therefore, economic (or political) conditions that lead to strong immediate demands for domestic oil may encourage more rapid extraction and consequently a smaller ultimate yield.

The image and influence of the resource scientists (mainly geologists) engaged in the energy debate have been damaged by the controversy and disagreement over the seemingly objective "fact" of ultimate petroleum resources. The apparent failure of geologists and other experts to agree on the magnitude of ultimate reserves has discredited all attempts to establish the crucial supply side of the energy equations invoked in the energy debate.

Since the 1930s, attempts to estimate how much petroleum lies beneath out land and offshore areas have been subjected to severe criticism. In 1933 V. R. Garfias, a leading geological consultant, wrote that "estimates of possible and probable oil deposits are as a rule but idle conjectures."[34] The National Resources Committee decided in 1939 that it is useless to try to estimate the volume of petroleum available for extraction because ultimate reserves "are not known; they will not be known in advance to drilling."[35]

As a result of these criticisms, and the apparent failures of earlier estimates, very few estimates were attempted during the period 1922–42. Government and industry geologists were content to estimate "proved reserves," which consisted largely of petroleum known to exist in already discovered oil fields. As the volume of proved reserves fluctuated (a result of short-term economic and oil price changes, which influence drilling and pumping rates), "oil scares" arose and subsided with little consideration for petroleum availability in the long run.

The concern for oil sufficiency during World War II and the Korean War stimulated renewed efforts to estimate ultimate reserves, but these attempts again were criticized. Even some of the most prominent estimators were highly critical of the enterprise. M. King Hubbert, a noted geologist with Shell Oil and later with the U.S. Geological Survey, said in 1962 that "the preponderance of recent attempts to determine this quantity are grossly in error."[36]

The basis for most criticisms of ultimate-reserve estimates has been the examination of existing estimates, which have shown that there is considerable diversity in the volumes estimated in different studies, and that the earliest estimates of producible oil have already been exceeded by total actual production.[37] The great variation in estimates is taken to mean that some of them are

134

obviously very much in error; the fact that earlier estimates already have been exceeded is interpreted as proof that specific estimates are definitely wrong.

Such comparisons of ultimate-reserve estimates with one another and with actual production levels are extremely misleading. The problem is that definitions of ultimate reserves differ in nontrivial ways. When the estimates are adjusted to the point where they are indeed comparable, much of the disparity among estimates disappears. Furthermore, the earliest estimates, which appear to be ludicrously low in terms of the petroleum production already on record, become much more reasonable when we take into account the fact that such estimates were directed at the amount of petroleum producible *given the technology of recovery at the time*.[38]

There are two important distinctions in terms of what the ultimate-reserve estimates were trying to measure—differences in how ultimate reserves are defined. Many have been estimates of how much petroleum ultimately could be produced at the recovery rates prevailing in the year of the estimate. Some authorities have even attempted to establish this measure as *the* definition of ultimate reserves.[39] But another definition has been nearly as prominent: the ultimate volume of petroleum produced, allowing for the effects of future improvements in extraction technology and the economic attractiveness of recovering more oil at higher prices.[40] According to 1970 estimates of both quantities by Ira Cram for the National Petroleum Council, there is a tremendous difference in these definitions. Under identical assumptions of the incidence of oil deposits (inferred from geological formations), Cram calculated that ultimate oil production using *current* recovery techniques would be 258 billion barrels, whereas with improved recovery rates (60 percent compared with the current rate of 33 percent), total yield would be 432 billion barrels.[41]

Which definition is more useful is a matter of debate. The current-technology definition obviously underestimates the actual volume of petroleum to be produced (assuming accurate estimates of oil in place), since technology is bound to improve, but current-technology estimates are not intended to reflect technological change, and hence cannot err on that account.

The second difference in defining ultimate reserves concerns the area covered by the estimate. Obviously, ultimate U.S. reserves, excluding Alaska and offshore areas, will be considerably lower than the reserves of the whole country. The inclusion of these areas in estimates of ultimate reserves has only recently become common, in part because exploitation of these areas has only recently become feasible with existing technology.

Regardless of the merits of these definitions, the point is that estimates of very different things have been compared as if they were the same, thereby leading to a distorted impression of the extent of difference among ultimate reserve estimates. The earliest estimates, which have been subjected to the greatest criticism since they appear to be ludicrously inadequate, were almost always cast in terms of oil recoverable through the drilling and extraction methods *of that era.* Consequently, the fact that cumulative production reached this level, say, fifteen or twenty years later disproves the estimate *only if* the production was accomplished through means available in the year in which the estimate was made. In fact, dramatic advances were made in recovery rates and drilling depths between the time of the early forecasts (1909–31) and the period (around 1950) when these estimates were so scathingly criticized.[42] Hence, much of the oil produced after the early estimates could not have been recovered under the conditions that prevailed when the estimates were made. The implication is not that these estimates were correct, since subsequent exploration has shown that even production by means of the early technology would have exceeded the estimates; rather, it is that the early estimates were not as outrageously inaccurate as deprecators of the estimation task have made them out to be.

To evaluate contemporary estimates, M. King Hubbert, in an influential 1962 report sponsored by the National Academy of Sciences, labeled fourteen estimates (including one of his own) made between 1948 and 1962 as "estimated ultimate U.S. crude-oil reserves." Because the estimates ranged from 110 billion to 590 billion barrels, Hubbert concluded that most attempts at estimation are "grossly in error."[43] However, when the original sources of the estimates are carefully examined, it turns out that the lowest estimate (by Lewis Weeks of Standard Oil of New Jersey) was an estimate only of petroleum producible from the continental U.S. land area using 1948 recovery technology; eight other estimates were of oil extracted from both land and offshore areas (excluding Alaska) using the technology of the late fifties; and five were estimates for the same area but in terms of petroleum extractable by future technologies. Thus, these were not estimates of the same thing under different assumptions; estimates of oil recoverable through current technology do not imply that technology will stagnate and that this volume is all that will be recovered.

Of the estimates listed by Hubbert, the range for future-technology estimates was 300-400 billion barrels. All but one of the current-technology estimates for land and offshore areas were within the range of 145-250 billion barrels. Furthermore, the single anomalous estimate of 590 billion barrels attributed to A. D. Zapp of the U.S. Geological Survey was a totally incorrect interpretation of Zapp's figures. In his original report, Zapp explicitly stated that further exploration "under static economic and technologic conditions . . . would bring the ultimate recoverable quantity to 300 billion barrels."[44] The figure of 590 billion barrels referred to Zapp's estimate of the total volume of oil in the ground, rather than to how much he expected would be recovered. It is interesting to note that in a 1974 Senate hearing Hubbert reiterated his attack on Zapp's study, claiming that Zapp had assumed that future sites to be explored all were as promising as sites already explored.[45] The 1975 National Academy of Sciences study *Mineral Resources and the Environment*[46] picked up this attack in order to discredit the geological-inference approach used by Zapp, apparently without realizing the error of Hubbert's attribution and the fact that Zapp had actually dismissed the possibility of straightforward generalizing to unexplored areas.[47] Taking Zapp's figures explicitly, the range of current-technology estimates was 145–300 billion barrels. Thus, while the ranges Hubbert listed are not negligible, the discrepancies among estimates within each category are far less bleak than Hubbert's presentation implies.

Similar objections can be lodged against other comparisons of ultimate-reserve estimates that seem to demonstrate an *a priori* inaccuracy. In 1960 Milton Searl of the AEC included both current-technology recovery estimates and future-technology recovery estimates in one table, giving a range of from 140 to 1,000–2,000 billion barrels. His conclusion was that "the range of these forecasts is so great as to provide little real guidance as to what ultimate discoveries may be."[48] Of the eleven studies he cited, however, the eight current-technology estimates ranged from 140 billion to 250 billion barrels, the two future-technology estimates ranged from 300 billion to 460 billion barrels, and an extremely high estimate by Gustav Egloff, for the 1952 Paley Commission,[49] was of quite uncertain status.

Most recently, the 1975 National Academy of Sciences report *Mineral Resources and the Environment* contrasts nine estimates of "undiscovered recoverable oil resources," concluding that

estimation of resources of petroleum and natural gas is complicated by the fact that, while methods for the estimation of *proved reserves* are well established, there is no generally accepted method for estimating undiscovered resources. This is reflected in a considerable range in estimates for the latter.... Differences in estimates naturally lead to confusion over the availability of petroleum and natural gas from domestic sources.[50]

To make this point, however, the report includes current-technology estimates (e.g., Week's 1960 calculation), future-technology estimates (such as Hubbert's production-curve calculations, which allow for future advancements in extraction methods), and several anonymous corporate estimates of unspecified definition.

In short, the efforts to discredit the enterprise of estimating ultimate oil resources are themselves of dubious validity. Since 1970 several authorities have devised more careful definitional categories to account for differences in the meanings of ultimate-reserve estimates, although, unfortunately, they have not tried to dispel the prevalent negative image of ultimate-reserve calculations. V. E. McKelvey of the U.S. Geological Survey has devised a block diagram partitioned into various cells to accommodate estimates for different land areas (e.g., coterminous U.S., Alaska) and different categories of resource availability (e.g., already produced, proven reserve, speculative recoverable reserve, submarginal reserves, etc.)[51] This sort of classification, together with the careful compilations by Theobald, Schweinfurth, and Duncan[52] and T. H. McCulloh,[53] all of the U.S. Geological Survey, permits valid comparisons of ultimate-reserve estimates. By examining comparable estimates, one can determine the implications of different methods and evaluate their reliability.

TECHNIQUES OF ESTIMATING ULTIMATE RESERVES

Ultimate oil-reserve estimates have been developed through two basic techniques: geological inference and production-curve extrapolation.

Geological Inference. By considering that the areas in which oil has been found are samples of various types of "sedimentary basins" in the United States, forecasters can extend their experience with drilled areas to those not yet drilled. If a particular type of basin typically yields a certain volume of oil per unit area, this yield may be used to estimate the volume of oil expected to be found in as yet undrilled basins of the same type. This procedure can produce ultimate-yield or "oil-in-place" estimates, which may then be coupled with either the current recovery rate or suitable forecasts of future extractive capacity.

In recent years the estimates made by the geological-inference approach have been comparatively high, especially after the terrain of Alaska and the continental shelf proved to be so promising. A team of geologists with the U.S. Geological Survey has used this approach to estimate petroleum, gas, and other mineral resources.[54] The National Petroleum Council and several oil companies have used the same basic approach, with results of similar magnitude.[55] Their high estimates, if correct, imply that incentives for further domestic exploration and technological development in extraction would pay off handsomely in the discovery of domestic petroleum.

The geological-inference approach has been criticized on the grounds that petroleum geologists do not know enough about the geology of the unexplored areas or about the relationship between basin types and yields to justify yield estimates. Much of the terrain (particularly in Alaska and offshore) has not yet been surveyed adequately to provide secure geological data. Even when the geology is known, "promising" areas do not always yield the oil they are expected to yield. It is conceivable that the same types of basins in different parts of the country could yield quite different volumes of oil.

Production (or Discovery) Curves. By assuming that exploration and drilling are conducted first in the most likely areas, estimators can extrapolate the

138

decreasing yields per attempted well. This produces a "production" trend of diminishing returns and a means for estimating the ultimate volume to be found. Since the petroleum supply is finite, and earlier discovery in the most favorable areas is presumably easier, an S-shaped, logistic curve has been used as the cumulative production curve, just as Pearl applied the logistic curve to U.S. population under the assumption of basically unexpandable natural resources (see chapter 3). The production-curve approach is associated primarily with M. King Hubbert,[56] whose public prominence is due largely to his adamant opposition to the higher estimates produced by the geological-inference approach, particularly those by his own colleagues at the U.S. Geological Survey. If Hubbert's lower estimates of ultimate reserves (200 billion barrels ultimately recovered) are correct, more than half of our recoverable petroleum has already been consumed, and further domestic exploration will be less rewarding than is implied by the higher estimates (about 300–350 billion barrels) derived by the geological-inference approach.

Other estimators also have employed a logistic-curve approach, but with quite different results. C. L. Moore used the curve of cumulative discovered "oil-in-place" and coupled this estimate with an independent forecast of recovery rates to arrive at his much higher estimate of recoverable oil.[57] Elliot and Linden used an approach apparently quite similar to Hubbert's, yet they arrived at an estimate of 450 billion barrels.[58]

Because production curves are extrapolations of past production trends expressing historical improvements in exploratory and recovery techniques, their extrapolation to future production levels presumably encompasses the results of future improvements in technology, expansions in the area of drilling, and changes in the economic feasibility of recovering previously marginal oil. Many experts believe that this solution to the problem of forecasting the effects of technological advancement and economic change is too "pat." They question the underlying assumption that whatever technological and economic trends go into the historical record will necessarily continue into the future. Lovejoy and Homan criticize the Hubbert approach as follows:

By thus staking his whole analysis on the continued validity of the trend exhibited in one catch-all statistical series, cumulative gross additions to reserves, he evades the necessity of looking at any of the separate factors which might be relevant, such as rate of recovery, backdating extensions and revisions to the year of discovery of fields, intensity of discovery effort, and discoveries relative to discovery effort.[59]

APPRAISING ULTIMATE-RESERVE ESTIMATES

The ultimate-reserves debate poses the archetypical problem of the policy-maker's relationship to the expert input serving him. The experts have devised two approaches that yield quite different results of great importance to the appropriateness of energy policy options. Yet proponents of each approach deny the validity of the other; consequently, the policy-maker cannot resort to "expert opinion" to resolve the problem.

How can a policy-maker, a nonscientist, choose between these two approaches? It is futile for a nonexpert to enter into the scientific considerations of the appropriateness of competing approaches. This would simply add another opinion to the debate, and an amateur one at that. However, policy-makers can legitimately ask whether the *performance* of experts using each of the approaches provides any evidence beyond the scientific plausibility of the methods. Broadly speaking, this orientation is analogous to retrospectively evaluating the performance of previous forecasts, except for the important fact that the actual volume of ultimate reserves, however defined, is still unknown.

The geological-inference and discovery-curve approaches differ in the kinds of patterns that would dispute or support their validity. The discovery-curve approach is rigidly bound to the assumption that there is one and only one discovery curve which the historical pattern of additions to known reserves must follow. In other words, the validity of the method depends on the existence of a deterministic, knowable growth pattern. If the approach is valid, ultimate production is precisely inferable at any point in time. The geological-inference approach is, in a sense, more modest. Imperfect information on sedimentary basins and on the geological indications of the existence of oil leads to imperfect estimates. Theoretically, however, these estimates should improve over time as information becomes more comprehensive as a result of further surveying and better geological theory.

The pattern of existing production-curve estimates challenges the validity of the approach. There is no way that the theory underlying the discovery-curve approach can account for the fact that estimates derived through this method differ from one another, both among different authorities and among estimates by the same authority over time. Unlike the geological-inference approach, in which discrepancies among estimates can reflect differences of opinion or different states of geological knowledge, the discovery-curve approach requires consistency of estimates to support the presumption of a single deterministic growth curve. As figure 5.33 indicates, (a) some discovery-curve estimates are about 200 billion barrels of ultimate reserve, while others are around 400 billion; (b) the estimates by Moore (the three high estimates connected in the diagram) vary considerably, presumably as a reflection of shifts in the pattern of historical discoveries and production; and (c) the estimates by Hubbert (the four connected low estimates) also vary significantly. Hubbert's 1974 estimate reflects the breakthrough in the discovery of Alaskan oil in 1968–70, an event that was neither predictable nor explainable by means of discovery-curve assumptions.

In fact, Hubbert's simple discovery-curve estimates seem to develop their own trend over time. It appears that these estimates, based on the shaky

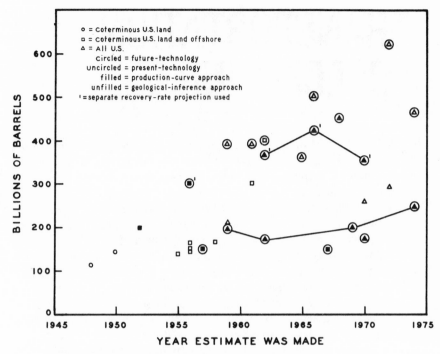

o = Coterminous U.S. land
□ = Coterminous U.S. land and offshore
△ = All U.S.
    Circled = future-technology
uncircled = present-technology
    filled = production-curve approach
    unfilled = geological-inference approach
' = separate recovery-rate projection used

5.33. Ultimate Petroleum-Reserve Estimates: Results
of Two Methods

assumption of constant rates of growth in exploration effort and technology,
are being adjusted upward in the face of real data, indicating greater-than-
constant growth rates. On the basis of this trend, it is not unreasonable to
expect that the simple discovery-curve technique will soon produce estimates
in the range of 300–350 billion barrels, which is not far from the 350–400
billion barrels estimated by Moore's discovery-curve and recovery-rate projections. Since 1960, the geological-inference approach has yielded estimates
between 350 billion and 500 billion barrels, with the one exception of the very
high Theobald estimate, which apparently has been disavowed by the U.S.
Geological Survey.[60] In other words, the crucial ultimate-resource estimates,
produced through very different methods, seem to be arriving at a consensus.
Convergence of results from different approaches that do not share common
presumptions is a strong argument for the validity of the results. This convergence will bring greater certainty to the debate on energy resource
availability. It may also restore the reputation of the expert in dealing with
energy policy issues.

CHAPTER 6

TRANSPORTATION FORECASTING

Transportation forecasting is an eminently practical task. There are few great or esoteric theories on how the demand for, and instruments of, transportation grow. Transportation forecasters openly search for more basic economic, technological, and social cues to inform them of how transportation will fit into the future context. Because of the potentially great variability in transportation forms, exactly what constitutes the future transportation system—landcraft, aircraft, mass transport, or individual transport—is a derivative characteristic of the socioeconomic milieu.

However, transportation forecasts are no less important for being derivative, nor are they less interesting intellectually. The volume of travel in the United States is an important determinant of the scope of social interactions that link the states into a single unit. It also affects the economic structure and prosperity of the country, which are so highly dependent on the flow of goods from one region to another. Intellectually, transportation forecasting in fascinating because it generally entails the construction of an edifice of more basic forecasts from which the transportation forecasts must be derived. The number of automobiles may not be as "basic" as the size of the population, but forecasting automobiles may very well rest on the population forecast. In other words, transportation forecasting is complex *because* it is derivative. Transportation forecasters usually perform many more "operations" than other forecasters in order to transform core assumptions on basic trends into projections. Thus, despite the derivative nature of transportation forecasting, core assumptions are essential. They may be about the surge in population, population composition (e.g., in terms of age and income breakdowns), prosperity and tastes, the structure of cities, or the technology of transportation itself. Whatever the basis of the core assumptions, the accuracy of transportation projections depends on these other projections.

Most transportation forecasting efforts have been directed at trends in specific travel modes, in terms of either the number of vehicles in operation or the volume of traffic. For most policy purposes, the overall volume of transportation (i.e., the sheer movement of people and goods) is less relevant to policy-making than are the specific modes of travel. Most transportation planning is concerned with anticipating the types of facilities required, and these, of course, are quite different for different modes of transport. Environmental problems also are quite different for different modes of transport. Since the bulk of intercity travel can be accomplished through several modes (plane, car, train, or bus), and since the choice of mode of transport is important, the question that has preoccupied transportation analysts since World War II is the *balance* of rail, sea, air, and road travel. The economic stakes involved, which include vast investments in highways, ports, airports, railroads, and manufacturing facilities for the vehicles themselves, are enormous.

The growth patterns of different modes of transportation are highly interdependent, since to a large extent they are substitutable and competitive. Because of the interchangeable nature of modes of travel, it would be somewhat redundant to examine the forecasting efforts for all transportation trends. For example, it is sufficient to project the rapid expansion in air travel as the primary cause of the contraction in rail travel. The failure, to date, of all-encompassing mass transit has virtually guaranteed the continued dominance of the automobile for intracity travel. Consequently, this study focuses on the forecasting records for only two of the primary types of transport, air and motor vehicle travel. The forecasting records in other areas are likely to be roughly similar, since inaccuracy in anticipating the relative importance of one mode of transport will usually mean inaccuracy in anticipating the role of alternative modes.

AVIATION FORECASTING

There are two quite different types of air travel, each of which has very different implications for public planners. *Airline* traffic is important in terms of the balance among transportation modes and the requirements for major facilities such as metropolitan airports. The post–World War II period has witnessed the great expansion of the airline industry (at least in terms of numbers of passengers, if not financially), the virtual collapse of the competing railroad industry, and governmental subsidization of airport facilities. Nevertheless, the inability to anticipate the volume of air travel in some localities has caused serious problems in air safety and in the adequacy of facilities.

The other type of air travel is known as *general aviation,* or the operation of private aircraft. As it turns out, the policy relevance of general aviation has been limited to providing modest local facilities for commercial, business, and recreational flying and to regulating air safety for unscheduled flights. However, during and immediately after World War II, many aviation experts considered as a serious possibility the massive shift to private planes as a substitute for automobiles. If private air travel on this scale ever does materialize, its relevance to public policy-making will become proportionately greater. It would affect the rationale behind maintaining or expanding the highway

143

system, the structure of cities if long-range commuting became feasible, and much more serious problems of air safety.

Aviation forecasting is one field in which the expectation of systematic biases according to forecasting institutions has been very strong. Many executives and officials in the aviation field presume that, of the two primary sources of aviation projections, the federal agencies (primarily the FAA, but occasionally the CAB) proceed with a deliberate conservative bias, whereas the aircraft manufacturers publish forecasts that are deliberately optimistic, presumably to encourage greater sales to airlines.

MOTOR VEHICLE FORECASTING

There are also two important types of automotive (or motor vehicle) forecasts, although this study focuses on only one of them. Automotive forecasts are usually stated in terms of sales (frequently of new vehicles alone) *or* in terms of the total "population" of motor vehicles. These are distinct because the total vehicle population does not increase directly with the purchase of each new car, since the scrappage of old vehicles to some extent offsets purchases. This study focuses on the total vehicle population. Sales are, of course, very important to automotive manufacturers and to the economy as a whole (although the connection between the success of the automobile industry and the health of the economy as a whole is a very complicated matter). However, forecasts of the total automobile population are of even greater importance to more decision-makers. The total number of vehicles is more directly relevant to the highway planners' problem of anticipating demand for highways, and to the pollution-control planners' need to anticipate automotive exhaust pollution. The balance of transportation modes, and all that this balance implies in terms of the structure of cities and the nature of life styles, is reflected more directly in the population of vehicles than in the turnover in vehicles represented by sales.

There is an interesting division among the people who undertake to forecast the motor vehicle population. On the one hand, there are forecasters in business or government who project automotive growth either as a matter of routine or for specific, rather narrow purposes, such as the calculation of future petroleum needs. On the other hand, there are forecasters, usually in academic or research institute positions, who forecast the growth of the motor vehicle population in order to expound on the broad influence of the automobile on the fabric of society. Bureau of Public Roads forecasters are an example of routine practitioners; Wilfred Owen[1] of the Brookings Institution is a good example of those who forecast in order to examine global implications.

These very different kinds of experts evoke the contrast between "technicians" and "intellectuals." The conventional wisdom of forecast users holds

that the routine forecasters tend toward careful conservatism, and perhaps reluctance to venture forecasts of high growth. The "intellectuals" are suspected of more flamboyance, especially when (as is usually the case) the social scenarios they project hinge on the greater proliferation of automobiles. As sociologists point out the long-range disabilities of automotive "overpopulation," suspicions arise that their fears might be based on exaggerations. Since the placement of each forecaster into one of these two categories is usually obvious, an analysis of forecasting records will establish whether this presumed bias really exists, just as an examination of the aviation forecasters' record will determine whether the presumed bias in governmental and aircraft-manufacturer projections actually occurs.

THE CHALLENGE OF TRANSPORTATION FORECASTING

If transportation forecasting seems mundane, it is because revolutionary technological changes in the modes of transport in America have *not* materialized. Some transportation experts believed that such changes would occur, and urged transportation forecasters to take them into account. The tremendous advances made in aviation during World War II might have presaged the mass use of private aircraft. Hovercraft, monorails, or even subterranean tubes might have made paved roads obsolete.

Thus, the pressure on transportation forecasters has been to decide how much attention to pay to technological predictions. For example, in presenting its 1956 aviation projections, the Civil Aeronautics Administration (precursor to the FAA) noted: "Late in May, 1956, Hall L. Hibbard, vice president-engineering for Lockheed predicted the eventual development of a twin-jet family type convertiplane which could be flown by anyone capable of driving an automobile. The jet engine makes such a plane possible, he said, and hinted it might come in 10 to 15 years."[2] If, indeed, there had been an aircar or convertiplane in every garage by the 1970s, the American highway system, the structure of American cities, and the problems of pollution and safety would have been dramatically altered. To be correct, forecasters have had to be somewhat blind to the alluring possibilities of technology that are entertained by authoritative experts in the transportation field. Predicting the steady growth of automobile ownership, and only modest growth in aviation, is a significant accomplishment.

TRANSPORTATION FORECASTING TECHNIQUES

Because of the unabashedly derivative nature of transportation forecasting, the most common short-term forecasting technique (to the extent that forecasters specify their methodology) has been *correlation*. Occasionally, simple extrapolation or straightforward judgment is used, but, usually, trends in the use and ownership of motor vehicles or aircraft are correlated with past trends in population and economic expansion, and then are projected on the basis of recently formulated projections of these demographic and economic trends. This approach reflects, and is predicated on, the assumption that the ownership and use of means of transportation are generally constrained by the ability to afford them; as the ability to afford automobiles and air travel increases, ownership and use increase accordingly.

The validity of this assumption, and consequently the appropriateness of the correlational approach, is weaker for long-term forecasting because the market for a particular mode of transportation may become saturated; i.e., demand may be satisfied despite greater ability to afford more.[3] Thus, one of the complexities of motor vehicle forecasting is the possible need to integrate the analysis of existing trends (i.e., the correlational analysis) with the eventuality of thresholds on ownership. Is there some point (say, one car for every adult) at which, even if the current requisite conditions for growth in automobile ownership (e.g., additional disposable income) were present, there would be no more growth simply because few people would want additional automobiles? Would the current constraint on ownership—namely, the ability to afford—be replaced by a completely different constraint, the desire to own? It should be noted that this saturation point or ceiling may actually occur at a level far lower than one vehicle per person; urban life styles may make automobile ownership undesirable, especially if mass transit becomes readily available.

Introducing the notion of saturation into transportation forecasting is a methodological problem first because it calls for the imposition of a theoretically based assumption onto the empirically based considerations of trends and correlations. Second, these theoretical assumptions are based on considerations of conditions not yet experienced. In other words, the dynamic nature of the trend would be quite different under conditions of near-saturation than it had been previously. Establishing the saturation level cannot be accomplished through an examination of the historical trend line alone, since, even if the curve appears to be leveling off, a number of possible shapes could lead the rest of the curve to different final levels; and, more fundamentally, the empirical leveling off may simply represent a lull in growth rather than the emergence of a real threshold.

It is the impossibility of formally connecting the short-term importance of historical trends and the long-term significance of theoretical thresholds that forces the methodology of transportation forecasting to rely on a heavy dose of nonexplicit judgment. Short-term and long-term projections are often spliced together without much description of where trend analysis ends and theoretical considerations begin.

Forecasters of general aviation trends face the same basic problem in a different guise. Projecting the total number of aircraft, once a trend line has been established, has been seen largely as a matter of tracing out changes in population and economic prosperity, which have their marginal effects, in the short run, on the number of planes affordable. However, the two broader constraints on the number of aircraft in use have to do with the proportion of the population with the skills and motivation to operate private aircraft, and with the basically technological question of whether the aircraft-manufacturing industry will introduce radically less expensive aircraft, which would change the meaning of affordability. Thus, the saturation point for the private aircraft market has some bearing on the long-term projections of aircraft ownership, and the level of saturation depends on the occurrence of particular discrete events such as wars (which boost the pool of potential civilian pilots) and engineering breakthroughs. It is interesting that the forecasts for general aviation made during World War II, when the vast number of trained pilots provided an unknown potential for future civilian air traffic, varied tremendously, and many turned out to be highly inaccurate. By the time of the Korean War, the aviation forecasters had apparently learned their lesson, because very few forecasts were hazarded. The Vietnam War produced a huge number of trained airplane and helicopter pilots; whether their familiarity and skills with aircraft will be translated into civilian ownership is still in question.

APPRAISAL PROBLEMS

Evaluating the accuracy of transportation forecasts presents no insurmountable problems, since the forecasted trends consist of discrete, easily characterized, and measured events. Two technical problems do arise, however.

One problem is that transportation forecasts often are expressed in terms that are useful to policy-makers, but that are not consistent with official statistics available for appraising the forecasts. For example, the number of motor vehicles "in use" is more relevant to policy-makers than is the number of registered vehicles, but the latter is the standard statistic gathered by governmental agencies. Obviously, the differences between forecasts and "actual" levels reflect inaccuracies only if the discrepancies do not arise out of different definitions of the forecasted and criterion trends. However, as long as these differences are recognized, and the ratio of forecasted magnitudes to actual magnitudes is known and is fairly constant, the official statistics can be translated into the terms of the forecasts, and appropriate measures of accuracy can be applied.

The second problem is that transportation forecasters, even within each area of motor vehicle forecasting or domestic airline travel forecasting, focus on somewhat different trends, albeit overlapping ones. Motor vehicle forecasts are sometimes cast in terms of passenger-car populations, sometimes in terms of all motor vehicles. Airline travel projections sometimes include only scheduled flights, sometimes only trunk flights. sometimes all domestic air travel on commercial liners. This makes comparisons of the accuracy of different forecasting efforts problematical. However, the problem is minimized to the extent that the differences in definition are minor in terms of the magnitudes of the trends. For example, although total airline revenue-passenger-miles will obviously be greater than scheduled airline revenue-passenger-miles, the bulk of the total operations are scheduled. Hence, the magnitude of errors in total airline revenue-passenger-miles, particularly when it is expressed in percentage terms, is comparable to that of errors in scheduled revenue-passenger-miles forecasts. Similarly, since the total number of motor vehicles "in use" is close to the total number of registered motor vehicles, errors in forecasting either trend are comparable. As long as the appropriate "real" datum is used to calculate the accuracy of each forecast, forecasts of somewhat different (but overlapping) trends can be examined together.

THE PERFORMANCE OF TRANSPORTATION FORECASTS

The appraisal of accuracy of aviation and motor vehicle forecasts was applied to all available forecasts of *domestic* totals from roughly around the 1920s, when such forecasts first appeared. Forecasts from all sources were relatively infrequent in the 1920s and 1930s, but became more common during and after World War II. It is interesting to note that fewer and fewer general aviation forecasts have been published by private manufacturers in recent years; the annual FAA general aviation forecasts have come to monopolize the published material in this field, although undoubtedly the manufacturers of personal and commercial aircraft also continue to forecast the growth of their markets.

GENERAL AVIATION FORECASTS

Forecasts of the general aviation fleet[4] show, unsurprisingly, a pattern of accuracy very similar to that of the long-range economic forecasts discussed in chapter 4. After the appearance of some wild errors during and immediately after World War II, the forecasts settled down to a fairly consistent level of accuracy. As indicated in table 6.1 and in figures 6.1–6.4, the forecasts made during the 1940s were gross overestimates,[5] reflecting most aviation forecaster's acceptance of the assumption that personal aircraft, transformed by technology into an affordable and convenient vehicle for middle-income Americans, would increase the total number of aircraft tremendously.

148

Table 6.1: Errors of General Aviation Forecasts, 1944–1974

Year	Source	Percentage of Error in Forecasts for								
		1950	1955	1960	1965	1970	1975	5 yrs.	10 yrs.	15 yrs.
1944	Damon/CAA	+223						+223		
	Kucher/Bendix							+224		
	Van Zandt/Brookings							+224		
	Burden/Commerce Dept.		+428						+428	
1945	CAA	+19	+385					+19	+385	
	Burden/Commerce Dept.		+369						+369	
1947	Dewhurst/Twentieth Century Fund	+8		+1310						+1310
	Doolittle/Shell		+369					+113		
	T. Wright/Commerce Dept.	+21	+381					+237		
	J. Wood		+373							
1949	CAA			+1				+1		
1955	CAA			+1				+1		
1956	E. P. Curtis/Pres. Comm.					−17				−17
1957	FAA						−24			−24
1960	FAA				−2	−23	−29	−2	−23	−29
1961	FAA				+1	−19		+1	−19	
1963	FAA				+1	−20		−13		
1964	New York Port Authority				+1	−13		−18		
1965	FAA					−10	−17	−12	−15	
1967	FAA					−2		+3		
1968	FAA					−2		−1		
1969	FAA					0	−1	−1		
	Business Week						−7	−7		
1970	FAA						+4	+4		
1971	FAA						−8			
1972	FAA						−11			
1973	FAA						−11			
1974	FAA						−2			

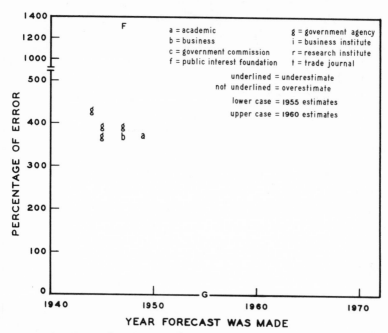

6.1. Errors of 1955 and 1960 Total Active Aviation
Fleet Forecasts, by Source

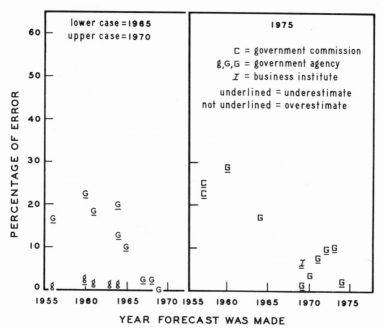

6.2. Errors of 1965, 1970, and 1975 Total Active
Aviation Fleet Forecasts, by Source

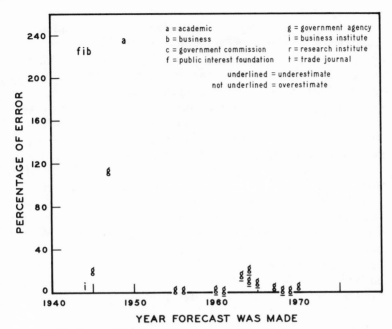

6.3. Errors of Five-Year Total Active Aviation Fleet
Forecasts, by Source

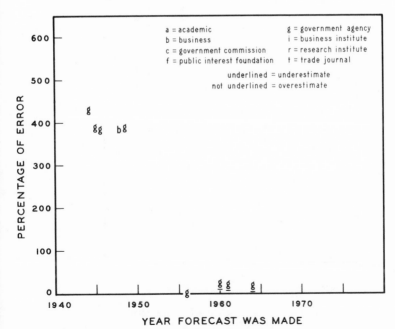

6.4. Errors of Ten-Year Total Active Aviation Fleet
Forecasts, by Source

After the Korean War (during which published general aviation forecasts were conspicuously absent), aviation fleet forecasts became far more accurate. Five-year forecasts are generally well under 10 percent in error. The few available ten-year forecasts for the period after the Korean War show errors ranging from 15 percent to 23 percent, compared to the ten-year forecasts of the 1940s, which had errors of nearly 400 percent. This marked improvement reflects the realization by the mid-1950s that, in addition to the relatively small fleet of high-capacity commercial airliners, civilian aircraft would be relegated to modest commercial use and even more limited pleasure flying.

It is significant that, once this conclusion was reached, it was reflected in forecasting efforts, regardless of the nuances of methodology employed. The more sophisticated FAA methodology now in use, which involves a model based on regression analysis,[6] has shown no improvement in accuracy for 1975 forecasts over their less formalized correlational analyses achieved for 1970 projections. Similarly, the five-year CAA and FAA projections made between 1955 and 1960 were as accurate as the five-year forecasts made between 1965 and 1970. Again, the most reasonable inference to be drawn from this pattern is that accuracy comes not from the maturation of forecasting

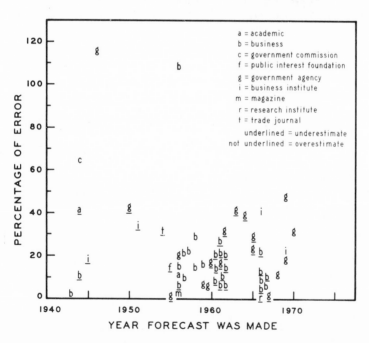

6.5. Errors of Five-Year Domestic Airline Revenue-Passenger-Miles Forecasts, by Source

techniques, but rather from correct choices of basic assumptions. The only poor five-year forecasts of the post–Korean War period were formulated between 1963 and 1965. Their underestimates cannot be explained on the basis of methodology, since the same methods were employed successfully just prior to this period; rather, they are explained by the fact that the continued boomlet of 1962–69 was unanticipated.

COMMERCIAL AIRLINE TRAVEL FORECASTS

Forecasts of commercial air travel have been relatively inaccurate *and* unreliable. For example, five-year forecasts of domestic revenue-passenger-miles since 1953 have a median error of about 15 percent. Ten-year forecasts, which cluster at different levels of accuracy in different eras, have a median error of around 40 percent, except for the period 1955–58, when the median error was about 20 percent. As seen in figures 6.5 and 6.6, no improvement over time can be detected in the accuracy of these forecasts.

Commercial air travel forecasts are unreliable in the sense that, even close to their target dates, some highly inaccurate projections occur. Since 1965, two five-year forecasts have been more than 40 percent in error, and five more

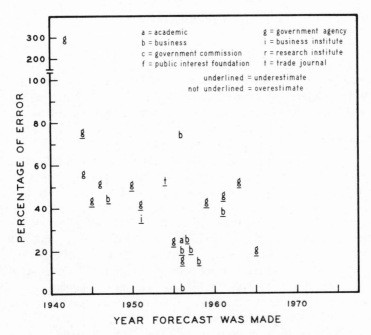

6.6. Errors of Ten-Year Domestic Airline Revenue-Passenger-Miles Forecasts, by Source

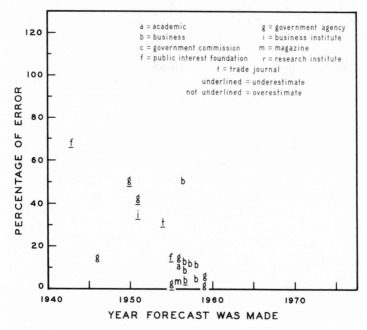

6.7. Errors of 1960 Domestic Airline Revenue-Passenger-Miles Forecasts, by Source

have had errors of greater than 20 percent. Figures 6.7–6.10 show that, as forecasters approach the most commonly used target dates (1960, 1965, 1970, and 1975), high levels of accuracy are not attained until two or three years just prior to the target date. The forecasts do improve as they approach the target dates, but they do so primarily through the elimination of extreme errors rather than through greater accuracy by all forecasters.

These figures also permit an examination of the presumed bias of governmental forecasters to underestimate—and that of private forecasters to overestimate— the volume of air travel. There is, in fact, no evidence from five- and ten-year forecast records that governmental forecasts are more "pessimistic" than the aircraft manufacturers' forecasts. When governmental forecasts are underestimates, business forecasts tend to be so also. When governmental forecasts overshoot actual levels, so do business forecasts. It is much more reasonable to presume that both governmental and private aviation forecasters are attuned to basically the same climate of opinion, and that, consequently, their errors are more likely to be in the same direction than they are to "straddle" the ultimately correct level. For any given forecast length or specific target date, there seems to be a pattern of short, alternating periods in which almost all forecasters, regardless of institutional affiliation or methodo-

154

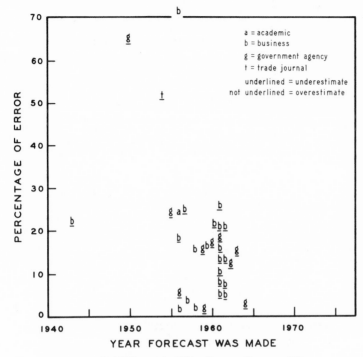

6.8. Errors of 1965 Domestic Airline Revenue-Passenger-Miles
Forecasts, by Source

logical detail, express a *consistent* bias of underestimation or overestimation.
For example, from 1956 to 1959, almost all five-year forecasts were overestimates; from 1960 to 1966, almost all were underestimates, followed by four
more years of overestimates.

For the long range (i.e., ten years or more), commercial air travel forecasts
have been consistently underestimating future growth. Of twenty-three
explicit ten-year forecasts made between 1940 and 1975, only six have been
overestimates. Apparently, the extent to which air travel would eclipse rail
travel in the long run was not fully appreciated by transportation forecasters
focusing on the very real short-term problems of the development of the
aviation industry.

The poor performance of commercial air travel forecasts must rest, in part,
on the nature of the trend. Unlike aircraft ownership, which represents a
major, fixed investment on the part of owners, the decision of a traveler to go
by plane rather than by bus, car, or train is relatively "unfixed" from the
traveler's point of view; it depends on a competitive balance of convenience,
price, and safety, which could result in shifts of large proportions of travelers

155

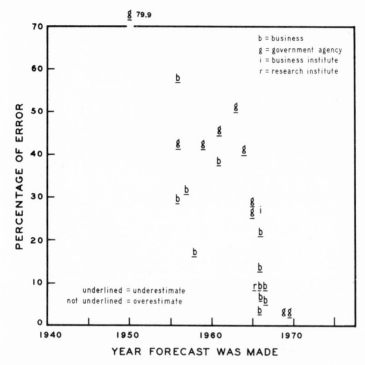

6.9. Errors of 1970 Domestic Airline Revenue-Passenger-Miles
Forecasts, by Source

from one mode to another because of only minor shifts in the balance of
attractiveness. The fact that a certain number of individuals and firms own
general aviation aircraft in a particular year provides a solid base for predicting aircraft ownership five years later, because many of the same aircraft will
still be operable and many of the same individuals and firms will still be
flying. In contrast, a given year's commercial air travel does not automatically
carry over to future years; each traveler's decision is made anew for each trip.

Another difficulty lies in the status of the airline industry in the overall
transportation picture. Technological forecasters often speak of "mature"
industries or technologies, by which they mean that the growth of an industry
or technology relative to competing forms has fulfilled its potential, and
therefore has leveled off. Before this point is reached (if it ever is), two
components of growth are encountered: increases due to the increased popu-
larity of that mode relative to others, and increases due to changes in the basic
economic and demographic factors that produce greater demand regardless of
mode. A perennial problem of airline forecasting is to combine the potential
of further *relative* growth with the potential for greater overall travel by a

156

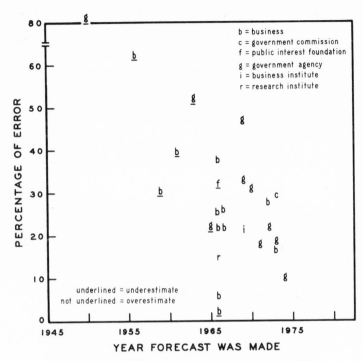

6.10. Errors of 1975 Domestic Airline Revenue-Passenger-Miles
Forecasts, by Source

larger and wealthier population. The point of "maturity" is in some respects
like a saturation level; it is a future event to which existing trends bring little
insight. Every airline forecaster has to face the possibility that existing trends
may deteriorate as indicators of future growth simply because the substitution
of aviation for land travel has run its course.[7] However, the underestimates
encountered in long-range airline forecasts demonstrate that, even when existing trends could have been simply extrapolated to accurately project future
growth, the forecasters' disbelief in the phenomenal potential of air travel has
held them to conservative—and inaccurate—forecasts.

MOTOR VEHICLE POPULATION FORECASTS
    Motor vehicle forecasts, whether expressed in terms of the total number of
passenger cars or the total number of motor vehicles in general, have the most
impressive post-1950 record of all the types of transportation forecasting
examined here. As with general aviation forecasts, the motor vehicle projections became much more accurate in the 1950s. The ten-year forecasts seem
to be consistently aroung 10 percent in error, the five-year forecasts about 5

157

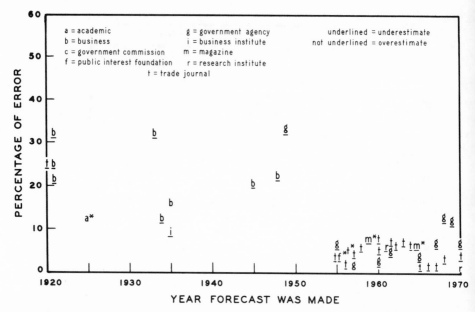

6.11. Errors of Five-Year Motor Vehicle Population
Forecasts, by Source

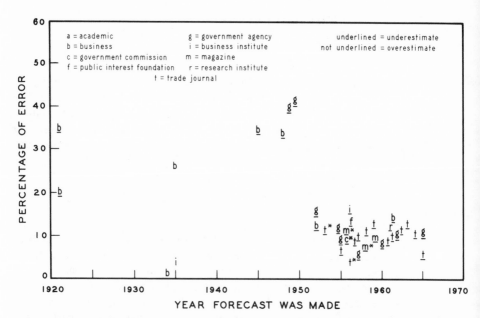

6.12. Errors of Ten-Year Motor Vehicle Population
Forecasts, by Source

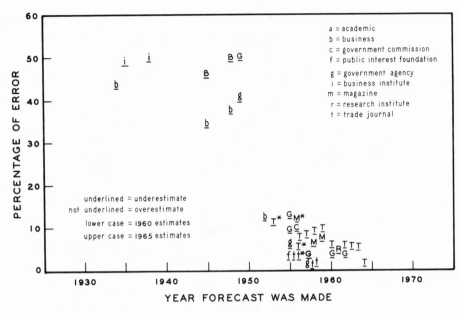

6.13. Errors of 1960 and 1965 Motor Vehicle Population
Forecasts, by Source

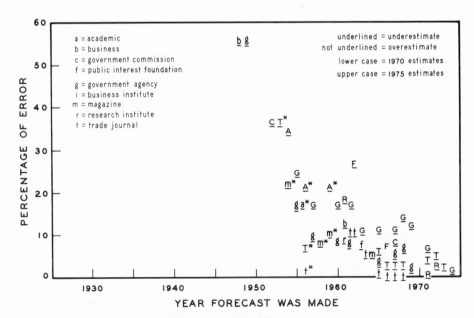

159

6.14. Errors of 1970 and 1975 Motor Vehicle Population
Forecasts, by Source

percent in error. Although very few post-1950 fifteen-year forecasts are now appraisable, these few show an average error of around 15 percent. The accuracy curves for 1960, 1965, and 1970 are all roughly linear, with the percentage of error again nearly equal to the number of years of remoteness of the forecast.

The bias to underestimate has been consistent over time and for all forecast sources. Apparently, after 1950 most motor vehicle forecasters came to accept a version of the American future that was *modestly* less growth oriented than the future actually turned out to be, but the forecasters were within reasonable limits such that the errors have been low (although this is less impressive if one takes into account the cumulative nature of the trend being forecast). However, it is striking that throughout the period from 1950 to 1970 the same slightly pessimistic bias was maintained. Forecasters apparently did not "learn" from the feedback of real statistics showing that previous forecasts indeed had been pessimistic. It is as if the forecasters were unwilling to believe the real data that indicated tremendous expansion in consumption and economic growth, and were expecting the bubble to burst at some time in the near future. Forecasters of the 1960s had access to the record of forecasts made in the 1950, which, using the methods still employed in the sixties, were too pessimistic. In other words, an examination of the earlier forecasts could have alerted the later forecasters that their methods and assumptions would lead to underestimates of future growth, but this sort of adjustment was not made. Indeed, the use of previous-error feedback is lacking in the forecasting efforts in every area except that of certain short-term econometric forecasting models. Even so, corrective adjustments *could* be introduced informally by modifying the core assumptions concerning future growth rates. The obstacle to adding this feedback adjustment seems to be that the forecasters believe their assumptions about the future already incorporate all the data that is pertinent to known trends. It is another case of forecasters being locked into the scientific outlook, which acknowledges only information relating to the phenomena studied rather than information on the behavior of the experts studying them.

The records of accuracy for motor vehicle forecasts also cast some light on the presumed biases of sociologically oriented forecasters as opposed to routine forecasters. The forecasts developed for broad studies on the impact of the automobile are designated in the figures of this chapter by asterisks. These projections have not suffered from exaggeration of the looming explosion in automobile growth; instead, they have been among the most conservative forecasts. In almost every case, such forecasts have shared the bias of underestimation that marks the overall pattern of motor vehicle forecasts.

The only difference in the motor vehicle forecast record that can be attributed to different institutional sources is the record of accuracy of recent short-term governmental forecasts. Five-year governmental forecasts made between 1967 and 1970 had greater errors (two exceeding 12 percent) than comparable forecasts made by the McGraw-Hill Economics Department and reported in the *National Petroleum News Factbooks*, the primary nongovernmental provider of motor vehicle forecasts. Fairly straightforward explanations for these inaccuracies have little directly to do with the fact that the institutional base was governmental. The worst five-year forecasts were produced by the Federal Power Commission[8] and the American Association of State Highway Officials,[9] in 1967 and 1968 respectively. In both cases the short-term predictions were just one aspect of longer-range projections to 1985 or 1990, which had been formulated with obviously more concern for long-range patterns than for short-term developments. The extrapolation of constant growth rate used in both studies was more appropriate for projecting beyond the short term. Moreover, in both cases the studies apparently used previously formulated forecasts that were not up-to-date. The FPC acknowledged that its data and projections were derived from other (unspecified) sources,[10] and the American Association of State Highway Officials study had been in preparation for four years.[11] Therefore, the difficulties of these forecasting efforts stemmed more from methodological problems—inappropriate techniques based on (probably) antiquated data—than from liabilities inherent in governmental forecasting.

TRANSPORTATION FORECASTING PROSPECTS

Judging by recent transportation forecasting and by the status of "new" modeling methods emerging in the field of transporation forecasting, the traditional magnitudes of error are likely to persist into the future. Motor vehicle forecasts are likely to remain relatively accurate, while commercial air travel forecasts will probably continue to be subject to their traditionally high levels of inaccuracy.

The continuation of these past patterns of accuracy is indicated first by the "dispersion" of recently compiled forecasts of motor vehicle registrations and air travel. A parallel examination of recent general aviation forecasts is not feasible, because of the scarcity of attempts by sources other than the Federal Aviation Administration. As seen in table 6.2, the range of recent air travel forecasts is very large. Air transport forecasts within each year are quite similar, but this only demonstrates, again, that forecasters operating from different institutional sites are usually attuned to the same cues and share the same "current" view of the future. The major differences occur over time; the forecasts prepared during 1972/73 are much higher for any given target year than are those prepared during 1974/75. If, indeed, the events of 1973—the energy crisis and economic downturn—affected the future of air transportation

**Table 6.2: Recent Air Transport Forecasts for
1980, 1985, and 1990**

Year	Source	Total No. of Domestic Airline RPMs (in billions)		
		1980	1985	1990
1972	Lockheed	262[a]	—	—
	CAB	258[b]	—	—
	Port Authority of NY/NJ	271[b]	—	—
	FAA[c]	229[a]	—	—
1973	Boeing	261	378	480
	Douglas	231[a]	—	—
	Air Transport Assoc.	241	343	455
	FAA[c]	259[a]	390	—
1974	Lockheed	190	266	—
	FAA[c]	222[a]	272[a]	—
1975	Boeing	189	259	—
	Air Transport Assoc.	176	236	308
	Lockheed	175	235	—
	FAA[c]	192[a]	273[a]	—
	Dept. of Transportation	207	280	372

SOURCES: George Sarames (Lockheed-California Company), "World Air Travel Demand, 1950–1980," paper presented at the 1972 summer workshop on Air Transportation Systems Analysis and Economics, Flight Transportation Laboratory, Massachusetts Institute of Technology, Cambridge, Mass., July 1972, fig. 2; Richard Vitek and Nawal Taneja, "The Impact of High Inflation Rates on the Demand for Air Passenger Transportation," Flight Transportation Laboratory, Massachusetts Institute of Technology, May 1975 (mimeographed), pp. 16, 21; U.S., Department of Transportation, Federal Aviation Administration, *Aviation Forecasts: Fiscal Years 1973–1984* (Washington, D.C.: Government Printing Office, 1972), p. 30; The Boeing Company, Boeing Commercial Airplane Company, Market Research Unit, *Domestic RPM Forecast: Trunks, Pan Am, and Local Service Carriers* (Renton, Wash., 1973), p. 42; Yves Aureille and Carl Norris, *Short and Long Term Forecasting Models of the U.S. Domestic and International Traffic and Forecasts to 1981*, 3rd ed., Report no. C1-805-3084 (Long Beach, Calif.: Douglas Aircraft Company, 1973), chart 4; Air Transport Association, Macro Forecast Subcommittee of the Industry Planning Committee, *Domestic Passenger Market Demand Forecast, 1973–2000: Trunk and Regional Carriers* (Washington, D.C., 1973), p. 39; U.S., Department of Transportation, Federal Aviation Administration, *Aviation Forecasts: Fiscal Years 1974–1985* (Washington, D.C.: Government Printing Office, 1973); Lockheed-California Company, *World Air Traffic Forecast* (Burbank, Calif., 1974), p. 12; U.S., Department of Transportation, Federal Aviation Administration, *Aviation Forecasts: Fiscal Years 1975–1986* Washington, D.C.: Government Printing Office, 1974), p. 19; The Boeing Company, Boeing Commercial Airplane Company, Market Research Unit, *Dimensions of Airline Growth* (Seattle, Wash., 1975), p. 21; Air Transport Association, *Executive Summary: Domestic Industry Passenger Demand Forecast, 1974–2000: Trunk and Regional Carriers* (Washington, D.C., 1975), p. 4; Lockheed-California Company, *World Air Traffic Forecast*, rev. ed. (Burbank, Calif., 1975); U.S., Department of Transportation, Federal Aviation Administration, *Aviation Forecasts: Fiscal Years 1976–1987* (Washington, D.C.: Government Printing Office, 1975), p. 31; U.S., Department of Transportation, *1974 National Transportation Report: Current Performance and Future Prospects* (Washington, D.C.: Government Printing Office, 1975), p. 32.

[a]Total figure derived from forecast of scheduled RPMs by adding 7 billion for 1980 and 10 billion for 1985 (estimated differences between total and scheduled-only levels according to Boeing, 1975).

[b]Average of two or more forecasts given.

[c]Calendar year figures derived from fiscal year forecasts by averaging adjacent fiscal year totals.

Table 6.3: Recent Motor Vehicle Population
Forecasts for 1980, 1985, and 1990

Year	Source	Total No. of U.S. Motor Vehicles (in millions)		
		1980	1985	1990
1971	Cole/General Motors	140	—	—
	Fed. Highway Admin.	139	151	163
	Park and Carbine/Nat. Planning Assoc.	148	—	—
	Intertechnology Corp.[a]	150	170	197
	Saul/Continental Oil[a]	155	—	—
	NPN/McGraw-Hill	151	—	—
1972	Predicasts, Inc.	154	178	—
	NPN/McGraw-Hill	147	—	—
1973	Fed. Highway Admin.	143	—	167
	Moore/Ethyl Corp.	141	—	—
	Darnton/General Motors[b]	141	—	—
	NPN/McGraw-Hill	—	—	—
	Field/SRI	—	160	—
1974	Fed. Highway Admin.	146	159	170
	Ford Foundation Energy Policy Proj.[a]	—	156	—
	Motor Vehicle Manufacturers Assoc.[a]	146	161	—
1975	Robinson-Humphrey Co.[c]	163	—	—
	Fed. Highway Admin.	146	159	170

SOURCES: Calvin S. Moore, "The United States Passenger Car Population through 1985," *SAE Transactions,* no. 730736 (1973), p. 2599; U.S., Department of Transportation, Federal Highway Administration, Highway Statistics Division, *Forecast of Motor Vehicle Distribution, Production, and Scrappage, 1971–1990* (Washington, D.C.: Government Printing Office, 1971); C. Park and M. Carbine, "Transportation Needs in the 1970's," *Projection Highlights* (National Planning Association) 2, no. 3 (October 1971); Intertechnology Corporation, *The U.S. Energy Problem* (Washington, D.C., 1971), p. N-7; *National Petroleum News Factbook,* issued mid-May 1971, p. 28; mid-May 1972, p. 33; mid-May 1973, p. 38; Motor Vehicle Manufacturers Association of the United States, Statistics Department, "Long Range Forecasts," 18 July 1975 (mimeographed), p. 3; U.S., Department of Transportation, Federal Highway Administration, *Guide for Forecasting Traffic on the Interstate System* (Washington, D.C.: Government Printing Office, 1973), p. A-8; Stanford Field, "The U.S. Energy Puzzle," paper presented at the Thirty-eighth Annual Mid-Year Meeting of the American Petroleum Institute, Division of Refining, Philadelphia, Pa., 17 May 1973, p. 26; U.S., Department of Transportation, Federal Highway Administration, *Highway Travel Forecasts* (Washington, D.C.: Government Printing Office, 1974), p. 32; Ford Foundation, *A Time to Choose: America's Energy Future* (New York: Ballinger, 1974), p. 442; Motor Vehicle Manufacturers Association of the United States, *World Motor Vehicle Data* (Detroit, 1974), p. 154; U.S., Department of Transportation, Federal Highway Administration, "Projections of Motor-Vehicle Registrations, Driver Licenses, and Motor-Fuel Consumption to 1990," in *Highways and the Petroleum Problem—Four Papers* (Washington, D.C.: Government Printing Office, 1975), p. 21.

[a]Total motor vehicle forecast derived from passenger-car forecast by applying given growth rate to 1975 total motor vehicle level of 132 million.

[b]Interpolated from 1982 forecast.

[c]Extrapolated from 1979 figure using 1979 growth rate given at 4.1 percent.

so profoundly as to make more than a 40 percent difference in forecasts for 1980 and 1985, and nearly a 50 percent difference in those for 1990, air transportation patterns are likely to be susceptible to such events in the future as well.

The range of automotive forecasts, even considering those made before and after the oil crisis, is characteristically small. As table 6.3 indicates, even the most extreme differences for a given target year are less than 20 percent of the lower figure. Moreover, there is no visible "trend" in the forecasts prepared from 1971 through 1975, which indicates that the status of motor vehicle ownership was not altered so radically by the oil crisis as to make a difference in forecasts for 1980, 1985, or 1990. However, the conclusions to be drawn from the consensus of motor vehicle registration forecasts must be tempered by three considerations. First, it may very well be the case that motor vehicle ownership—which is just one trend within motor vehicle forecasting—is much less sensitive to changing circumstances than other automotive trends, such as "vehicle miles traveled," which may be a more meaningful statistic in determining petroleum demand. Second, motor vehicle registration forecasts cannot convey or capture crucial contextual factors that "intervene" between car ownership and energy demand—e.g., how much a car is driven (which can be captured by "vehicle miles traveled" forecasts), fuel economy, the mix of city versus highway driving, and so on. Third, a consensus in motor vehicle forecasts does not guarantee that they will be correct; they may all be wrong. It is an encouraging sign, though, since a lack of consensus (as in the case of air travel forecasts) precludes accuracy and reliability.

Another perspective on future accuracy is provided by recent attempts to develop mathematical models of travel patterns. In their review of formal modeling approaches in air transport forecasting, Vitek and Taneja of the MIT Flight Transportation Laboratory summarize the projections generated by several of these mathematical models. One of the most striking attributes of the models is the great variation in outcomes produced by different—but plausible—sets of assumptions. For example, two 1972 models, one developed by the Port Authority of New York and New Jersey and the other by the Civil Aeronautics Board, generated revenue-passenger-miles forecasts for 1980 ranging from 207 billion to 335 billion, and from 210 billion to 306 billion miles respectively.[12] The magnitudes of difference mean that the models rest on assumptions that involve considerable uncertainty. Even if the models are valid (i.e., if putting in the correct values for external variables would produce the correct values for variables predicted by the model), the choice of values for external variables, which often include projections of the broad economic context, leads to divergent results. Thus, the choice of core assumptions is terribly important to air travel forecasting, yet the certainty or predictability of "appropriate" assumptions is quite low.

CHAPTER 7

TECHNOLOGICAL FORECASTING

Technological forecasting, which covers all efforts to project technological capabilities and to predict the invention and spread of technological innovations, deals directly with scientific breakthroughs and has shared in the excitement that such breakthroughs engender. Indeed, it has been lauded as the "vanguard" of the forecasting movement. No other area of forecasting has generated greater optimism with regard to the ability to forecast or greater glorification of the diversity and sophistication of forecast techniques. Since technological forecasting generally requires a grasp of the scientific or engineering principles involved in the technology under investigation, technological forecasters are often scientists or engineers, a fact which has reinforced the scientific aura of most technological forecasting.

Yet, recently, the enthusiasm of the technological forecasters has given way to a more sober outlook. In the 1960s, technological forecasters displayed a rather remarkable confidence that their methods work. One of the most widely published technological forecasting theorists, Marvin Cetron, expressed the general sentiment: "Future technical possibilities aren't hard to project, but forecasters find their most difficult job is getting planners to use the predictions effectively."[1] What makes this confidence remarkable is that there was so little evidence, positive *or* negative, that technological forecasts had been successful. Instead of evaluating the past performance of technological forecasting, forecasting theorists generally analyzed past growth trends in the technologies themselves, which usually implied that a given technology *would have been* forecasted accurately because it is now known that its growth trend followed some identifiable curve or formula. This conclusion makes sense, of course, only if that specific curve or formula (i.e., the appropriate forecasting method) definitely was used by the hypothetical earlier forecasters. It does not provide any real justification for optimism. The mood in the 1970s is captured in the assessment given by Harold Linstone, senior editor of *Technological Forecasting and Social Change:* "We have already learned quite a bit about our needs and capabilities, about forecasting and planning. The best minds today are less arrogant and narrow, far more cognizant of the *problematique* than they were a decade ago. They understand the limitations of the state of the art. . . ."[2] Yet there still is very little empirical evidence on where the limitations of technological forecasting lie.

This chapter evaluates the actual performance of the limited range of *appraisable* technological forecasting efforts. A number of obstacles stand in the way of evaluating technological forecasts, but, for those forecasts which are amenable to appraisal, evaluation reveals that technological forecasting is quite erratic. In light of this poor performance, a critique of the technological forecasting enterprise is offered, along with some suggestions for the development of a general theory to guide technological forecasting away from *ad hoc* improvisation.

THE MEANING OF TECHNOLOGICAL FORECASTING

All forecasting may involve technological components, inasmuch as any trend is conditioned by related technology. For example, population projections may take into account the technology of birth control, since population growth depends on that technology. Energy projections may integrate technological progress in energy conversion, petroleum extraction, appliance efficiency, and so on. It is therefore necessary to restrict the definition of "technological forecasting" to efforts focusing primarily on changes in technology, rather than efforts to project other kinds of trends, even if they involve a technological component. As often happens, however, a forecast of a basically nontechnological trend will rest on the assumptions or conclusions provided by related technological forecasts. Thus, the policy-maker evaluating that basically nontechnological forecast must judge whether the related technological forecasts provide a firm enough basis to justify the forecast he plans to use. Despite this limitation in definition, technological forecasting still covers an enormous range of subjects. Medicine, weaponry, transportation, communications, information-processing, industrial production, agriculture, energy, and innumerable other fields have been subjected to technological forecasting efforts.

Two qualities of technological forecasting are generally useful for policy-making and are *essential* for forecast appraisal. The first is the expression of technological improvement in terms of *functional capacity* rather than the specific configurations of inventions. Policy-makers usually require insight into what machines and techniques will be able to accomplish, rather than how they will look or work. The implications of technology for social and economic processes depend primarily on emerging capabilities rather than on the precise nature of the inventions providing the capabilities. If specific inventions rather than capabilities are predicted, the implications of technological progress may be missed because of the failure to capture the development of *parallel* inventions serving the same functions.[3] For example, whether rapid transit is accomplished through monorails or through subways, the significance of technological improvement in mass transit lies more in capability than in form. Yet, occasionally, the specific nature of an innovation is indeed important for policy-makers, since each configuration may convey peculiarities that have their own effects. The functional capacity of efficiency in energy production, for instance, does not convey all of the environmental, social, and economic implications of specific technologies like solar or nuclear energy.

For appraisal purposes, the functional-capacity format is indispensable. The unique challenge of technological forecasting is to anticipate the consequences or capabilities of inventions not yet fully conceived or imagined. Consequently, predictions of specific inventions, particularly if they are detailed predictions, are likely to be wrong in at least some respects, no matter how accurate they are in anticipating what can be done with the invention. For example, S. C. Gilfillan predicted in 1912 that a combination of projector, telephone, and movie screen would be widely used in American homes of the future to serve the same function that television eventually fulfilled.[4] The prediction of the specific invention was wrong—televisions do not have separate projectors and movie screens, and programs are not transmitted through telephone wires—but the prediction ought to be rated as largely correct.

The second desirable characteristic of technological forecasts is that they explicitly specify the *timing* of technological innovations. The prediction that an invention will emerge at some unspecified time in the future is less useful to the policy-maker, who must make decisions for specific, time-bound situations. Yet here again the lack of a specific target date does not totally cancel out the usefulness of the forecast for policy-makers; forecasts without specific target dates can nonetheless sensitize policy-makers to potential opportunities or dangers.

Harold Lasswell calls these expectations about the future "developmental constructs," and points out that, even if they do not have the status of scientific propositions, they can serve as working hypotheses to aid in the search for, and evaluation of, other information relevant to the future.[5] A good example is Lasswell's 1941 prophecy of the "garrison state," one of the earliest predictions of a "military-industrial complex" that allows "specialists on violence" to dominate.[6] The prediction bears no date, yet it effectively underscored the potential danger of the encroachment of the military and "national security affairs" on national policy-making. Even science fiction, which does not pretend to predict reality precisely, can have this effect. Nevertheless, the *appraisal* of technological forecasts absolutely requires specific dates, simply to establish which point of actual technological development is to be used as the criterion for evaluating forecast accuracy.

Because of the importance of the timing of technological breakthroughs, many forecasts are presented in terms of dates rather than quantities over time.

Date-of-breakthrough predictions usually *can* be converted into projections of the quantity of products produced with that sort of technology or of the demand engendered by new innovations facilitated by that technology. For example, instead of forecasting the date of the development of a performance- and cost-competitive electric car, one could project the number of electric cars or the demand for electric battery rechargers. However, in many cases the breakthrough to a new level of technology is so abrupt in terms of its consequences that the timing of the change is more important than the specific quantities involved. Therefore, many date-of-breakthrough forecasts must be evaluated in their own terms—by the accuracy of the predicted dates. They require, then, a different appraisal technique, since the appraisal technique used so far is based on the similarity between forecasted and real *quantities* over time.

APPRAISAL PROBLEMS

Establishing the worth of general techniques in technological forecasting turns out to be a very difficult undertaking. Three distinct problems face the appraiser of technological forecasting. First, few specific technologies have received as much intensive attention as have the trends in energy, transportation, population, or economics. Since each type of technology has received only limited attention, a comparison of the success of different methodologies is precluded except for a very few technological categories.

Second, for most types of technological forecasts, few independent forecasts have been made in terms that allow for sophisticated comparisons. Particularly in the case of forecasts of technological breakthroughs, the specification of what fulfills the prediction varies from one study to another. In effect, such studies forecast the occurrence of somewhat different breakthroughs, thereby setting for themselves tasks of varying difficulty. Independent technological forecasts also differ considerably in terms of whether they refer to the initial discovery, practical introduction, or widespread use of a particular innovation. Therefore, except in a few rare cases, there are too few forecasts of the same innovation to evaluate their improvement over time or to reliably compare the results of forecast methodologies.

Third, most technological forecasts address events that have yet to occur. Consequently, the hindsight evaluation of their accuracy cannot be accomplished. This problem was encountered in an interesting attempt by Grabbe and Pyke to evaluate date-of-breakthrough computer forecasts.[7] While it was feasible to measure the errors of forecasts for events which had already taken place by the time of the Grabbe-Pyke study (1972), it was impossible to determine the magnitudes of error for the predictions of breakthroughs that still had not materialized. Grabbe and Pyke's tentative conclusion that, in general, the forecasts had been pessimistic may still prove to be wrong, if the unfulfilled innovations are not realized for many years, in which case their bias would be one of optimism rather than pessimism.

Because of these obstacles to hindsight evaluation of most technological forecasts, this study concentrates its direct appraisal efforts on only two technological areas, the development of nuclear energy and the progress in computer capabilities. Due to the longstanding interest in both of these areas, enough forecasts exist to permit a meaningful hindsight analysis. In addition, by examining the extent of disagreement among experts forecasting the same innovations, a less direct appraisal approach is employed to analyze forecasting for a broader spectrum of technological topics.

NUCLEAR ENERGY FORECASTS

The future role of nuclear energy is one of the most crucial and problematic aspects of the persistent energy-environmental crisis. Since the mid-1950s, forecasters have been trying to anticipate the magnitude of the nuclear contribution, with, as we shall see, very limited success.

Forecasts of nuclear electrical capacity first appeared in the mid-1950s, after the technical feasibility of uranium fission reactors was demonstrated. At stake were the funding of research-and-development projects on nuclear generators, the development plans for uranium extraction, and the future of all the conventional fuels used in electricity generation. Projections were authored by a wide diversity of institutions, including research institutes, trade associations (such as the Atomic Industrial Forum), individual corporations, governmental agencies, and public commissions.

Forecasts of nuclear energy really have two different aspects, both of which are useful for policy-making addressed to either the short or long term. Forecasts of energy actually produced by nuclear reactors are required to determine the adequacy or shortfall of energy supply in the target year of the forecast. On the other hand, forecasts of nuclear capacity pertain to the potential for nuclear energy production under the condition of full operation of the plants—it is a forecast of *installed capacity.*

It turns out that nuclear electricity generation is generally regarded as a derivative of installed capacity. Despite the wide variations in the performance of individual plants, overall generation can be calculated from capacity and an average load factor, often set at 80 percent of full-time production.[8] Consequently, for those studies that project both capacity and generation, we have focused primarily on the capacity forecasts in the following analysis. Studies projecting only nuclear generation also are considered, however. Since the capacity-generation relationship is relatively constant, the errors of either quantity have the same meaning and significance.

Projections of nuclear capacity have particularly important technological aspects. Although the development of nuclear capacity is superficially an economic question—whether nuclear energy costs less than conventional energy, and whether capital for high initial construction costs is available— **169** the economics of nuclear energy production has depended directly on the solution of engineering problems that keep atomic energy production expensive: the costs of repurifying and remachining the uranium rods, disposing of radioactive wastes, and so on. Eugene Ayres and Charles Scarlott, engineers prominent in analyzing energy needs and resources, noted in the early 1950s that "nuclear fuel, having been demonstrated to be capable of producing large amounts of energy and to be available in important quantities, still has another obstacle to hurdle before it becomes competitive with other energy forms. These are the engineering problems—which boil down to cost."[9]

The key assumption behind nuclear energy forecasts has been that the rate of engineering improvement, directed at reducing the cost of nuclear energy as compared with that of conventional fuels, is the limiting factor; as engineering obstacles are removed, growth will occur. Most forecasts of nuclear capacity have not considered other potential limiting factors, such as the supply of fissionable material or political difficulties. Since technological progress is generally considered to occur at an accelerating, exponential rate (i.e., a constant proportion of improvement over the current base, which itself increases), this focus on technology as the primary constraint has led to forecasts assuming exponential growth. These forecasts have tended to ignore the fact that what makes a given technology feasible and acceptable often depends on the political climate, as in the case of increasingly stringent demands for exhaustive site-safety tests and nonpolluting waste disposal.

TECHNIQUES OF NUCLEAR FORECASTING

For strictly short-term forecasting, a very simple approach relying on announced construction plans has been widely used. Nuclear plants in the 1960s required at least a five-year lead time, and currently require a nine-to-ten-year lead time.[10] Therefore, it is feasible to anticipate the volume of nuclear capacity in future (but not too distant) years on the basis of current plans and commitments.

The straightforward simplicity of this approach is deceiving, however. The completion and start-up of nuclear plants on schedule is by no means automatic. Delays may be caused by technical problems of design and construction, by labor problems or other nontechnical, "socioeconomic" problems, and, most importantly, by lawsuits or other forms of resistance by groups antagonistic to nuclear power plants. The latter two types of problems make short-term nuclear forecasting as much a matter of social forecasting as it is technological forecasting.

For long-range projections, nuclear forecasters have generally employed a component approach.[11] The rate of growth in nuclear capacity is partitioned into two components: the growth rate of *total* electrical capacity, and the proportion of new capacity provided by nuclear reactors. James A. Lane of the Oak Ridge National Laboratory began forecasting in this vein in 1954,

170

when he assumed that total electrical capacity would increase eight times in the next fifty years, and that half of the new plants built in the year 2000 would be nuclear.[12] Working backward, Lane calculated for the 1960–2000 period the annual rate of growth in nuclear capacity required to reach this level, assuming a constant proportional rate of increase on a base of half a million kilowatts of nuclear capacity in 1960.

Forecasters of the growth of an infant industry and technology face peculiar obstacles. The earliest nuclear forecasts had to be made without the benefit of a real-data baseline, since prior to 1960 the existing nuclear capacity was negligible. Thus, the starting level to which the proportional growth rate was applied was itself a predicted, rather than an actual, figure. In the long run the choice of baseline level is not very important, since subsequent additions to nuclear capacity are naturally of much greater magnitude. But for short-term forecasts a bad guess at the baseline level could produce considerable error. Lane's prediction of 500,000 kilowatts for 1960 nuclear capacity overestimated the real capacity by more than 60 percent, and the ten-year forecast calculated from this inflated base was four times greater than the actual figure.

Similarly, in the early days of nuclear forecasting, no trend had been established for the rate at which nuclear designs for new plants would be chosen over conventional designs. Lane's assumption that half of the new plants built in 2000 would be nuclear was not anchored in real data; he had to rely solely on his evaluation of the very long-range promise of nuclear power. His projection is quite sensitive to this evaluation; an alternative assumption that all plants built after 1990 would be nuclear leads to a prediction more than twice as great as Lane's projection for nuclear capacity in the year 2000.

As the construction and operation of nuclear plants proceeded, real trends in the growth of nuclear capacity and in the substitution of nuclear for conventional installations emerged. However, the most common method of forecasting nuclear development after 1960 still was to project the same components the earlier forecasters had used in a more conjectural way. The rate of substitution, sometimes called the "nuclear capture" rate, was derived either from further projections of trends in the costs of nuclear and conventional fuels, or from unitary, theoretical growth curves. An example of the use of cost extrapolations to derive capture rates was described by Richard Tarrice of the Stanford Research Institute in 1962.[13] By 1965 the AEC had adopted this approach in order to forecast beyond the dates of known installation plans.[14] In contrast, a 1962 forecast by Atomics International, a division of North American Aviation, falls into the theoretical growth-curve category, in that an S-shaped curve was presumed to describe future capture rates because, it was argued, S curves hold "in the case of any new product."[15]

A further elaboration on the component approach involves dividing the country into regions in order to apply different capture rates to different areas according to the cost of conventional fuels, which sets the nuclear capture rate. Each region's growth in electricity consumption and nuclear capture rate are calculated separately, then aggregated for the national total. This approach was first used explicitly in 1957 by Karl Mayer in a study for the National Planning Association.[16] The AEC, FPC, and several nongovernmental forecasters have been using this method regularly since 1964.[17] It is important to note that this sort of elaboration, as unquestionably "valid" as it is, does not circumvent the need to accurately anticipate the "national" factor of the efficiency (i.e., cost) of nuclear energy. Just as the cohort and component elaborations of population forecasting are sensitive to nationwide attitudes toward family size, nuclear forecasts for different regions are still sensitive to national (and international) developments in nuclear technology.

EVALUATION OF NUCLEAR FORECASTS

The errors of nuclear capacity and nuclear generation forecasts are displayed in figures 7.1–7.4. They are expressed as "factors of error" rather than as percentages, so that overestimates (which could be several hundred percent greater than real levels) will not be artificially calculated as having

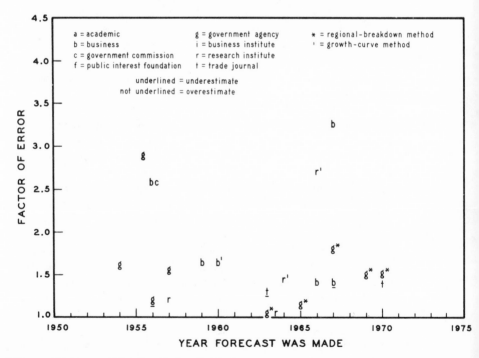

7.1. Errors of Five-Year Nuclear Energy Forecasts

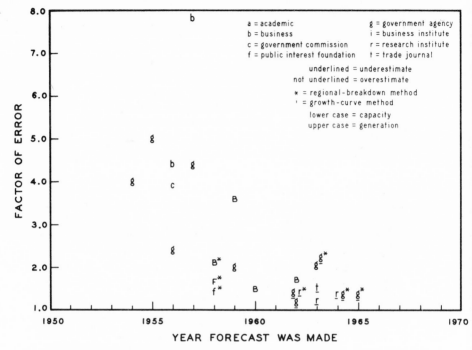

7.2. Errors of Ten-Year Nuclear Energy Forecasts

greater errors than underestimates (which in percentage terms cannot be more than 100 percent less than the real values). An "error factor" treats high and low forecasts without this bias, by dividing the forecast into the actual level if the actual level is larger, or dividing the actual level into the forecast level if the forecast is larger:

$$\text{error factor} = \begin{cases} \text{actual level} \div \text{forecast level,} & \textit{if } \text{actual} > \text{forecast.} \\ \text{forecast level} \div \text{actual level,} & \textit{if } \text{actual} \leqslant \text{forecast.} \end{cases}$$

Thus, for example, the error-factor measure would regard forecasts that are four times larger than the actual level, and forecasts that turn out to be one-fourth as large as the actual level, as equally in error—by a factor of four.

Despite the fact that nuclear technology has advanced in the past twenty-five years from infancy to technical sophistication, the quality of short-term nuclear forecasts has hardly improved. Figure 7.1, which shows the error factors of five-year forecasts of on-line nuclear power capacity, reveals that the post-1965 forecasts have been no better than the earliest forecasts on record. The median forecast error of the pre-1965 projections is the same as

173

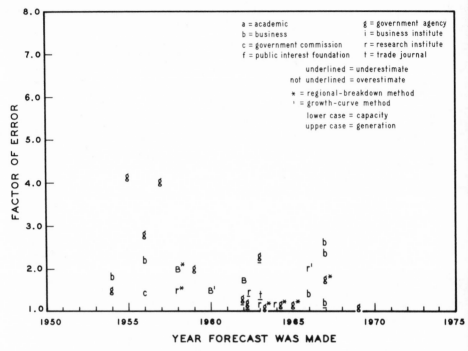

7.3. Errors of 1970 Nuclear Energy Forecasts

the median error for post-1965 projections, a factor of 1.5 (i.e., a 50 percent error).

There has been considerable improvement in long-term nuclear forecasts, however. Figure 7.2 reveals that post-1960 predictions have a median error factor of 1.4, while the pre-1960 forecasts had an average error factor of approximately 4.0. This huge difference is discounted to some extent by the fact that forecasts made between 1960 and 1965 were relatively accurate, regardless of forecast length. Furthermore, even the most recent forecasts leave much to be desired in terms of accuracy, since nearly half are more than 50 percent in error, while two "official" forecasts predicted twice as much nuclear capacity as actually materialized. Nevertheless, the more recent ten-year forecasts are certainly far better than the earlier forecasts, which prior to 1960 had no errors of less than 100 percent. Regardless of the forecast method or the institutional site of the forecast, early long-term forecasts reflected no real insight into the future rate of development of nuclear power, which is not surprising in light of the newness of the technology and the industry.

The fact that ten-year nuclear forecasts have improved, while five-year forecasts have not, reveals an important difference between technological and

174

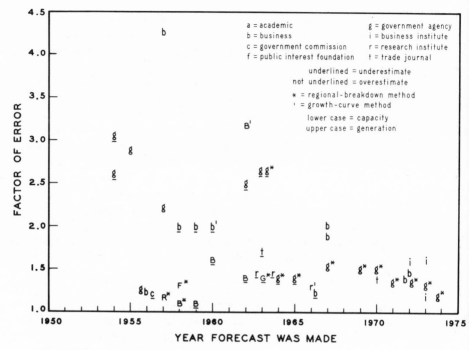

7.4. Errors of 1975 Nuclear Energy Forecasts

social forecasting. The longer forecasts, which are in large measure technological, do improve as the technology advances. In contrast, the short-term, primarily social predictions have thus far maintained the same level of uncertainty throughout the course of nuclear development.

The difficulty of predicting short-term economic, social, and political aspects of nuclear power growth also accounts for one of the most glaring failures of nuclear forecasting—its inability to take advantage of up-to-date information and greater certainty to improve forecast accuracy as the target date approaches. As figure 7.4 indicates, up until 1973 the forecasts of 1975 nuclear capacity were still off by more than 35 percent. In fact, after 1964 these forecasts gained very little advantage from increasing proximity. Similarly, the more recent forecasts for 1970 (see figure 7.3) gained nothing after 1962 in terms of increased accuracy. This implies that the same level of uncertainty remains in nuclear power forecasting until two or three years before the target date. Post-1965 forecasts of 1970 nuclear capacity were actually worse than the forecasts made between 1960 and 1965, as ambitious plan announcements apparently swayed the later forecasters to overestimate short-term nuclear growth. However, the forecasts of 1970 nuclear capacity are in a sense less significant than the forecasts for 1975, since even by 1970 nuclear capacity was still quite modest. The approach curve to the 1975 target date is probably more typical of the pattern we can expect of future nuclear forecasts—an almost horizontal line reflecting only minimal (if any) improvement until the target date is nearly reached.

Effects of Forecast Sources. Forecasts of nuclear capacity have been made by individuals in diverse institutional settings, including governmental agencies, commissions, businesses, trade journals, industry associations, and research institutes. There is little to distinguish among these institutional sources in terms of their performances. All institutional sites seem to share the same direction of error peculiar to each era. Early ten-year forecasts were overly optimistic, while later ones were pessimistic. Practically all of the short-term forecasts have been optimistic. This indicates that forecasters from all institutional sites are exposed to common cues and preconceptions; they all seem to share a common *Zeitgeist* which overshadows whatever differences might arise from differences in peculiar institutional perspectives or motives for presenting forecasts.

The only notable institutional difference in terms of forecast accuracy is that in some respects the governmental forecasts have been more successful than other forecasts of the same era and length. Although all pre-1960 ten-year nuclear energy forecasts were highly inaccurate, the three non-governmental ones were considerably worse than the six governmental projections. For 1970 capacity, governmental forecasts were generally better than other forecasts made at the same time. In other words, although some governmental forecasts are no better than other forecasts (e.g., in forecasting 1975 capacity), governmental agencies (particularly the AEC) are the only sources to show any advantage in reliability over other sites.

Another aspect of the forecast source to consider is the personal orientation and background of the individual forecaster or team of forecasters, regardless of institutional site. The authors of pre-1960 nuclear energy forecasts were primarily scientists directing or engaged in basic atomic energy research. Several forecasts were put forth by luminaries of the Oak Ridge National Laboratory. In the early years the Atomic Energy Commission's forecasting was dominated by research scientists rather than by the economics-oriented specialists of the formal AEC forecasting office established to routinize the forecasting process. We cannot attribute the magnitudes of error of these early forecasts to naïveté on the part of the scientists, since generally the progress of new technologies is more difficult to predict, regardless of who the forecasters are. The direction of their error, though—consistent overoptimism—fits the proposition that scientists would err on the high side in projecting technical growth.

Effects of Techniques. For projections beyond the short term, nuclear forecasters have shown two differences in their methodology. First, the option of analyzing nuclear growth regionally rather than nationally has been adopted by some, but not all, forecasters. In figures 7.2–7.4 those studies explicitly using regional breakdowns are designated by asterisks. Second, nuclear capture rates can be derived either from cost extrapolations or from growth curves. The few studies using growth curves are designated by apostrophes.

The regional-component forecasts were not very different from the projections that relied solely on national trends. The 1957–58 forecasts by the National Planning Association, the first agency to use the regional-component refinement, were superior to other forecasts of the same era. It is misleading, however, to consider these three forecasts as independent "tests" of the component technique, since all shared the same assumptions as part of a joint effort. The 1963 Federal Power Commission forecast, another application of the regional-component method, was worse than other forecasts of the same date in its ten-year and 1975 projections, although it was the best 1963 forecast for the 1970 target year. From 1964 onward, the regional-component forecasts were about as accurate as other forecasts.

It is important to analyze why this more sophisticated, refined method did not appreciably improve the accuracy of the projections. After all, a refinement like the application of regional substitution rates is a very sensible and cost-free way of incorporating additional information of obvious relevance into the forecasting procedure. Yet the "refined" forecasts are not much better than simpler forecasting results that ignore this distinction. The answer seems to be that, as we found for population forecasts, the validity of the basic, "core" assumptions carries more weight than methodological refinement in determining the level of accuracy. In this case, the core factors are the rate of progress in nuclear technology (both in efficiency and in safety), and the strength of the opposition expressed by antinuclear groups. Errors in projecting these factors swamp the improvements brought by superior methodology.

The regional-component method does seem to have one important advantage, even if it is still vulnerable to inaccurate core assumptions. Even though regional-component forecasts are not superior to many forecasts that forego the regional breakdown, none of them is drastically inaccurate. The worst regional-component forecasts are in error by a factor of just over 2, while a number of other forecast methods are in error by a factor of 4 or 5. Although the limited number of cases precludes conclusive generalizations, this finding is consistent with the proposition that the closer scrutiny required for region-by-region analysis can at least avoid some important discrepancies between assumptions and reality that might escape notice at the aggregate level.

177

The few applications of growth curves were as successful as other forecasts of the same eras, except in the case of five-year forecasts, for which the only two growth-curve applications, in 1960 and 1966, produced greater errors than comparable cost-extrapolating forecasts. This is not surprising, since the shape and parameters of theoretical growth curves are chosen more with an eye to long-term patterns than to the fit for the years immediately following the year in which the forecast is made.

FORECASTING COMPUTER CAPABILITIES

The prediction of computer capabilities is an especially significant focus of technological forecasting. Improvement in computer technology is the most frequently cited example of technological progress in the literature on technology and the future. The progress made in computer technology has been regarded as remarkable, and has been cited as a demonstration that technological forecasting is manageable even for "exploding technologies." Robert U. Ayres has used the trend in computer progress to demonstrate the feasibility of envelope-curve forecasting.[18] Joseph Martino used computer improvement for his demonstration of trend extrapolation using regression analysis.[19] Therefore, computer-capability forecasting is an important test case in the technological forecasting enterprise.

Computer forecasting has also been an important practical undertaking. Even though summary measures of computer capability have become less adequate for computer-facility planners choosing computer systems for increasingly specialized needs, these measures do indicate the general level of available technological sophistication and the performance levels to be expected in specialized applications. Thus, for example, the number of additions executed per second by a computer system cannot be converted directly into a measure of the speed at which logical operations or information retrieval are performed, but the addition rate does reflect effective circuit speeds and the sophistication of machine organization ("architecture"), which are relevant to the whole range of performance.

Even today's computers operate at speeds almost unimaginably fast. Is the question of whether future computers will operate one hundred or one thousand times faster of any real policy significance? In fact, it is. Willis Ware points out that computer models for long-range weather forecasting, arms-limitation monitoring through photoreconnaisance analysis, simulations of neurological systems for medical research, and numerous other tasks require computer capacities far beyond those in existence today for their results to be achieved within feasible time limits.[20] Ware concludes that the laws of physics *probably* do not preclude the development of computers with processing speeds adequate for these tasks, but whether or when these capacities will be reached is problematic.[21] The question is a matter for *public* policy; not only has much of computer development to date been financed through the Defense Department and other governmental agencies, but the development of computers capable of accomplishing these tasks will require such huge investments that government will of necessity be the major source of financing if such machines are to be built.

Of the more than two hundred articles and books I found listed in bibliographies as relevant to future computer developments, less than fifteen contained explicit forecasts of future computer capabilities in any appraisable form. Many studies pointed out that future computers would be "very fast." Some predicted the capabilities of the "next computer generation," without specifying when this generation would arrive. A few even predicted computer capabilities in specific years in terms of "instructions per second," but failed to specify what types of instructions they had in mind, which makes a tremendous difference in the meaning and the ultimate accuracy of the prediction.

It is interesting that forecasts explicit enough to evaluate did not appear until the mid-1960s, when what computer industry analysts called the "third generation" computers appeared.[22] Apparently, earlier computer specialists were aware of the impressive progress made in computer development throughout the late 1950s and early 1960s, but were still unsure of the tempo of operational improvement. With the introduction of integrated circuits in the machines of the mid-1960s, a discernable pattern of roughly five-year generations appeared. Because each generation brought a consistent proportional increase in computer speed, some brave specialists and a few nonspecialists became convinced that growth in computer technology can be accurately anticipated.

Furthermore, some of the appraisable forecasts are not adequately explicit in themselves, but can be evaluated because information in the accompanying text reveals which specific measures were involved. For example, a forecast of "number of additions per second" may refer to "32-bit fixed additions," which would be relatively simple additions of short numbers; or to "64-bit rounded, normalized floating-point additions," which would be complicated and more precise additions of longer numbers, requiring more time on any computer. Fortunately, such forecasts either cited the speeds of existing computers, which revealed the nature of the capability measures, or were expressed in terms of factors of speed improvement over time, which permit the use of any of the conventional measures of computer speed. Unless a different measure of computer capability was explicitly stated in a forecast or is inferable from other information provided, the forecasts studied here are expressed in terms of the number of 64-bit fixed additions performed per second by the fastest operational computer under optimal programming conditions.[23]

COMPUTER-CAPABILITY FORECASTING TECHNIQUES

Few studies are very explicit about how they forecast computer advances, but three basic approaches can be discerned. There is no indication that one method is more "primitive" than the others, or that one method is beginning to dominate.

One computer forecasting method, used in numerous other areas of forecasting, is simply to average the results of several existing or elicited expert forecasts. The 1965 Diebold forecasts stem from a study in which more than eighty American and European corporations participated. The forecasts were apparently developed from the input of experts employed by the computer-supply companies involved in the study.[24] In 1966 the Naval Supply Systems Command gathered multiple expert opinions by creating a large data bank of available publications and reports. Its forecasts presumably represent the center of the range of opinions gathered in the data bank.[25] The 1971 Bernstein-Feidelman forecast was one outcome of a Delphi study and thus reflects the median opinion of numerous experts asked to speculate about future computer developments.[26]

The second method, also commonly used in all realms of forecasting, is trend extrapolation. For computer-speed growth, however, an exponential rather than linear trend has been extrapolated. Projections by Armer and Joseph extended the straight-line trend that appeared when past growth was plotted on a graph whose vertical scale (operating speed) was given in units of tenfold increases (i.e., semilog paper).[27] The results of these studies are not identical, however, because the straight lines obtained varied with the year in which the forecast was made and the authors' interpretations of what the trend points actually had been.

The studies by Hobbs and Ozbekhan involved a two-step procedure of first predicting the nature of devices available by the target date and then estimating the capabilities of such devices.[28] This method would appear to be most suitable for short-term forecasting, because it requires anticipation of the specific nature of the devices, which is not known for more remote innovations. Rein Turn, for example, analyzes imminent memory and logic devices to forecast short-term computer-speed advances, but relies on extrapolation to project trends beyond the first five-year period.[29] However, Ozbekhan attempts to forecast eight-year growth (1967–75) on this basis.

The methods adopted for computer-capability forecasting are based on, and convey, the core assumptions that each forecaster held with respect to his expectations of future computer developments. The cues available to computer-capability forecasters in the late 1960s were mixed and somewhat confusing. On the one hand, physicists were pointing out that, while previous improvements in computer speeds had been achieved through advancements in electronic components, the speeds of individual components were approaching ultimate physical limits.[30] On the other hand, computer engineers were launching development projects for machines that would process numerous instructions simultaneously, either by overlapping the execution of several instructions ("pipelining") or by using several processors in concert ("array processing"). Designers of these systems spoke of *theoretical* computer speeds far greater than the single processor's theoretical limits, and considerably greater than the actual *operational* speeds achieved by 1975.[31] However, there was no guarantee that these new architectures would succeed in terms of engineering and economic feasibility.

Therefore, the forecasters had to decide whether the rapid past trend of speed improvement would level off because of physical limits, or would be extended by the breakthroughs to new configurations. If they predicted that the new architectures would be successful, they also had to decide whether the rate of improvement would be the same as that achieved through progress in electronic components. By using trend extrapolation, Armer and Joseph were expressing confidence in continued rapid technological progress despite the potential physical limits. The device-analysis technique and the multiple-opinion approach do not commit the forecaster to the assumption of continued trends, but instead put the burden of establishing core assumptions on the judgment of the forecasters or the experts he calls upon.

EVALUATION OF COMPUTER FORECASTS

Only forecasts for 1965, 1970 and, 1975 are included in this analysis because the decade and half-decade dates happen to coincide with the advent of new computer "generations." Therefore, ambitious forecasts for these dates do not miss out on new breakthroughs by a year or two, as would forecasts for, say, 1968 or 1972–73. Between 1964 and 1968 work was under way on the CDC 7600, which, however, was not delivered until 1969; between 1970 and 1974 several very fast new computer architectures were under development, such as the CDC pipeline processor (CDC STAR-100) and the Burroughs–University of Illinois array processor (ILLIAC-IV), but these machines did not become operational until 1974 and 1975 respectively.

The accuracy of these forecasts of operating speed (number of operations per unit of processing time) is summarized in table 7.1. Inaccuracy is expressed as "factor of error," as it was for nuclear forecasts.

The short-term forecasts, ranging from two to five years in length, are reasonably accurate for gauging the technological "state of the art," showing an average error factor of 1.6. As an estimate of technological progress, this 60 percent average error is not drastic, considering the range of performance available within a single technology and the tenfold increase historically associated with five-year periods. However, the error may be serious for

Table 7.1: Accuracy of Computer-Capability Forecasts

Date	Source	Forecast Method	Target Date	Forecast	Actual	Factor of Error	Bias
1965	Diebold group	Multiple opinions	1970	20 million fixed adds./sec.	18 million	1.1	Optimistic
1966	Naval Supply Command	Multiple opinions	1970	33 million fixed adds./sec.	18 million	1.8	Optimistic
			1975	900 million fixed adds./sec.	262 million	3.4	Optimistic
1966	Hobbs	Device analysis	1970	15 million fixed adds./sec.	18 million	1.2	Pessimistic
1966	Armer	Trend extrapolation	1970	48 million fixed adds./sec.	18 million	2.7	Optimistic
			1975	760 million fixed adds./sec.	262 million	2.9	Optimistic
1967	Ozbekhan	Device analysis	1975	3.3 billion fixed adds./sec.	262 million	12.6	Optimistic
1968	Joseph	Trend extrapolation	1970	15 million instructions/sec.	12.5 million	1.2	Optimistic
			1975	105 million instructions/sec.	173 million	1.6	Pessimistic
1971	Bernstein and Feidelman	Multiple opinions	1975	180 million fixed adds./sec.	262 million	1.5	Pessimistic

decision-makers who must decide when to purchase new computer systems. Furthermore, when these short-term forecasts were made, the most advanced computer systems for the target years were already well along in their development and construction, making the estimation task more a question of intelligence than one of projection. In this respect, the short-term forecasting performance is hardly impressive.

The long-term forecasts, ranging in length from seven to nine years, are far less reliable. It is not true, as several computer experts say,[32] that forecasting computer developments beyond five years is impossible—the simple extrapolation by Earl Joseph was quite accurate. However, several of the forecasts show very large errors, indicating that long-term computer-capability prediction has been at best unreliable.

The optimistic bias is somewhat surprising in light of all we have heard about the amazing growth of computer technology and the computer industry. Nevertheless, most forecasts, whether short-term or long-term, overestimated the rate of progress of computer technology. Perhaps the experts themselves fell prey to the popular image of their own field. This error is reminiscent of the 1940–55 demographers' failure, in the face of public dismay about the prospects of declining population, to incorporate the upward change in fertility rates into their forecasts (see chapter 3).

Effects of Techniques. Trend-extrapolation forecasts reflect considerable variability in terms of accuracy, ranging from Joseph's slightly pessimistic forecast for 1975 to Armer's rather optimistic forecast. This presents a paradox: if trend extrapolation is the most mechanistic, objective approach used, how can forecasts produced at almost the same time (i.e., 1966–68), with the same target date of 1975, have such completely different results? The problem appears to be that different forecasters define and measure *the* trend in quite different ways. In this case, Armer's 1966 forecast was based on the assumption that, historically, computer speed increased by a factor of ten every four years, and the Joseph forecast in 1968 was based on a factor-of-ten improvement every ten years. If this much variation can be introduced by arbitrary factors, such as the starting point of the data used to establish the trend line, the objectivity and reliability of trend extrapolation must be questioned.

No definitive conclusions can be drawn from the performance of device-analysis forecasts, since only two forecasts are available for appraisal. It is interesting, though, that the short-term use of this method by Hobbs was quite successful, whereas the long-range prediction by Ozbekhan was the worst forecast of all. This difference supports the logic of restricting device analysis to the short run, since the nature of distant technology is largely unknown.

The performance of multiple-opinion forecasts points to a strength of *ad hoc* opinion-averaging that is often overlooked. Most forecasting theorists regard methods that solicit *ad hoc* opinions, such as the Delphi technique, as "intuitive," implying that such methods are little more than guesses.[33] Yet we have seen that in many instances the accuracy of forecasting depends more on the validity of core assumptions than on the elaborateness of method. Studies that rely on multiple *ad hoc* opinions are perhaps better able to establish a balanced view of future growth than are single-expert projections, no matter how sophisticated. The Diebold group and Bernstein-Feidelman studies do quite well in comparison with other forecasting attempts. Another "survey" forecast, carried out by the trade journal *Datamation* in 1966, though not strictly comparable in that it projects circuit speeds rather than execution speeds, also is extremely accurate in terms of 1972–73 capabilities.[34] Of the three multiple-opinion studies, the Naval Supply Command study was least accurate. It relied on written publications and technical reports, which in effect stocked the opinion pool with somewhat less up-to-date opinions. This information lag may be what accounts for the relatively poor forecasts obtained by this study in comparison with the other multiple-opinion forecasts.

Effects of Sources. The most consistent and interesting finding with respect to forecast sources accounts for bias rather than accuracy. While it is *not* true that the experts on computer hardware (Hobbs, Joseph, Armer, and presumably many of the participants of the Diebold and Navy Supply Command studies) have been more pessimistic than the nonexperts, the forecasts designed to explore the *implications* of the "computer explosion" are consistently more optimistic than the others. Thus, the "implications for management" studies by Ozbekhan, Diebold and the Naval Supply Command, and Armer's study of the socioeconomic implications of computer innovations, overestimate the computer-capability growth rate more than do the studies by Hobbs, Joseph and Bernstein and Feidelman provided as "technical information" to the community of computer designers and users. Whereas exaggeration by forecasters preoccupied with the impact of the forecasted trend was absent in the motor-vehicle forecasting efforts examined in chapter 6, it is in evidence for computer-capability forecasts. The difference may be that while the transportation forecasters, regardless of the purposes of their projections, conformed to a well-established conventional wisdom that brought uniformity in bias to their forecasts, forecasts of the more volatile developments of computer technology have had no such source of uniformity.

TECHNOLOGICAL-BREAKTHROUGH
FORECASTING

Nuclear and computer forecasts are unusual because of the fairly large number of appraisable predictions available for each trend. Most technological innovations have not been subjected to such extensive forecasting efforts. Therefore, at this point, the appraisal of technological forecasting must depart from the approaches used to evaluate other forecasting attempts. Not only are technological forecasts generally expressed in terms of dates rather than magnitudes, but there are rarely enough forecasts of the same technological breakthrough to do the sort of analysis feasible for projections of nuclear capacity, computer speed, population, GNP, energy use, or transportation. It is not often that many independent forecasters over a span of years develop forecasts of the same item. Furthermore, since explicit technological forecasting is a relatively recent phenomenon, there have been few technological forecasts for which the confirming events have already occurred. Most technological forecasts made during the 1960s and 1970s relate to scientific breakthroughs expected in the late 1970s, the 1980s, or even beyond; hence, their accuracy cannot be evaluated through *post hoc* comparison.

However, some joint efforts at technological forecasts by many experts have been attempted, and they comprise, in a sense, a "natural experiment" through which we can estimate the dispersion and variation in technological forecasts of the same scientific events *as if* such forecasts had been made independently. This opportunity is provided by various types of experiments with directed forecasting. The most fruitful of these methods has been the Delphi technique as developed at the Rand Corporation.[35]

The Delphi technique was designed to structure systematic interchanges among experts in order to produce the greatest possible "legitimate"[36] convergence to a consensual estimate or forecast. The most general use of Delphi, then, has been to establish the middle range of the experts' opinions—*the* single most likely guess.

However, Delphi results can be interpreted in a radically different way. Despite the fact that the Delphi procedure, in exposing each expert to the opinions of the others, tends to create convergence in opinions, some differences invariably remain. What do these differences represent? A Delphi result may be considered an analog to a set of independent efforts of experts exposed to the divergent opinions of other authorities. Since most independent forecasters do make some effort to discover what other forecasters are saying, the Delphi feedback and the "natural" information search of an independent forecaster are not very different. Therefore, the divergence remaining among Delphi estimates is analogous to the divergence of independent forecasts. In short, a Delphi exercise involving thirty experts may be regarded as thirty separate forecasts.

The shortcoming of this convenient fiction is that the Delphi procedure may instill a different level of conformity among its participants than the natural environment would bring to bear upon independent forecasters, making the level of Delphi divergence open to question as a measure of "natural" divergence. However, if Delphi results alone are used to compare the difficulty of forecasting in different technological areas, we still can compare results, for the possible lack of correspondence between independent and Delphi forecasts will not be a confounding factor.

Most of the innovations considered by Delphi studies, and by technological forecasts in general, are distant events. For example, it has been noted that, of six major pre-1969 Delphi studies involving some developments in computer technology, only two involved computer events forecasted to occur prior to 1972, and two included no computer forecasts with target dates earlier than 1975.[37] Therefore, the evaluation of these forecasts must rely on indicators of *likely* accuracy rather than on direct hindsight measures.

The best indicator of likely accuracy for forecasts of future trends is the dispersion, or spread, of the predictions made for the same target date or event. We may not know which forecast is correct, but we do know that among different forecasts of precisely the same trend, only one can be correct. Indeed, it may be that none is correct, and, even if all forecasts are very close in their predictions, the reality may be quite different, despite the lack of dispersion in the forecasts. Therefore, the dispersion measures the *minimum level* of inaccuracy (or error) that characterizes a set of projections. If the actual trend turns out to be within the range of the forecasts, the dispersion among forecasts reflects most of the inaccuracy; if the actual trend is quite different, an even greater degree of inaccuracy must be attributed to the forecasts.

To determine precisely what the minimum inaccuracy would be for a set of forecasts, we first must establish the median forecast (i.e., the forecast that is greater than half of the forecasts and less than the other half). The median is significant because, if the actual trend value turns out to be the same as the median forecast, the average error for the whole set of forecasts would be minimized. This would not occur if the mean, or some other measure of the central tendency of the forecasts, were used.[38]

Consider the hypothetical forecasts of table 7.2. If the actual level is at the median value (i.e., 9), half of the forecasts have negative errors and half yield positive errors, except, of course, for the median. If the actual level is lower than the median (say, 7), lower forecasts will gain in accuracy, but the median and above-median forecasts will lose at least as much accuracy. If the actual level exceeds the median (say, 12), the accuracy gained by higher forecasts will be more than offset by the greater inaccuracy of the lower forecasts. Thus, if the real trend turns out to be either higher or lower than the median, the sum of the differences of the forecasts from this real value could only increase. Therefore, the *minimum* error of forecasts will be their average **186** difference from the median forecast.

Table 7.2: **Magnitudes of Error of Hypothetical Forecasts, Given Different Actual Values**

	Forecast Value	Forecast Error if Actual Value is			
		Low (e.g., 7)	Median (i.e., 9)	Mean (i.e., 10)	High (e.g., 12)
Forecast 1	5	2 (−)	4 (−)	5 (−)	7 (−)
Forecast 2	8	1 (+)	1 (−)	2 (−)	4 (−)
Forecast 3	9	2 (+)	0	1 (−)	3 (−)
Forecast 4	13	6 (+)	4 (+)	3 (+)	1 (+)
Forecast 5	15	8 (+)	6 (+)	5 (+)	3 (+)
Median	9				
Mean	10				
Total absolute error		19	15	16	18
Avg. absolute error		5.8	5.0	5.2	5.6

Of the several alternative ways of defining this "average," the most useful for calculating minimum errors is to designate the median "high" forecast and the median "low" forecast as typically different from the median of the whole set of forecasts. That is, the forecast that separates the top 25 percent from the rest is a typically high forecast (in terms of the overall median), and the forecast that separates the bottom 25 percent from the rest is a typically low forecast. Their average difference from the median is half of the "inter-quartile range" (i.e., the range encompassed by the middle 50 percent of the forecasts), which may be termed the "minimum typical error," or "MTE." This measure is superior to such alternatives as the standard deviation or the arithmetic average (the mean), in that the median and the interquartile range do not require the averaging of all forecast values, which would prove impossible if any forecasters predicted that an event would never happen.

A peculiar problem of evaluating date-of-innovation forecasts is that the actual "forecast length" is unknown until the events actually occur. For date-of-innovation forecasts, unlike fixed-year trend forecasts (e.g., total energy use in 1980), the "forecast length" is precisely what is to be predicted. Although the forecast length is an unknown for date-of-innovation forecasts, events still may be usefully regarded as relatively more imminent or more remote. Our estimate of remoteness is simply the median length of available forecasts of that event. The median forecast length is superior to the mean (or arithmetic average) length because determining the mean will be impossible whenever any of the forecasts predict that the event will not occur at all. Using the available forecasts' median length as a stand-in for the actual forecast length is not at all unreasonable, even if the actual date is not the same as the median date, since the policy-makers themselves have only the forecasts on which to base their opinion on the likely remoteness of the event.

The policy-maker can take into account the median forecast length in order to estimate the likely accuracy of the forecasts.

Even with the MTE measure, the large sets of forecasts provided by the Delphi technique and similar panel forecasting methods are not very illuminating in their raw form. To compare the dispersion (and hence the likely level of accuracy) of forecasts of different technological areas, we must standardize for the differing lengths of the median forecasts encountered. The remoteness of forecasted events does make a difference in terms of forecast accuracy; therefore, more remote forecasts of one technology would appear worse in a comparison with less remote forecasts of another. If only those forecasts of standard lengths (such as ten, fifteen, or twenty years) are examined, intermediate-length forecasts would have to be discarded, as would those outside the range.

To incorporate the whole range of forecasts and at the same time control for the differing remoteness of forecasts of different technological fields, *adjusted* MTEs for ten-, fifteen-, and twenty-year forecasts are used. The adjusted MTEs for each technological field are calculated from the regression line that best fits the relationship between the lengths and the MTEs of forecasts in that field. For example, one of the Gordon-Helmer panels in their pioneering *Report on a Long-Range Forecasting Study*[39] attempted to forecast the dates of twenty-three innovations in automation. In some cases the panel's experts were in agreement—the smallest interquartile range was 5 years. For other future innovations the experts' forecasts of when the innovation would occur diverged greatly from one another—the greatest interquartile range was 615 years, which meant that even the middle 50 percent of the forecasts of one innovation ranged over six centuries. The median forecasts for each of the twenty-three innovations ranged from 10 to 62 years. The correlation between each innovation's median forecast length and its range of estimates (reflecting the extent of experts' disagreement) was very high ($r = 0.8$). Figure 7.5 shows that the straight line fitting the twenty-three points (each representing the median forecast length calculated from the time of the study [1967] and the MTE for one of the forecasted innovations in automation) slopes upward, reflecting the fact that higher ranges correspond to higher median lengths. Where this line intersects the median forecast lengths of ten, fifteen, and twenty years, the adjusted MTEs are found. Thus, the adjusted MTE for ten-year forecasts of automation innovations is 4.6 years, for fifteen-year forecasts is 6.6 years, and for twenty-year forecasts is 8.6 years.

In effect, this adjustment method estimates what the average MTE would be if a very large number of items were forecasted for the ten-, fifteen-, and twenty-year periods. The only limitation on the use of this adjustment is that it will not necessarily be meaningful for forecast lengths outside the range included in the studies examined. That is, the MTEs of automation forecasts

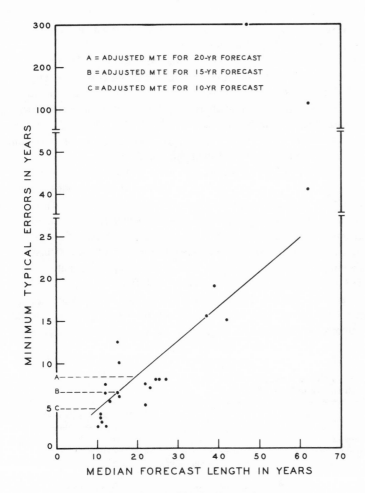

7.5. Forecast Lengths and MTEs for Twenty-three
Automation Innovations

with median lengths of less than 10 years or more than 47 years may not be
"predictable" from the line based on existing data, since the slope of the line
that best fits this range of forecasts may be quite different.

It is interesting to note that this adjustment method makes sense regardless
of the correlation between the interquartile ranges and the median forecast
lengths. If the correlation is high, the MTE forecast-length points fall closely
along the best-fitting line (estimated by least-squares). A low correlation
means that the effect of forecast length on the size of the interquartile range is
189   low, and the adjusted estimates of MTEs for each forecast length will tend

toward the average MTE for the whole set of innovations, which is consistent with the irrelevance of forecast length in this case.

These measures and techniques have been applied to those Delphi studies which provide enough information to calculate median lengths and interquartile ranges.[40] The results are given in table 7.3. To the extent that generalizable patterns can be derived from an analysis of the specific categories examined here, these insights can be applied to technologies not specifically included in the Delphi studies discussed here. Do consistent relationships obtain between the nature of the topics and their precision?

Indeed, the ordering of topics according to the MTEs of their forecasts is quite revealing. As seen in table 7.3, the categories of technologies can be grouped into three clusters, each having a different MTE level. The first cluster consists of technical areas in which advancement depends on engineering refinements and the diffusion of such innovations. The fields of communications, educational technology (which centers on computer-aided instruction), and automation fall into this group. With the exception of automation, these topics have the lowest MTEs, which indicates, first, that experts in these fields are in general agreement about the direction and pace of progress, and, second, that a representative forecast has the *potential* for being fairly accurate. The automation innovations covered in the Gordon and Helmer study

Table 7.3: Adjusted MTEs of Technological Forecasts by Category and Median Length of Forecast

Source	Category	10 yrs.	15 yrs.	20 yrs.
Trans-Canada Telephone System	Medical communications	2.5	3.4	4.3
Šulc	Communications	2.6	3.4	4.2
Parsons and Williams	Computers	3.2	4.4	5.7
Trans-Canada Telephone System	Educational technology	3.3	4.0	5.7
Trans-Canada Telephone System	Business communications	3.7	4.6	5.8
Smith, Kline, and French	Health care systems	3.8	4.8	6.0
Gordon and Helmer	Automation	4.6	6.6	8.6
Smith, Kline, and French	Medical education	4.8	—	—
Gordon and Helmer	Space exploration	4.8	5.4	6.0
Smith, Kline, and French	Biomedical research	6.1	7.4	8.8
Smith, Kline, and French	Medical diagnosis	6.3	9.8	14.8
Gordon and Helmer	All scientific breakthroughs	6.8	7.8	8.8
	Physics and chemistry	6.6	7.0	7.4
	Biology and medicine	6.6	7.8	9.0
Smith, Kline, and French	Medical therapy	7.0	8.6	10.1

MTE for Forecast Length of

have somewhat higher MTEs, indicating less agreement and certainty about the timing of automation changes.

The second cluster of topics involves advances implemented through large-scale, official programs. Innovations in health-care systems, medical education, and space exploration all require "official" (though not always governmental) policy decisions at a high level. In other words, future events in these fields require not only engineering refinements, as do the topics of the first cluster, but also discrete, fairly high-level decisions, as opposed to the multiple, disaggregated decisions on the individual or firm level which are relevant to the first cluster. Apparently, there is less certainty (or at least less agreement) in predicting discrete official policies than in anticipating summary patterns of many smaller decisions. For predictions of advancement in large-scale programs, the political aspect adds an additional degree of uncertainty to that surrounding the technical feasibility of the programs.

The third cluster consists of fields in which the accomplishment of predicted innovations requires basic scientific breakthroughs. The greatest divergence, and hence the largest MTEs, holds for the timing of accomplishments in these fields. Scientific breakthroughs in both the physical and biological sciences fall into this category. Medical innovations depend on both laboratory and theoretical breakthroughs. Thus, forecasts of medical therapy, which entail predictions of when various diseases would become curable, have the largest ten-year MTEs. However, Gordon and Helmer's panel on scientific breakthroughs diverged as much on the breakthroughs in physics and chemistry as on the biological and medical breakthroughs, indicating that the difficulties in predicting were due to the basic breakthroughs required, rather than to the fact that the fields were related to medicine.

In summary, forecasts of engineering innovations are likely to be more precise than forecasts of large-scale, policy-dependent programs, while scientific breakthroughs are the most difficult of all to predict. The differences are quite large: the MTEs of policy-dependent program forecasts are roughly one and a half times as great as those of engineering innovations, while the breakthrough forecasts' MTEs are twice as great as the engineering MTEs.

There is a consistent and expectable relationship between the remoteness of events and the spread of predictions. Dr. Joseph Martino has shown that more remote events have higher interquartile ranges. Working from Martino's analysis of many Delphi studies, which showed highly significant correlations between median forecast lengths and interquartile ranges, we find that, on the average, each 5-year increase in remoteness (i.e., median forecast length) is associated with a 2.2-year increase in the MTE.[41]

It is easy to speculate about what kinds of topics will be more sensitive to differences in remoteness than others. Less distant breakthroughs in technologies involving cumulative progress, or requiring lead time (such that more imminent events can be anticipated from plans and commitments), would in theory be much easier to forecast than more distant events. However, there are several indications that the nature of the technology does not systematically affect the accuracy-remoteness relationship. As seen in table 7.4, the ordering of topics according to the magnitude of MTE increments does not reveal any pattern that corresponds to plausible distinctions among types of topics. Certainly, the distinctions of engineering applications, policy-dependent programs, and scientific breakthroughs, which accounted for the absolute MTE levels, do not explain the differences in the impact of forecast lengths. Some engineering-application topics are not sensitive to forecast length (e.g., Šulc's communication predictions), while others are quite sensitive (e.g., Trans-Canada's educational technology forecasts). Similarly, some scientific-breakthrough forecast topics are sensitive (e.g., medical diagnosis), while others are not (e.g., Gordon and Helmer's scientific breakthroughs). The same holds for policy-dependent topics, in that the accuracies of health-care-systems forecasts were relatively insensitive to forecast lengths, while a TRW panel on urban and international developments showed considerably less dispersion for short-term forecasts.

Furthermore, several independent Delphi studies on the same topic yield different forecast length–MTE relationships. For example, the Parsons and Williams information-processing forecasts give a 1.2-year MTE increment for five-year forecast length increases, while a TRW study on the same topic gives a 3.4-year MTE increment. The Šulc communications study shows a very low increment (0.8 years per five-year forecast length increase), while one TRW Delphi panel on communications shows an increment of 2.1 years.

The strongest conclusion we can draw concerning the length-accuracy relationship is that for *all* topics, greater forecast lengths correspond to greater MTEs, but that the amount of uncertainty resulting from a given increase in forecast length varies from one topic to another with no discernable pattern in terms of the kinds of topics involved.

IMPROVING TECHNOLOGICAL FORECASTING

Technological forecasting is distinct from other forecasting tasks in that, almost always, specific foci of technological forecasting quickly become obsolete. Forecasts of particular breakthroughs obviously lose importance as soon as the innovations involved are abandoned, actualized, or surpassed by superior innovations. For example, predictions of the development of breeder reactors or desalination methods competitive with conventional fresh-water supply methods will become obsolete once these innovations are achieved or after better means of accomplishing the same ultimate ends are found.

This does not mean that forecasting these and other technological breakthroughs is unimportant. It does mean that there is limited utility in refining a

Table 7.4: Average MTE Increment for Any Five-Year Addition in Forecast Length

Source	Category	MTE Increase	Source	Category	MTE Increase
Sülc	Communications	0.8	TRW Aerospace Systems	Manufacturing	1.9
Gordon and Helmer	Scientific breakthroughs	1.0	Trans-Canada Telephone System	Business communications	2.1
	Physics and chemistry	0.4	Gordon and Helmer	Automation	2.2
	Biology and medicine	1.2	TRW Aerospace Systems	Personal and medical	2.2
Smith, Kline, and French	Health-care systems	1.1	TRW Aerospace Systems	Materials	2.3
Parsons and Williams	Computers	1.2	Gordon and Helmer	Space exploration	2.4
TRW Aerospace Systems	Aerospace	1.2	Trans-Canada Telephone System	Educational technology	2.5
TRW Aerospace Systems	Electronics	1.3	TRW Aerospace Systems	Urban and international	3.0
Smith, Kline, and French	Biomedical research	1.3	TRW Aerospace Systems	Information-processing	3.4
TRW Aerospace Systems	Transportation	1.4	TRW Aerospace Systems	Mechanics and hydraulics	3.4
TRW Aerospace Systems	Power	1.5	Smith, Kline, and French	Medical diagnosis	3.5
TRW Aerospace Systems	Plant automation	1.6	TRW Aerospace Systems	Ocean	3.6
Smith, Kline, and French	Medical therapy	1.6	TRW Aerospace Systems	Instrumentation and controls	4.0
Trans-Canada Telephone System	Medical communications	1.8	TRW Aerospace Systems	Environmental controls	4.1

technological forecasting technique that focuses on one specific application. In contrast, refining forecasting techniques that are specific to projecting many of the nontechnological trends, such as population, GNP, or energy consumption, does make sense because these trends are of permanent interest. For technological forecasting techniques to be of equal utility, they must be generalizable to the projection of several technologies.

However, very few attempts have been made to develop *general* techniques of technological forecasting. Technological forecasting techniques have been largely *ad hoc* applications whose validity in specific cases has been gauged through hindsight rather than *a priori* reasoning. This is reflected in the proliferation of technological forecasting techniques, which, ironically, has been held by technological forecasters as a sign of the vitality of their field. As early as 1967, Erich Jantsch, in a review of technological forecasting in OECD countries, reported that more than a hundred distinct technological forecasting techniques, falling into twenty broad categories, had been employed by the organizations covered in his study.[42] While many of the methods enumerated by Jantsch may have enough in common to be considered variants of a smaller number of "basic" methods, the arsenal of methods is large enough to be bewildering because no guidance is offered on the choice and application of techniques. Since 1967, refinement in methodology has progressed, but has not been accompanied by much progress on a general, "metatheory" to guide forecasters in this choice of methodology for specific applications.

In fact, technological forecasting theorists have not confronted the cold fact that there are no decent guidelines for selecting the appropriate forecasting method from among the great diversity of possibilities. Via hindsight they have demonstrated that particular approaches would have been appropriate for specific technological patterns, but this in itself does not establish what sorts of approaches, growth models, or formulae should be applied to current problems. Such guidelines ought to be the goal of a general theory of technological forecasting, which could relate the choice of specific method to pertinent characteristics of the technology and the context under consideration.

What we mean by a general theory of forecasting is quite distinct from the rather common general "integrative approaches" that have engaged much of the time of technological forecasting theorists. Based on the premise that the forecasting task, narrowly defined, is relatively easy, and that the real difficulty lies in applying forecast results to decision-making, these approaches provide intricate procedures for linking *already* developed forecasts with optimality critiera in order to make management decisions. But these approaches take for granted that the forecasts themselves will be produced via the most appropriate technique in the broad arsenal of methods.

194

The difference is illustrated very well in an article by Marvin Cetron and Thomas Monahan, who competently analyze thirty of what they call "various approaches to technological forecasting." Prior to listing these approaches, Cetron and Monahan make the conventional distinctions among forecasting methods: various types of extrapolation, trend correlation analysis, and analogy.[43] However, when Cetron and Monahan begin to categorize the thirty approaches, these distinctions are entirely absent; the approaches are classified according to whether the system is computerized, what sort of optimality criteria are used, what factors constrain decisions, whether the procedures can flag problem areas, and so on.[44] It is clear that the "approaches" do not provide guidelines for selecting from among what Cetron and Monahan (and almost all other technological forecasting theorists) consider to be the alternative forecasting *methods*. In other words, the "approaches" are addressed to a further stage of *applying* forecasts rather than to the actual production of forecasts. The question, then, is whether or not the production of forecasts is a "solved problem" for which enough confidence exists to justify moving to the next step, elaborate implementation.

In treating the specific forecasting methods of intuition, extrapolation, correlation, and analogy, Cetron and Monahan are strongly, but characteristically, *ad hoc* and noncommittal:

There is *considerable merit* in a forecast made by a single individual who is expert in his special area . . . [but] it *may be well* to combine the judgments of several individuals who are active in the field. It is presumed that a realistic forecast can be obtained by cancelling out the errors of individual predictions, *but this may not necessarily be true.* . . . Technological progress . . . *more than likely* proceeds in an exponential manner. . . . *Several* types of trend curves may be described. . . . To calculate and project trends quantitatively, *one or more* empirical equations *can* be used. . . . The trends of the primary variables *may be* projected on the basis of *any techniques which appear appropriate.* . . . To study the impact of a new technology on functional capability, it *may be desirable* to consider lessons from history. . . .[45]

Cetron and Monahan then conclude that

the technique which is best depends upon the circumstances under which the forecaster is working; his needs; the reliability, completeness and quantitative precision of the data base; the purpose of the forecast; the length of the forecast period; and the time available for generating the forecast.[46]

It is significant that Cetron and Monahan do not include in this lengthy list of "circumstances" the nature of the technology or the premium put on forecast accuracy. Whereas they consider "an understanding of available forecasting techniques and how and when to apply them" as a major requisite of good forecasting, they provide no insights into this understanding except to say that the other requisite (along with good data) is "astute judgment and common sense on the part of the forecaster."[47]

What confronts a forecaster trying to use his astute judgment and common sense? Let us consider the choice of method to project the future growth of nuclear energy. In terms of the sheer availability of plausible methods, there is an embarrassment of riches. Several types of standard curves, such as Pearl curves (symmetric S-shapes) or Gompertz curves (S-shapes with longer "future" tails than "past" tails), could be supported as potentially fitting the growth of the nuclear share of total electrical generation. Joseph Martino[48] shows that Gompertz curves and Pearl curves can be equally well fitted to the historical trends of a number of different technological growth patterns. Envelope curves (exponential curves encompassing several cumulative technological breakthroughs) could be proposed as best for describing future progress in reactor efficiency, which in turn determines the extent to which nuclear plants may replace conventional-fuel plants. On the other hand, appropriate analogies may be drawn concerning other technologies that grew according to nonstandard patterns.

What does the choice of "method" signify? Embedded in this choice is a preconception of the shape of future growth. Envelope curves are chosen not because all growth patterns can be described that way, but rather because of the forecaster's preconception that the relevant technology will "explode" in capability under the spur of cumulative breakthroughs. This obviously does not happen to all technologies. The decision to use any form of curve-fitting methodology embodies an assumption that *some* commonly encountered growth pattern will occur. The choice of *specific* curve type commits the forecaster to more stringent assumptions and in effect imposes narrower boundaries for expected growth patterns. Pearl curves are, after all, shaped differently from Gompertz curves. The decision to fit a Pearl curve commits the forecaster not only to a framework of procedure (fitting standard curves) but also to a more specific position on what the growth will be. Similarly, the choice of forecasting via analogy commits the forecaster to equating the forecasted growth pattern to a *specific* historical experience of some other technology.

The significance of this analysis is that the selection of a broad method and of more specific techniques is much more than a technical choice or a matter of convenience. Specifically, the choice of basic method *is* important. An unfortunate choice of method type (e.g., curve-fitting, extrapolation, trend correlation, or analogy) could lead irremediably to inaccurate forecasts (though the "correct" choice of basic method does not in itself guarantee accurate forecasts). Moreover, no method is optimal for all applications of technological forecasting. Since any method presumes some nonuniversal aspects of technological growth, no method can be most appropriate for all forecasting tasks.

These points are supported by the technological growth patterns that have already occurred and that hence can be examined as history. Some technological growth patterns do not fit any standard curve; some deviate sharply from previous trends; some do not correlate closely with other, basic trends; and some depart sharply from the patterns suggested by apparently relevant analogies. The errors that have *sometimes* been encountered with the use of each of these methods indicate that none is *the* answer to technological forecasting. Debates over which method ought to enjoy *exclusive* use are therefore misguided.

The same holds for the specific decisions made within the boundaries of any broad method. Since the growth patterns of different technologies are often fundamentally different, no single curve or family of curves could possibly be correct for all technologies. Similarly, numerous analogies are provided by other technologies, not all of which can be appropriate for a given technology. If trend extrapolation is the method of choice, the differences resulting from using different lengths of time to establish the baseline trend can be enormous. Or, if the basic decision is to forecast through trend correlation, the selection of one or more specific trends to correlate with the technology under investigation is by no means obvious—selection of the wrong trends will result in very poor forecasts.

The first step toward a general theory of technological forecasting is to establish the sociological determinants of technological progress. S. C. Gilfillan's interesting book, *The Sociology of Invention,* which enumerates thirty-eight "principles of invention,"[49] can serve as a basis for a more integrated and comprehensive theory to account for the effects of external influences on technological development. A modest literature already exists on the economic factors affecting technological change.[50] There are also numerous case studies and broader empirical works on the diffusion of technological innovations, the impact of competition on technological innovation, and the impact of public policy.

A sociological "context" theory is not a forecasting method in itself, nor is it sufficient for selecting a method, since obviously the "nature" of the technology (including such aspects as the physical limitations of improvement, the difficulty of theoretical and practical advances for a given level of effort, etc.) also is relevant. A context theory can, however, establish the core assumptions of future growth, whose validity is essential for accurate forecasts, regardless of methodology.

The second step toward a general theory of technological forecasting is to establish a framework for analyzing and categorizing those aspects of the technology *per se* that make one methodology superior to another. The list of potential factors includes: (*a*) dependence on basic scientific breakthroughs for progress; (*b*) relevance of physical limits to the rate of development; (*c*) maturity of the science and application of the technology; (*d*) relevance of high-level policy to the pace of innovation; (*e*) relevance of research-and-development funding; (*f*) extent of substitutability by other products or by parallel innovations; (*g*) relevance of diffusion; and (*h*) relevance of the opportunity to borrow advances from related technologies.

Whether or not each of these factors will prove useful in predicting what type of forecasting methodology is most appropriate for a given technology is of course open to question; the point is that the variety of differences in the nature of different technologies (and at different stages in the development of a single technology) is great enough for us to suspect that *some* factors will point to the most appropriate methodology for each specific application. A purely empirical approach to the search for such factors could begin with an exploratory search for characteristics that correlate with particular growth patterns. For example, we may ask what types of technologies or stages in technological development are associated with Gompertz curves, or with Pearl curves, or with any other explicit growth patterns. Once the growth pattern is identified with certain technological characteristics, these characteristics will be known to call for the application of methods embodying that pattern. Or, more directly, we may search for characteristics that correspond to technologies for which a particular method has been shown to be successful. The correlation of these factors to particular forecasting methodologies will not in itself accomplish the projection. It will, however, enable the forecaster to use the most appropriate methodology along with the most plausible core assumptions provided by his sociological model of how society, science, and technology work.

CHAPTER 8

CONCLUSION

This review of relative forecast accuracy has provided some general conclusions on the correlates of accuracy. First, the time horizon of the forecast is the most important factor: the more distant the forecast target date, the less accurate the forecast is expected to be. Second, different results are obtained by different institutional sites of forecasting efforts, primarily in terms of systematic biases rather than absolute accuracy. Even so, the most common pattern is the appearance of the same bias in all forecast sources at a given point in time. Third, the choice of methodology in practice is not generally linked to differences in accuracy, in part because several methodologies are often used in combination, but also because the presumed advantages of sophisticated methodologies simply have not materialized. Fourth, forecasts which do appear to be much less accurate than others often turn out to rest on antiquated information, or to have been influenced by major events in the course of the trend in a way not at all anticipated by the forecaster.

These examinations of different forecasting areas permit both "diagnosis"—why are *some* forecasts so bad?—and "prognosis"—what will happen to the modes and performance of forecasting in the future? Many of the problems encountered are specific to each forecasting area, and are therefore covered in each chapter. The following discussion of *general* problems focuses on different aspects of the one central difficulty of providing good core assumptions, the most crucial requisite of ccuracy. The discussion of the future of forecasting concentrates on the poιential of likely developments in forecasting modes to improve performance, and on the applicability of this study's appraisal conclusions to the future performance of forecasting.

THE IMPORTANCE AND IMPLICATIONS OF CORE ASSUMPTIONS

The findings on the correlates of accuracy are consistent with a simple proposition: The core assumptions underlying a forecast, which represent the forecaster's basic outlook on the context within which the specific forecasted trend develops, are the major determinants of forecast accuracy. Methodologies are basically the vehicles for determining the consequences or implications of core assumptions that have been chosen more or less independently of the specific methodologies. When the core assumptions are valid. the choice of methodology is either secondary or obvious. When the core assumptions fail to capture the reality of the future context, other factors such as methodology generally make little difference; they cannot "save" the forecast.

The primacy of good core assumptions in determining forecast accuracy is neither tautological nor trivial. It is certainly conceivable that accurate assumptions could be coupled with inappropriate methods to produce inaccurate forecasts, and there are a few actual exceptions of this nature. For example, lower levels of accuracy were achieved in ten-year electricity consumption forecasts prepared through judgmental methods rather than other methods, despite the fact that forecasters using all the methods shared a common outlook. There are also a few examples of incorrect core assumptions leading to accurate forecasts for at least some span of the projection. Raymond Pearl's logistic-curve population forecasts were accurate for up to twenty years, even though the assumption of S-shaped population growth leveling off below 200,000,000 was obviously incorrect.[1] There are a few cases of several incorrect core assumptions offsetting one another. One such instance was the 1935 American Petroleum Institute forecast of 1945 passenger-car registrations: their population forecast was too low by almost four million, but the ratio of automobiles per person projected for 1945 was too high, resulting in a forecast within four percent of the actual total.[2] These rare cases demonstrate that the *usually* greater importance of core-assumption accuracy is not a matter of definition, but rather is an empirical fact resulting from the variation in conceivable core assumptions, the practical differences that competing core assumptions make in forecast outcomes, and the relatively small practical effects of differences in methodology or source.

The cruciality of correct core assumptions is a basis for orienting the forecasting disciplines to achieve better results. It calls for a better balance between the development of more sophisticated techniques—which has been the major preoccupation of leading forecasters—and the currently neglected search for ways to establish core assumptions and to test their validity. Too often the emphasis on methodology masks the fact that assumptions really do underlie any forecast, and allows the forecasters to neglect the validity of these assumptions. Since forecasters usually are not interested *per se* in the background conditions and trends that they must incorporate in the preparation of their forecasts, assumptions on such trends and conditions are often adopted without the careful scrutiny they warrant by virtue of their importance to ultimate accuracy. Frequently, an elaborate and painstaking analysis is employed to forecast a given trend, but the other trend projections on which it depends are casually lifted from existing (and often out-of-date) sources without an examination of their validity.

A few aspects of the forecasting process make a difference in the likelihood that core assumptions will prove to be accurate. These include the interconnectedness of forecasting tasks, the problem of "assumption drag," and the backwardness of sociopolitical forecasting. Progress in forecasting can be attained by efforts addressed to any of these areas. Examining the connections between different forecasting tasks permits the identification of crucial core assumptions; rectifying assumption drag eliminates one of the main sources of error in core assumptions; and advances in sociopolitical forecasting are important because so many core assumptions are social or political in nature.

THE INTERCONNECTEDNESS OF FORECAST TASKS

The fact that no forecasting task stands isolated from all others has been demonstrated in the examinations of forecast methodologies. All trends reflecting human activity are interrelated; consequently, the ability to forecast in one area depends on the ability to foresee how trends in other areas may impinge. Thus, the core assumptions involved in population forecasting are social, economic, and technological; the core assumptions in long-range energy forecasting are demographic, economic, social, and technological; and so on. Very often these interconnections are made explicit in the forecasting methodology, but even when they are only implicit they are nonetheless crucial in determining the accuracy of the forecast.

The dependence of each forecasting task on several others is, of course, discouraging to many forecasting specialists, who find that their own expertise is not sufficient to accurately project the trends with which they are so familiar. There is no way to reduce this dependence through the selection of sophisticated and clever methodology, because it is inherent in the interdependence of social activity. Hence, the only constructive approach to the fact of interconnectedness is to determine the best allocation of effort for the forecasting tasks that would make the greatest improvement in other areas of forecasting.

Two factors determine how important a particular background forecast will be in determining the accuracy of anotner forecast. The first factor is the relevance of the background forecast to each of the trends aggregated in the forecast being developed, since not all of the aggregated trends are necessarily dependent on the same background forecast. The importance of each component that is dependent on a particular background forecast is, of course, measured by its proportional contribution to the aggregate. For example, in the case of forecasting water demand, industrial use outweighs residential use; therefore, an error in projecting industrial growth would have more serious consequences than an error in population projection.[3]

The second factor, less obvious but probably of greater importance, is the magnitude of potential error of each background forecast or assumption, which may be carried over to the final forecast. If a particular background forecast or core assumption is more likely to be in error, or if its error is likely to be greater than the inaccuracies of other background factors, its actual accuracy will have a greater impact on the final forecast. In other words, background forecasts or core assumptions of greatest uncertainty are—unfortunately—of greatest importance.

Both of these factors permit a clear-cut identification of the forecasting tasks that deserve the greatest preliminary attention before work on a given final forecast is undertaken. The determination of which component trends involve particular background forecasts or core assumptions is straightforward. Nor is it difficult to identify the trends of greatest volatility and uncertainty. For example, comparisons of the assumptions underlying energy forecasts reveal that more uncertainty is introduced via background assumptions on population growth than by the assumptions on economic growth (see the introductory pages of chapter 3). By determining which background factors make the greatest difference, forecasters can decide where to devote resources to improve the core assumptions on which their projections must be based.

THE PROBLEM OF "ASSUMPTION DRAG"

The need for appropriate core assumptions makes the problem of "assumption drag"—the reliance on old core assumptions—particularly important. It has been the source of some of the most drastic errors in forecasting. The worst overall population forecasts were made in the late 1930s and early 1940s after the assumption of declining birth rates had been invalidated (though it remained the basis for the forecasts of the period). Similarly, the electricity demand forecasts of the 1960s continued to project fairly low electricity-use increases even when the actual rates of increase contradicted this assumption. As one critique of these forecasts points out: "Utility planners persisted in their forecasting course even after it began to look askew. So committed were they to traditional theories of load growth that the deviations were rationalized as weather aberrations."[4]

Assumption drag occurs for several reasons, and these are helpful in understanding why the problem is chronic and not completely soluble. The reasons include aspects of the forecasting disciplines which could be corrected, but they also include intractable problems created by the uncertainty inherent in forecasting.

The specialization of most forecasters is one reason why out-of-date assumptions are often retained. A specialist in one forecasting area (e.g., energy forecasting) must rely implicitly or explicitly on forecasts in areas that are beyond his own expertise (e.g., population forecasting). Since his knowledge of appropriate assumptions outside his specialty is limited, he will not produce definitive forecasts in these other areas. More importantly, he may not be able to appraise the continued validity of the older forecasts, which lie around so conveniently. Unless the resources are available to mount new studies in these supportive areas, forecasters will often rely on existing studies, whose assumptions are "frozen" at the dates the earlier studies were made.

Indeed, resources often are lacking. Thus, another source of assumption drag is the high cost of most forecasting efforts, which forces forecasters in other areas (as well as forecast-users) to rely on whatever has been produced, even if it is obsolete. Yet, although some effort is required to generate forecasts using any methodology, some methods require much less expense, and therefore can be completed more frequently for the same amount of money. Since the choice of methodology, which is the most important determinant of the cost of a study, is not as crucial to forecast accuracy as is the appropriate choice of core assumptions, recent inexpensive studies are likely to be more accurate than older studies, even though the latter may be more expensive and elaborate. It may be recalled that multiple-expert-opinion forecasts, which require very little time or money, do very well in terms of accuracy because they reflect the most up-to-date consensus on core assumptions. Thus, when the choice is between fewer expensive studies and more frequent inexpensive studies, these considerations call for the latter.

The final major source of "assumption drag" is a more profound and intractable problem. It is the persistent uncertainty as to whether recent data actually represent a new pattern that will negate the old assumptions. There is danger in taking every deviation from the past pattern seriously; the deviation may turn out to be a minor, short-lived "quirk" in the basic pattern. Pearl's population projections suffered from the presumption that a very minor decline in population growth signified a new pattern of continual declines. To avoid this danger, forecasters at times *choose* to ignore a departure from the assumptions on which their forecasts are based, because the departures are believed to be only temporary. When with hindsight they see that the departures from earlier assumptions were not temporary quirks at all, but rather the beginnings of major changes, they appear to have been inattentive and overly conservative. However, equally extreme errors could arise if every short-lived shift were regarded as the start of a new pattern of future growth.

THE STATUS OF SOCIOPOLITICAL FORECASTING

Social conditions and political acts are relevant to every forecast covered by this study. Social and political core assumptions are inevitable, if only because forecasters must assume either that the sociopolitical context will remain the same or will change in some specified way. Yet, for these appraisable projections, social and political conditions are part of the context rather than the primary focus; sociopolitical predictions are subsidiary. Social and political predictions do exist in their own right, but the problem is that in their typical forms they are not appraisable. Of course, a forecast need not be appraisable to have impact or to be useful if it happens to steer believing policy-makers to the "correct" policies. Nevertheless, appraisability is, first of all, an indication of preciseness and an aid (if not a *sine qua non*) to utilizing existing forecasts. A social forecast that is so lacking in specificity that it cannot be verified is a hazardous base for other forecasting tasks that rest on social core assumptions. Appraisability is also a quality that permits experts to choose the most suitable approaches (on the basis of their performance), to assess progress in their field, and to assign confidence limits for the forecasts they are developing. Hence, any approach that would enhance the meaningfulness, precision, and appraisability of social forecasting would benefit forecasters who must rely on sociopolitical core assumptions, as well as policy-makers who must use sociopolitical forecasts directly.

Social and political forecasts are scattered throughout the literature of the social sciences and the popular writings on social conditions and politics.[5] They vary in specificity, scope, and audacity. They may pertain to the election outcome of the following week or to the future of Western civilization.

Any observer of social and political forecasting is immediately struck not by the lack of predictions, nor by their accuracy or inaccuracy, but rather by the impossibility of appraising the record. Predictions abound, but are rarely expressed in a form that permits evaluation. Predictions of discrete events often lack specific dates or sufficient definition to be scored as correct or incorrect. Other predictions are couched in vague conditional terms, such as "if the situation does not change," which preclude the verification of the prediction.

Of course, vague predictions can be found in any field of forecasting. The problem peculiar to social forecasting is that, even if these requisite conditions of specificity are met, a more fundamental difficulty arises. The correctness of an isolated prediction of unspecified importance (relative to the universe of social or political predictions) is of correspondingly unspecified significance to the general success of sociopolitical forecasting. There is no "typical" sociopolitical prediction. Nor is there an overarching, comprehensive trend whose predictability could summarize or faithfully reflect the difficulty of making other specific social predictions.

Gathering a *sample* of social predictions does not provide an answer to this problem. Any attempt to infer the general predictability of sociopolitical events on the basis of a particular sample of predictions would be prejudiced by its peculiar mixture of important and trivial events, of obvious and challenging predictions. Surely the well-publicized attempts at social predictions, which establish the popular impression of the success of social forecasting, would constitute a very misleading sample, because many of them are well known precisely because they represent unusual examples of either prescience or short-sightedness.

It is difficult to pinpoint why social and political forecasting is qualitatively different from other forecasting tasks. All trends relating to human behavior, from population growth to the demands for energy, are obviously "social," so that a distinct boundary between social forecasting and other forecasting does not exist.[6] Moreover, although social and political predictions are often vague (and hence untestable even with hindsight), they can be as concrete as any other type of forecast. Predicting the degree of income inequality in 1988 (as measured by the Gini index, which is a specific measure of the difference between an actual distribution of some possession and the theoretical distribution of complete equality), or the victorious party in the 1988 presidential election, would be as specific as any forecast of energy demands.

One insight into what is distinctive about social and political forecasting is that it generally refers to actions and attitudes pertaining to the broad concerns of respect, rectitude, affection, and power—the "deference values."[7] Projections of actions related to wealth, well-being, enlightenment, and skill—the "welfare values"—are usually considered to be outside the realm of social forecasting *per se,* and rather are encompassed by the tasks of economic, resource, demographic, and technological forecasting.

The activities devoted to the pursuit of deference values have several distinguishing characteristics. First, they are in general highly alterable through human volition, because few constraints are imposed by limited material resources. While material resources can be and have been used to enhance the respect or affection for a particular individual, or to enhance his power or rectitude, these results *also* emanate from attitudinal changes that can be free of material constraints in a way that material trends never can be. Heroes can be created overnight, by an act of will on the part of people who want heroes, but an increase in electrical capacity can be accomplished only through the investment of time and money. Elections can swing dramatically from one candidate to another, whereas changes in attitude alone cannot budge the GNP.

Second, there is seldom a consensus on the preferred direction of the development of social activities and attitudes. Consequently, even the direction of future social change is highly uncertain in contrast with the unidirectional nature of many material trends such as industrialization, technological progress, or economic growth. In contrast to the material values, for which there is usually a broad consensus that, *ceteris paribus,* one direction of development is preferable, there rarely is agreement on desirable social change— which political group should gain power, how resources ought to be distributed (as a separate question from the concern to increase the total level of resources), who deserves respect, what sorts of beliefs deserve approval or disapproval, and so on. Disagreement on the direction that such trends ought to take provides the potential for radical changes in the actual direction of social

205

trends. Thus, the probable direction of future social developments is far less certain than the direction of material trends such as energy use or the growth of GNP.

Third, social attitudes, because of their relative independence from material resource bases, are usually less cumulative than material growth patterns. Population or demographic growth provides the resource base for further growth, just as technological advancement sets the scene for further advancement. In contrast, the predominance of a social attitude does not necessarily enhance the chances for its further acceptance this often means simply that the pendulum of social attitudes is on the verge of swinging back again in the opposite direction.

Fourth, social forecasts often entail single, discrete events. While all forecasts involve events of one sort or another, the prediction of single crucial events (such as election outcomes, the outbreak of wars, etc.) presents special problems. Unlike the aggregate trends that summarize a multitude of somewhat independent events such as energy use by thousands of firms and households, social forecasts often succeed or fail utterly on the basis of single events.

Finally, a political or social condition or event is really a configuration of many conditions or events, because the *meaning* of one aspect depends crucially on the nature of the others. For example, the prediction that the Democratic party will win the presidential election of 1988 is not very meaningful unless it is known what the Democratic party will stand for more than a decade from now, or whether elections will still have any importance. If more subtle, "functional" terms are used to characterize the prediction—for example, whether in 1988 the balance of political power will be maintained or will be captured by the more change-oriented of the moderate groups seeking political office—meaningfulness may be enhanced. To accomplish this, however, more than just the name of the victorious party must be involved in the forecasts.

There are two reasonable approaches to making sociopolitical forecasting both more meaningful and more appraisable. One is the specification of *scenarios* that consist of integrated sets of events or conditions. Often a particular probability or range of probability is attached to each scenario, and sometimes one is casually labeled "most likely."

The advantage of sociopolitical forecasting through scenarios is that it permits the forecaster to convey enough of the social context to make each element of the forecast meaningful. Richness in detail makes the forecast more comprehensible and useful as a basis for core assumptions or as a basis for policy-making.[8]

However, the fact that scenario forecasts are "stories" involving numerous points complicates their interpretation if one or more point is doubted or turns out to be incorrect. To what extent does the accuracy of one aspect of the scenario depend on the accuracy of another? Rarely are these relationships specified in the scenario forecasts being developed today.

Moreover, the multiple nature of the events and conditions of a scenario also makes its appraisal difficult, since the scenario forecast can be partially correct and partially wrong, and usually there are no explicit indications of which elements are more important or by how much. If accuracy is judged simply on the basis of the proportion of events and conditions related in the scenario that actually turn out to be correct, these differences in importance are disregarded without any justification for doing so. Furthermore, since many events or conditions can be divided into any number of "subevents" or less general conditions, the number of events and conditions chosen to describe a scenario is arbitrary, but the number chosen will affect the ratio of correct to incorrect predictions.

These problems can be overcome by additional effort on the part of social and political forecasters. The elements of a social or political scenario can be "nested"; the aspects that depend on other events or conditions can be designated as such. Since probabilities (usually of a subjective nature) are generally assigned to the scenario as a whole, it is also feasible to assign probabilities to each aspect, both conditional probabilities (i.e., the probability that the prediction of a particular aspect is correct, given that predictions of the more basic aspects within which it is nested also are correct) and absolute probabilities (i.e., the probability that the prediction of a particular aspect is correct, taking into account the uncertainty of the enabling conditions and events). On occasion the same outcome may be an element of more than one scenario, in which case the probabilities can be suitably combined. The result of these efforts would be an *organized* set of scenarios and their elements, with clearer indications of relatedness to ease interpretation and of levels of importance to aid appraisal.

The second promising mode of sociopolitical forecasting is the projection of *aggregate* measures of social interaction or conditions, which are often called "social indicators." Social indicators are summary measures, usually of society-wide phenomena, such as the distribution of wealth, levels of satisfaction or alienation, consumption patterns, and broad aspects of the "political climate." Efforts devoted to developing social indicators have focused on the need for universally applicable measures, precisely because of existing difficulties in comparing and differentiating social contexts. Thus, social indicators are analogous to the functional capabilities projected in technological forecasting, in that social indicators standardize the outcomes of diverse social structures just as functional capabilities standardize the performance of diverse inventions. When a social indicator is projected, the problem of deciding whether the actual result is very much different from the forecast is eliminated as long as the indicator can be measured.

207

The shortcoming of social indicators as opposed to scenarios is that social indicators generally do not paint a full contextual picture that would clarify the relationships among elements of the context. A scenario such as George Orwell's *1984* is a far more explicit and vivid depiction of relationships among totalitarian rule, surveillance, the nature or scope of dissent, and the meaning of war than are projections of citizen participation levels, oppositional activity, and war casualties.

The advantages of social indicators are that they are generally widely applicable, they can be used with relatively little additional contextual information (because they encompass enough of the meaningful context themselves), they are explicit, and they are straightforwardly appraisable and interpretable. As long as they can be measured unambiguously for each case and time period, they are valid forecasting tools.

It may seem strange that social indicators are employed for social forecasting; they are usually regarded as instruments of appraisal. The first large-scale governmental attempt to compile recent social indicators, the Department of Health, Education, and Welfare's *Toward a Social Report,*[9] was designed "to set up a set of social indicators for measuring the performance of the society in meeting social needs."[10] However, it was recognized much earlier that the study and measurement of social *change* presupposes the capacity to study and measure existing social conditions. In fact, attempts to develop social indicators for the purpose of aiding social forecasting date back to the work of William F. Ogburn in the 1920s through the 1940s.[11] Daniel Bell points out that this work has been "neglected for thirty-five years."[12]

The social-indicators approach and its application to social forecasting have developed very slowly, apparently for two reasons. First, the development of the indicators themselves has been slow because of the difficulty of obtaining appropriate data. Data appropriate for social indicators are not usually the same as the official data already collected by governmental agencies, and special efforts to collect new data or to transform official statistics into meaningful social indicators are very costly. Historical data necessary for establishing trend lines are often very difficult or impossible to obtain, especially those based on survey results.

Fortunately, these problems face the United States less than most other countries because of the federal government's extensive data collection capacity and the advanced capabilities of American commercial and academic survey organizations. As the social-indicators approach becomes more widely known and used, there will be a greater incentive to invest in more sophisticated data-gathering and in the development of a wider assortment of social indicators. Besides the government's interest, attention to social indicators in academic circles has been reflected in several conferences.[13] The Social Sci-

208

ence Research Council has shown some commitment by establishing a Center for Coordination of Research on Social Indicators.

The second reason for the slow development of forecasting with social indicators is the lack of means to relate social indicators to either their causes or their consequences. Otis Dudley Duncan points out that the social-indicators approach, far from being ready to forecast levels of social indicators, is not even certian about which specific measures to develop.[14] This uncertainty, however, has the same origin as the almost universal problem of selecting the right variables to develop theories and explanations: one must first have a theory. Theories are needed to explain and predict the levels of social indicators. Other theories are required to determine the effects that forecasted levels of social indicators will have on other trends, so that the social indicators can be used as meaningful core assumptions. The problem is not any inherent vagueness in the social indicators themselves, but rather that most current theories in the social sciences are rarely addressed to explain summary outcomes cast in the same broad terms as are the social indicators. This problem is again parallel to that of technological forecasting, wherein specific innovations are of course acknowledged to occur, but theories explaining the growth of functional capabilities are hardly developed. Ironically, the ''grand social theory'' of the nineteenth century, associated with such theorists as Durkheim, Weber, Pareto, and Mosca, is more suitable to linking social indicators to their correlates than is the more specific level of theory developed in the social sciences of today. Unless theories are cast in terms of outcomes that can be related directly to social indicators, the incorporation of social indicators into any forecasting effort beyond simple extrapolation—probably a poor choice of method, considering the volatility of most social trends—is likely to remain rudimentary.

FUTURE TRENDS AND DEVELOPMENTS IN FORECASTING

In speculating on future developments in forecasting, it is important to note that the impetus for further refinements comes from two sources. Not only do demands arise from the needs of forecast-users, but they also stem from the professional aspirations of forecasters who are developing their discipline. The demands of the discipline are likely to force forecasting to become both more technical and more ambitious, even beyond its utility for its users. Moreover, professional demands usually culminate in greater specialization, which from the forecast-user's point of view is a very promising development, since forecasts are used for specialized purposes. In addition to the developments in social forecasting already covered in this chapter, the interesting developments emerging from increased technical elaboration, ambition, and

209

specialization will be expressed in three areas: modeling, surprise-sensitive forecasting, and normative forecasting.

MODELING

Future developments in forecast methodology in all areas will be influnced by "modeling," the mathematical expression of structural relationships between the forecasted trend and other factors. Models are technically refined in that they explicitly represent existing relationships. Moreover, they serve as accounting devices that trace the implications of growth assumptions, reducing the possibilities of inconsistencies within a model and allowing for finer disaggregation of data and assumptions. Because of these advantages over less sophisticated or less explicit methods, mathematical modeling stands as the "great hope" for forecasting in almost every area.

The advantages of modeling, however, must be tempered by the implications of the importance of core assumptions. The improvements brought about by modeling are useful only to the extent that the structural relationships, brought into each model from the forecaster's experience with existing and historical conditions, endure into the future. Models or accounting techniques can at best only draw out the implications of these structural relationships. If and when the structure changes in some unanticipated way, the most technically sophisticated, elaborate, and consistent model will be little better than the crudest sort of extrapolation. This is, of course, another way of saying that models reflect core assumptions, which must anticipate fundamental (i.e., "structural") changes in the context.

How likely are "structural changes"? Obviously, this depends on the nature of "structure" for any particular model. What may be a structural relationship in one model, in that it is held to be a constant relationship, may not be considered so in a more elaborate model that contains factors which explain and predict changes in the initial relationship. Even so, every functioning model, having a finite number of relationships, has only so many relationship-modifying factors, and always must have some invariant relationships, however complicated. There is reason to believe that the turnover in "structures" defined at any level is increasing in this rapidly changing and changeable world. Significant changes in international relations, social attitudes, and technology alter the context in which trends emerge and impinge upon basic needs and resources. This has always been true; it is the rapidity of these changes and of their effects that is new. It has become trite to point out that one of the most important changes from the traditional to the modern world is the preeminence of change itself. In this context of change, the likelihood of unanticipated structural changes in the long run (i.e., ten years or more) is high, so the usefulness of progress in forecast methods relying on

210

any level of fixed structure is minimized for long-term forecasts. For short-term forecasts, however, the improvements and refinements in technique are likely to result in some improvements in results, since the short term is obviously less likely to encompass significant structural changes.

SPECIALIZED SURPRISE-SENSITIVE FORECASTING

The most important area of specialization in forecasting will be the development of methods designed to be highly sensitive to potential surprise outcomes, even if they are not the most likely outcomes. The rationale for such forecasts is the need to anticipate and avert future problems and crises that may not be apparent from considerations of what is *most likely* to happen. This is the potential gain in establishing specialized operations—sometimes called "lookout institutions"—designed to call attention to future problems before it is too late to avert them. Such operations would require forecasting techniques that are particularly sensitive to the possibilities of future crises.

The sensitivity of a forecasting technique to future "surprise" outcomes can be enhanced in several ways. First, the techniques can be made sensitive to very recent departures from old patterns by establishing trend lines from the most recent data. What for other methods might be considered ephemeral deviations from the long-range pattern may be given more credence by a technique that is explicitly designed to catch even the most minute indications of new and surprising patterns.

Second, surprise-sensitive forecasting methods would have to be free of the imposition of plausibility checks external to the assumptions that go into the forecast's development. Very often a hidden step in the development of a standard forecast is to ask whether the results emerging from the application of the best technique are nonetheless implausible and therefore incorrect. This sort of plausibility check is even made routinely by many of the short-term economic forecasters relying on econometric models—if the models do not produce plausible results, the forecasters will go back and modify the model. Whether this turns out to be wise or foolish depends, of course, on whether implausible conditions (from the perspective of the forecasters) actually occur. The problem is that conditions that would have seemed highly implausible years ago exist today and are taken for granted as normal. It is very doubtful that anyone living in 1900 or 1920 would find an annual automobile fatality rate of more than 50,000 for the 1960s plausible. The imposition of plausibility testing on projections guarantees a certain conformity of the forecasts to the forecaster's intuitive notions. It thereby reduces the potential of

211 methods besides judgment to reveal surprising potential implications that are

hidden from judgment. It reduces the chance that startling, dangerous conditions will be anticipated.

Third, surprise-sensitive forecasting must not resort to consensus amalgams of the forecasts of others. Consensus, or the procedure of averaging numerous different forecasts, counters "high" surprises with "low" surprises, and generally produces the most middle-of-the-road projections. If, indeed, the average forecast were to anticipate a crisis, that crisis would not be very surprising.

However, high sensitivity to the possibilities of surprise conditions is likely to be costly—it requires forecast techniques that do not perform as well as other methods when the world runs smoothly. A technique that is very sensitive to short-term deviations, unbound by intuitive plausibility, and oblivious to conventional wisdom, will often be extreme when moderation is more accurate. Consequently, surprise-sensitive forecasting is likely to have problems of credibility and accuracy. The boldest forecasts are often not only the most exciting, but also the most ludicrous after the outcomes are known. The institutions that employ such techniques, regardless of the importance of the service they are providing, may be ridiculed when their warnings turn out, on many occasions, to be unwarranted. It is therefore very important that the specialized function of lookout institutions be made quite explicit, and that their surprise-sensitive forecasts be clearly labeled as "dangerous possibilities" rather than as likelihoods.

NORMATIVE FORECASTING

The forecasting apparatus used to predict what *will* happen can be adapted to recommend what *ought* to be done. "Normative forecasting" is one of the numerous labels for decision-making procedures, involving some projections of policy implications, designed to determine either how a given set of goals can be achieved or what sorts of goals can be achieved. In other words, normative forecasting seeks to identify appropriate policy rather than to assume particular policy choices as givens.[15]

One motivation behind the development of normative forecasting is the recognition that forecasting is intertwined with the policy decisions made by forecast-users. If actual trends depend on the policy choices of forecast-users, whose judgment is in theory suspended during their consideration of the forecasts and other data, a forecast that *assumes* their policy choices is hardly meaningful or welcome. This problem is highly visible in company-level technological forecasting, where the company's ultimate decision to pursue a particular technology will have an impact on progress in that technology. It is also obvious in providing forecasts to top public policy-makers in areas such as pollution control, where governmental choices on the strictness of antipol-

212

lution regulation will make a huge difference in the trends that forecasters are expected to project. It is much safer for forecasters to generate a series of *conditional forecasts,* each based on a policy alternative, than to presume what the policy-makers are going to do. A safe *and* active role for forecasters in this situation is to work backward from desired "end-states" (such as an acceptable level of air pollution) to the policies required to bring them about.

In addition, the spread of normative forecasting means that the scope of the forecasting disciplines will expand. This is true not only on the academic level, where forecast theorists can develop the procedures of normative forecasting, but also in application. Indeed, normative forecasting really carries forecasting as a specialized discipline far into the whole realm of decision-making. Joseph Martino notes that "it must be clearly understood that exploratory and normative methods are not competitive with, or replacements for, one another."[16]

However, for this reason, the acceptance of normative forecasting on the part of policy-makers introduces all the limitations of the explicit decision-making routines described in chapter 2. To the extent that normative forecasting penetrates into decision-making, the prerogatives of technically competent but formally powerless forecasters are challenged. When a formerly technical function is reinterpreted very broadly, giving it expanded scope (which usually reflects the ambitions of its technical practitioners), it ceases to be considered as technical. Normative forecasting, it turns out, is simply another metaphor for decision-making. It will not be dominated by specialists in forecasting.

FUTURE APPLICABILITY OF FINDINGS

An inherent limitation of any appraisal is that it can be based only on the past. The appraisal methods employed in this study consist of three techniques: (1) direct performance evaluation of forecasts with target dates that have already passed; (2) indirect performance evaluation of forecasts with future target dates, which is based on the dispersion or variation among projections of the same trend and (3) theoretical evaluation of the strengths and weaknesses of various forecasting techniques, which is based on the "logic" that underlies them. The first method is obviously strictly retrospective. The second is limited to forecasts already made, and the third rests on generalizations about what has worked, no matter how abstract the reasoning. Given this unavoidable dependence on the performance of forecasts already made, the question is how well this (or any other) appraisal will apply to the forecasting efforts of the future.

The only way to answer this question is to determine whether the period on which this study is based has peculiarities that would affect forecasting performance in an atypical fashion. In this light it is interesting to note one of the

213

most common reasons forecasters have given for the inaccuracies of forecasts made during the past several decades. The forecasts themselves were reasonable; the extremely rapid expansion of the post–World War II period was unreasonable!

As perverse as this explanation or excuse for forecasting errors may be, it does point to one of the difficulties of generalizing from this study. The economic expansion of the United States since World War II and the "booming" trends that accompanied it have been "surprisingly" great, causing projections to be underestimates on the whole. Therefore, it may be that some of the generalizations on appropriate methods and time horizons are applicable only for periods that turn out to have high growth rates. If particular forecasting methods have distinctive biases, some periods may simply be more congenial for some methods than for others. For example, the fact that simple extrapolation has been able to hold its own against more complicated methods such as correlation or modeling may be a result of the relative smoothness of American economic, transportation, and energy growth since World War II. On the other hand, the other methods do not do appreciably better in forecasting those short periods in which growth was not very smooth: the prewar period and the very recent recession.

The direction of biases of the forecasts taken as a whole are time bound. However, the relative biases of institutional sources are built into the roles of their forecasters, which have no clear connection to any specific characteristics of this historical era. Therefore, the few institutional differences found in this study are likely to endure into the future.

Finally, there is the question of whether the overall magnitudes of error already found are likely to be typical of the errors found in the future. In this regard it is important to note that most of the forecast sets examined here begin at least as far back the 1930s. The United States has experienced periods of high stability and certainty, but also periods of flux and uncertainty. Thus, this appraisal does not rest on necessarily unique experiences. The magnitudes of error encountered in this study constitute the "best guesses" at future levels of inaccuracy. The fact that this is the best that can be done is a strong argument for the idea of *ongoing* appraisal of forecasting and all other aspects of the decision-making process.

NOTES

CHAPTER 1: INTRODUCTION

1. Peter deLeon, "Scenario Designs: An Overview," *Simulation & Games* 6, no. 1 (March 1975): 39–60, esp. 48.

2. This argument is cogently stated in Joseph Martino, *Technological Forecasting for Decisionmaking* (New York: American Elsevier, 1972), pp. 11–13.

3. U.S., Federal Power Commission, *The National Power Survey, 1964* (Washington, D.C.: Government Printing Office, 1964), pt. 2, p. 132.

4. Harold D. Lasswell, *World Politics and Personal Insecurity* (New York: McGraw-Hill, 1935), chap. 1.

5. Mihajlo Masarovic and Eduard Pestel, *Mankind at the Turning Point* (New York: E. P. Dutton, 1974), p. 34.

CHAPTER 2: THE IMPACT OF EXPERT FORECASTING

1. The process of agenda-building and the determination of what constitutes "issues" and "nonissues" are considered in Matthew Crenson, *The Unpolitics of Air Pollution* (Baltimore and London: The Johns Hopkins University Press, 1971), and Roger W. Cobb and Charles D. Elder, *Participation in American Politics: The Dynamics of Agenda Building* (Baltimore and London: The Johns Hopkins University Press, 1972).

2. Harold D. Lasswell discusses "mood" and "climate" in "The Climate of International Action," in *International Behavior: A Socio-Psychological Analysis*, ed. H. C. Kelman (New York: Henry Holt & Co., 1965).

3. Robert Dahl and Charles Lindblom, *Politics, Economics, and Welfare* (New York: Harper & Bros., 1953), p. 73.

4. Antony Jay, in his *Management and Machiavelli* (New York: Holt, Rinehart & Winston, 1967), vividly catalogues the political confrontations that can occur in corporations. See also Harry Levinson, "Management by Whose Objectives?" *Harvard Business Review*, July/August 1970, which points out that, in practice, long-term goals and short-term goals may conflict. What is important, however, is the presumption that in theory there are clear ultimate goals.

5. Erich Jantsch, *Technological Forecasting in Perspective* (Paris: Organisation for Economic Cooperation and Development, 1967), p. 256.

6. Thomas Naylor and Horst Schauland, "A Survey of Users of Corporate Planning Models," *Management Science* 22, no. 9 (May 1976): 927–37, esp. 932.

7. Jantsch, *Technological Forecasting*, p. 271.

8. U.S., Department of Labor, Bureau of Labor Statistics, *National Survey of Professional, Administrative, Technical, and Clerical Pay, March 1975*. Bureau of Labor Statistics Bulletin no. 1891 (Washington, D.C., Government Printing Office, 1975), p. 2.

9. Based on subscription to two outside services and some contract work. Some firms, of course, pay much more. A *New York Times* article of 19 October 1975 (Soma Golden, "Forecast: Profits for Prophets," p. 1 and 4, financial sec.) states that one firm spends $500,000 for outside forecasting services.

10. A high ratio of in-house to outside forecasting in economics is reasonable because the macroeconomic trends projected by the outside services must be extensively "processed" before they become relevant for a specific firm's products and financial situation. Corporate planners use the forecasts of broad trends not only as "background" information, but also to forecast specific trends (e.g., the sales growth of particular products) that are correlated historically with one or more of the macroeconomic trends. The specific-trend projections are derived from projections of the macroeconomic trends through regression analysis, which in effect determines the historical relationship between the specific trend and the macroeconomic trends, which then permits the prediction of the specific trend from the projections of the others. The forecaster does not have to know *a priori* how these trends relate—he chooses the basic trends and the equations relating

them to the specific trend on the basis of past experience. The growth trend of any product, service, or price can be approached by this method, since any trend will be found to correlate to some extent with some of the macroeconomic or demographic trends. Of course, this correlational method ties the accuracy of the specific-trend projection to that of the macroeconomic projections on which it is based. Consequently, unexpected fluctuations in economic conditions can have a widespread effect on the accuracy of forecasts made for all types of products throughout American industry.

11. Personal communication to the author.

12. Naylor and Schauland, "Users of Corporate Planning Models," p. 931.

13. Ibid., p. 928.

14. Ibid., p. 932.

15. Ibid., p. 936.

16. See Harper Q. North and Donald L. Pyke, "Technology, the Chicken—Corporate Goals, the Egg," in *Technological Forecasting for Industry and Government: Methods and Applications,* ed. James Bright (Englewood Cliffs, N.J.: Prentice-Hall, 1968), p. 424.

17. Ralph Sprague and Hugh Watson, "MIS Concepts," *Journal of Systems Management,* January 1975, p. 36 (emphasis added).

18. Edward Roberts, "Exploratory and Normative Technological Forecasting: A Critical Appraisal," *Technological Forecasting* 1, no. 2 (1969): 122.

19. U.S., Congress, House, Committee on Science and Technology, Subcommittee on the Environment and the Atmosphere. "Long-Range Planning in the Private Sector," in *Long Range Planning* (Washington, D.C.: Government Printing Office, 1976).

20. The politics and structure of the NRPB is discussed in Charles Merriam, "The National Resources Planning Board," in *Planning for America,* ed. George B. Galloway (New York: Henry Holt & Co., 1941), pp. 489–506. Galloway also discusses the NRPB in his chapter "Psychological Obstacles to Planning" see esp. pp. 74–77.

21. Galloway, "Psychological Obstacles to Planning," p. 76.

22. Of the large body of literature on PPBS, the most useful sources for understanding the problems of implementation are: Allen Schick, "The Road to PPB: The Stages of Budget Reform," *Public Administration Review* (26 December 1966): 243–58; Aaron Wildavsky, "The Political Economy of Efficiency: Cost Benefit Analysis, Systems Analysis, and Program Budgeting," ibid., pp. 292–310; Allen Schick, "A Death in the Bureaucracy: The Demise of Federal PPB," ibid. (March/April 1973): 146–56; and the collection of appraisals in David Novick, ed., *Current Practice in Program Budgeting* (New York: Crane Russack, 1973).

23. Alain C. Enthoven and K. Wayne Smith, *How Much Is Enough: Shaping the Defense Program* (New York: Harper & Row, 1971), p. 45.

24. Schick, "A Death in the Bureaucracy," p. 147.

25. Ibid. Schick summarizes the potential causes of PPBS failures.

26. David Novick, "Program Budgeting, 1971," in Novick, ed., *Current Practice in Program Budgeting,* p. 36.

27. Edwin Harper, Fred Kramer, and Andrew Rouse, "Personnel Limitations of 'Instant Analysis,'" in ibid., p. 204.

28. Jack W. Carlson, "Recent U.S. Federal Government Experience with Program Budgeting," in Ibid., p. 212.

29. Charles Lindblom, "The Science of Muddling Through," *Public Administration Review* 19 (Spring 1959): 79–88.

30. Edwin Harper, Fred Kramer, and Andrew Rouse, "Implementation and Use of PPB in Sixteen Federal Agencies," ibid. 29, no. 6 (November/December 1969): 623–32 and Stanley B. Botner, "Four Years of PPBS: An Appraisal," ibid. 30 no. 4 (July/August 1970): 423–31.

31. Ralph E. Strauch, "'Squishy' Problems and Quantitative Methods," *Policy Sciences* 6 no. 2 (June 1975): 175–84.

32. This problem is also analogous to the well-known "Hawthorne effect": subjects of an inquiry may behave differently *because* they are under scrutiny. See George Homans, "Group Factors in Worker Productivity," in *Readings in Social Psychology,* ed. E. Maccoby, T. Newcomb, and E. Hartley, 3rd ed. (New York: Henry Holt & Co., 1958), pp. 583–95.

33. Donald J. Bogue, *The Population of the United States* (Glencoe, Ill.: The Free Press, 1959), p. 764.

34. These are published in the several series of the U.S. Bureau of the Census' *Current Population Reports*.

35. J. Frederic Dewhurst et al., *America's Needs and Resources* (New York: Twentieth Century Fund, 1947); idem, *America's Needs and Resources: A New Survey* (Twentieth Century Fund, 1955).

36. U.S., President's Materials Policy Committee, *Resources for Freedom* (Washington, D.C.: Government Printing Office, 1952).

37. *Resources for Freedom* sold roughly 13,000 copies; *America's Needs and Resources* sold about 22,000 copies of the first edition alone.

38. According to the *New York Times Index*, the first Dewhurst study was cited eight times in articles in 1947; the Paley Report was cited once in 1951 and seven times in 1952.

39. Donella H. Meadows et al., *The Limits to Growth* (New York: Universe Books, 1972).

40. Martin Greenberger, Matthew Crenson, and Brian Crissey, *Models in the Policy Process: Public Decision Making in the Computer Era* (New York: Russell Sage Foundation, 1976), chap. 5; John Clark and Sam Cole, *Global Simulation Models: A Comparative Study* (New York and London: John Wiley & Sons, 1975), esp. chap. 1.

41. Greenberger, Crenson, and Crissey, *Models*, p. 165.

42. Aurelio Peccei, *The Chasm Ahead* (London: Macmillan & Co., 1969).

43. Mihajlo Mesarovic and Eduard Pestel, *Mankind at the Turning Point* (New York: E. P. Dutton, 1974), p. 1.

CHAPTER 3: POPULATION FORECASTING

1. Ali Bulent Cambel et al., *Energy R & D and National Progress* (Washington, D.C.: Government Printing Office, 1965), p. 20.

2. H. S. Pritchett was president of the Massachusetts Institute of Technology, H. Gannet was a member of the National Resources Planning Board, and C. S. Sloane was a geographer for the U.S. Bureau of the Census. See H. S. Pritchett, "A Formula for Predicting the Population of the United States," *Quarterly Publication of the American Statistical Association* 2, no. 14 (June 1891): 278–86; idem, "The Population of the United States during the Next Ten Decades," *Popular Science Monthly* 58, no. 4 (November 1900): 49–53; H. Gannet, "Estimates of Future Population," *Report of the National Conservation Commission* (Washington, D.C.: National Conservation Commission, 1909), 2: 7–9; and for Sloane's estimates, C. E. Woodruff, *Expansion of the Races* (New York: Rebman, 1909). p. 476.

3. Raymond Pearl and L. J. Reed, "On the Rate of Growth of the Population of the United States since 1790 and Its Mathematical Representation," *Proceedings of the National Academy of Sciences* 6, no. 6 (15 June 1920): 275–88; Raymond Pearl, *The Biology of Population Growth* (New York: Alfred A. Knopf, 1925), p. 14. Pearl and Reed were members of the faculty of The Johns Hopkins University.

4. P. K. Whelpton, "Population of the United States, 1925 to 1975," *American Journal of Sociology* 34, no. 2 (September 1928): 253–70; W. S. Thompson and P. K. Whelpton, *Population Trends in the United States* (New York: McGraw-Hill, 1933); idem, *Population Statistics: National Data* (Washington, D.C.: National Resources Committee, 1937); idem, *Estimates of Future Population of the United States, 1940–2000* (Washington, D.C.: National Resources Planning Board, 1943).

5. See Herbert Simon, *The Sciences of the Artificial* (Cambridge, Mass.: The MIT Press, 1969), pp. 66–73.

6. Thompson and Whelpton, *Estimates, p. 3.*

7. *L. I. Dublin and A. J. Lotka, "The Present Outlook for Population Growth," American Sociological Society Publications* 24, no. 2 (1930): 106–14.

8. The following reports of the U.S. Bureau of the Census contain national population projections: P-3, no. 15 (1940); "Forecasts 1945–75" (1947); P-25, no. 18 (1949) P-25, no. 43 (1950); P-25, no. 78 (1953); P-25, no. 123 (1955); P-25, no. 187 (1958); P-25, nos. 241 and 251, (1962); P-25, no. 286 (1964); P-25, no. 329 (1966); P-25, no. 381 (1967); P-25, no. 448 (1970); P-25, no. 470 (1971); P-25, no. 476 (1972); P-25, no. 493 (1972).

9. H. F. Dorn, "Pitfalls in Population Forecasts and Projections," *Journal of the American Statistical Association* 45, no. 251 (September 1950): 311–34; and H. Hajnal, "The Prospects for Population Forecasts," ibid. 50, no. 270 (June 1955): 309–22.

10. See, for example, U.S., Bureau of the Census, *Current Population Report,* P-25, no. 381 (Washington, D.C.: Government Printing Office, 1967).

11. Hajnal, "Prospects for Population Forecasts," p. 311.

12. Otis Dudley Duncan, "Social Forecasting: The State of the Art," *The Public Interest,* no. 17 (Fall 1969), pp. 91–92.

13. Pearl and Reed, "On the Rate of Growth," p. 281.

14. T. J. Gordon and Olaf Helmer, *Report on a Long-Range Forecasting Study,* Rand Corporation, Paper no. P-2982 (Santa Monica, Calif., 1964).

15. A. D. Bender et al., *A Delphic Study of the Future of Medicine* (Philadelphia: SK & F Laboratories, 1969); and George Teeling-Smith, *Medicine in the 1990s* (London: Office of Health Economics, 1970).

CHAPTER 4: ECONOMIC FORECASTING

1. The Federal Reserve Bank of Richmond summarizes numerous annual and quarterly forecasts of prominent sources in its annual *Business Forecasts;* together the American Statistical Association (ASA) and the National Bureau of Economic Research (NBER) do the same for about fifty anonymous sources, and publish the median forecasts in the *American Statistician* and the NBER's *Explorations in Economic Research.*

2. John Kenneth Galbraith, *The Great Crash, 1929* (Boston: Houghton Mifflin, 1961), p. 90. It should be noted, though, that a generally incorrect method may occasionally produce correct results.

3. Geoffrey H. Moore, "Forecasting Short-term Economic Changes," *Journal of the American Statistical Association* 64, no. 325 (March 1969): 1.

4. Ibid., p. 2. The specific forecasts are reviewed in several sources, including Edwin B. George, "Gross National Product Projections for Full Employment: II. Contrasting Estimates: Range and Reasons," *Dun's Review,* May 1945, pp. 9–14; Everett E. Hagen, "Postwar Output in the United States at Full Employment," *The Review of Economic Statistics* 27, no. 2 (May 1945): 45–59; and J. Frederick Dewhurst et al., *America's Needs and Resources* (New York: Twentieth Century Fund, 1947), pp. 26–27.

5. Stephen K. McNees, in "How Accurate Are Economic Forecasts?" *New England Economic Review,* November/December 1974, p. 4, points out that General Electric Co. forecasts, which are purchased by many other corporations, have relied on econometric models less since 1971 than before. The ASA-BNER compilation (see n. 1 above) also shows a dip in reliance on econometric models in the past two years as compared with the early 1970s.

6. *Fortune,* March 1975, p. 154.

7. Stephen K. McNees, "The Forecasting Performance in the Early 1970s," *New England Economic Review,* July/August 1976, p. 29.

8. Martin Shubik, "The Nature and Limitations of Forecasting," in *Toward the Year 2000: Work in Progress, Daedelus,* Summer 1967, p. 945.

9. Ibid., p. 945.

10. This order of current useage was derived from the self-characterizations of forecasters included in the ASA-NBER sample of forecasting operations. See Vincent Su and Josephine Su, "An Evaluation of ASA/NBER Business Outlook Survey Forecasts," *Explorations in Economic Research* 2, no. 4 (Fall 1975): 588–618, esp. 600.

11. See for example, Ronald L. Cooper, "The Predictive Performance of Quarterly Econometric Models of the United States," in *Econometric Models of Cyclical Behavior,* ed. Bert G. Hickman (New York: National Bureau of Economic Research, 1972), 2: 813–925, in which certain econometric-model forecasts are found to be inferior to "naïve" schemes based on the projection of GNP at constant rates.

12. Jan Tinbergen, *Business Cycles in the United States of America, 1919–1932* (New York: Columbia University Press for the League of Nations, 1939).

13. Publication of the model in Lawrence R. Klein and Arthur S. Goldberger, *An Econometric Model of the United States, 1929–1952* (Amsterdam: North-Holland Publishing Co., 1955), was the catalyst for econometric modeling and subsequent efforts to forecast with such models.

14. For an elaboration of this position, see James S. Duesenberry and Lawrence R. Klein, "Introductory Essay," in *The Brookings-SSRC Quarterly Econometric Model of the United States,* ed. James S. Duesenberry et al. Chicago: Rand McNally, 1965).

15. See the discussion of the development of econometric models in Martin Greenberger, Matthew Crenson, and Brian L. Crissey, *Models in the Policy Process: Public Decision Making in the Computer Era* (New York: Russell Sage Foundation, 1976).

16. Irwin Friend and Paul Taubman, "A Short-Term Forecasting Model," *Review of Economics and Statistics* 46, no. 3 (August 1964): 229-36; Ray C. Fair, *A Short-Run Forecasting Model of the United States Economy* (Lexington, Mass: Heath-Lexington, 1971), chap. 1.

17. Leonall C. Anderson and Keith Carlson, "St. Louis Model Revisited," *International Economic Review* 15 (June 1974): 305-27.

18. Lowell E. Gallaway and Paul E. Smith, "A Quarterly Econometric Model of the United States," *Journal of the American Statistical Association,* June 1961. The model's heavy reliance on the money supply is noted in Irwin Friend and Robert C. Jones, "Short-Run Forecasting Models Incorporating Anticipatory Data," in *Models of Income Determination,* Studies in Income and Wealth, no. 28 (Princeton: Princeton University Press for the National Bureau of Economic Research, 1964), p. 287.

19. Michael Evans, Yoel Haitovsky, and George I. Treyz, "An Analysis of the Forecasting of U.S. Econometric Models," in Hickman, ed., *Econometric Models,* 2: 1033; Herman O. Stekler, *Economic Forecasting* (New York: Praeger, 1970), p. 55; and Victor Zarnowitz, "Forecasting Economic Conditions: The Record and the Prospect," in *The Business Cycle Today,* ed. Victor Zarnowitz (New York: National Bureau of Economic Research, 1972), p. 222.

20. Bert G. Hickman, "Introduction and Summary," in Hickman, ed., *Econometric Models,* 1: 17.

21. Fair, *Short-Run Forecasting Model,* chap. 1.

22. See D. J. Daly, "Forecasting with Statistical Indicators," in Hickman, ed., *Econometric Models,* 2: 1159-83, esp. 1160-61.

23. A brief summary of the development of the indicators approach is given in Geoffrey H. Moore and Julius Shiskin, *Indicators of Business Expansions and Contractions,* National Bureau of Economic Research, Occasional Paper no. 103 (New York, 1967), pp. 1-2.

24. Ibid., pp. 8-28.

25. Zarnowitz, "Forecasting Economic Conditions," p. 194.

26. Jacob Mincer and Victor Zarnowitz, "The Evaluation of Economic Forecasts," in *Economic Forecasts and Expectations: Analyses of Forecasting Behavior and Performance,* ed. Jacob Mincer (New York: National Bureau of Economic Research, 1967), pp. 7-11.

27. For example, errors of 1 and 9 yield an average absolute error of $(1 + 9)/2 = 5$, as would errors of 5 and 5. But the root-mean-square error of 1 and 9 is $([1 \times 1 + 9 \times 9])/2)^{1/2} = 6.4$; for errors of 5 and 5 it is $([5 \times 5 + 5 \times 5]/2)^{1/2} = 5$.

28. There is another error measure, the inequality coefficient (called Theil's U), which is the square root of the ratio of the sum of squared errors and the sum of squared actual changes. See Henri Theil, *Applied Economic Forecasting* (Chicago: Rand McNally, 1966), pp. 27-28. While this ratio coefficient is useful for making accuracy comparisons between forecasts of different trends, it is unnecessarily complex for comparisons of forecasts of the same trend.

29. This point has been made by many analysts. For example, see Stekler, *Economic Forecasting,* p. 16; or R. Agarwala, "Comments on the Meeting," in Hickman, ed., *Econometric Models,* 2: 1209.

30. Moore and Shiskin, *Indicators,* p. 2, note that "it had always been recognized that leading, coincident, and lagging indicators by themselves comprise an incomplete basis for current business analysis."

31. Rendigs Fels, "The Recognition Patterns of Business Analysts," in Rendigs Fels and C. Elton Hinshaw, *Forecasting and Recognizing Business Cycle Turning Points* (New York: National Bureau of Economic Research 1968), pp. 5-6.

32. Victor Zarnowitz, *An Appraisal of Short-Term Economic Forecasts* (New York: National Bureau of Economic Research, 1967), p. 80.

33. See Su and Su, "Evaluation of ASA/NBER"; and Stephen K. McNees, "An Evaluation of Economic Forecasts," *New England Economic Review,* November/December 1975, pp. 3-39. In both cases the nominal-GNP forecast errors are converted to 1958 dollars by multiplying by the implicit price deflator for 1970-1971 for the 1968-1973 period and by the implicit price deflator for 1972-1973 for the 1970-1975 period.

34. The "actual" data are taken from the most recent revision of the national accounts and

income statistics published in U.S., of Commerce, Bureau of Economic Analysis, *Survey of Current Business,* January 1976, pt. 2.

35. McNees, "Evaluation of Economic Forecasts," pp. 3–39.

36. Fels, "Recognition Patterns," p. 47.

37. Ibid., pp. 54–57. Note that this result was derived from Fels's scoring system, which does not explicitly state success and failure in these terms.

38. Ibid., pp. 47 48. Also, from Table D, Appendix I, p. 52, it can be inferred that the *maximum* number of correct turning-point forecasts by the eclectic analysts for the eight peaks and troughs was 13 out of 64 for the 1948–1961 period and 9 out of 32 for the 1957–1961 period. Since Fels reports only average scores, the precise number of correct predictions cannot be deduced from his figures.

39. Zarnowitz, *Short-Term Economic Forecasts,* p. 80. The fact that the annual test (which in theory is less stringent than the half-year test) incurred greater errors can probably be explained by the time periods involved. Zarnowitz's sample covers more of the period prior to 1957, when turning points were more difficult to anticipate than in the 1957–61 period, according to the figures in Fels, "Recognition Patterns," p. 52.

40. Su and Su "Evaluation of ASA/NBER," pp. 597–605.

41. "ASA–NBER Business Outlook Survey: Second Quarter 1976," *Explorations in Economic Research* 3, no. 2 (Spring 1976).

42. Sources for the error analyses are: McNees, "Evaluation of Economic Forecasts"; Gary Fromm, "Forecasting, Policy Simulation, and Structural Analysis: Some Comparative Results of Alternative Models," *Proceedings of the American Statistical Association* (Business and Economics Section), December 1964, esp. p. 15; Gary Fromm and Lawrence Klein, "The NBER/ NSF Model Comparison Seminar: An Analysis of Results," *Annals of Economic and Social Measurement* 5, no. 1 (January/February 1976): 1–28; Evans, Haitovsky, and Treyz, "Forecasting of U.S. Econometric Models," pp. 186–92; Carl F. Christ, "Judging the Performance of Econometric Models of the U.S. Economy," *International Economic Review* 16, no. 1 (February 1975): 54–74; Yoel Haitovsky, George Treyz, and Vincent Su, *Forecasts with Quarterly Macroeconomic Models* (New York: National Bureau of Economic Research, 1974); *The Economic Outlook for 1975,* Twenty-Second Annual Conference on the Economic Outlook, University of Michigan, 12–13 December 1974, p. 2. All of the errors reported in these sources have been converted to 1958 dollars by multiplying by the appropriate implicit price deflators for their mid-year period.

43. Sources for these judgmental accuracy levels are: Zarnowitz, *Short-Term Economic Forecasts,* for nominal and real GNP average absolute errors for the 1947–63 period; idem, "Forecasting Economic Conditions," for root-mean-square errors of quarterly nominal GNP forecasts for 1953–69; Haitvosky, Treyz, and Su, *Forecasts,* for average absolute errors of nominal and real GNP forecasts for 1967–69 (based on Zarnowitz's series A [nominal only], G, and S, and on the record of General Electric's MAPCAST forecasting service); Stekler, *Economic Forecasting,* for 1960–64 root-mean-square errors of quarterly nominal-GNP forecasts; Su and Su, "Evaluation of ASA/NBER," for root-mean-square errors of quarterly nominal- and real-GNP forecasts for 1968–73; and McNees, "Evaluation of Economic Forecasts," for average absolute errors of quarterly nominal- and real-GNP forecasts for 1970–75. Again, all error levels have been converted to 1958 dollars.

44. *Annual* errors of econometric and judgmental forecasts have not been evaluated recently, but approximate error levels can be calculated from the multiperiod analyses that have been made. The error in an annual forecast will be very close to the average error in the forecasts made near the end of the previous year for the GNP levels of each of the target year's quarters. The absolute annual error and this average error for the four quarters will not necessarily be identical, because of the possibility of offsetting errors in the latter case. The annual forecast errors for 1970–75 reported here were calculated in this manner.

45. The size of an econometric model can be expressed by the number of equations, the number of structural equations, or the number of variables. These standards are obviously related, and the relative magnitude of different models is consistent, regardless of the definition of size. The number of equations is the measure of size employed here. "Very small" models have less than 15 equations; "small" models have 15–29; "medium" models have 30–59; "large" models

have 60-174; "very large" models have at least 175. This classification is consistent with the terminology used by most forecasters in describing their models, and with the categorization given in Greenberger, Crenson, and Crissey, *Models*.

46. Examples of econometric policy simulations can be found in Gary Fromm and Paul Taubman, *Policy Simulations with an Econometric Model* (Washington, D.C.: Brookings Institution, 1968), which describes simulations with the Brookings model; and Yoel Haitovsky and Neil Wallace, "A Study of Discretionary and Nondiscretionary Monetary and Fiscal Policies in the Context of Stochastic Macroeconomic Models," in *The Business Cycle Today*, ed. Victor Zarnowitz (New York: National Bureau of Economic Research, 1972), which examines results of the Wharton, FRB-MIT, and Michigan models.

47. Dewhurst, et al., *America's Needs and Resources;* and idem, *America's Needs and Resources: A New Survey* (New York: Twentieth Century Fund, 1955).

48. The NPA's methodology has been described in detail in *NPA Methodology for Long-Term National Economic Projections*, Report no. 69-N-1 (Washington, D.C.: National Planning Association Center for Economic Projections, 1969); and *An Econometric Model for Long-Range Projections of the United States Economy*, Report no. 71-N-1 (Washington, D.C.: National Planning Association Center for Economic Projections, 1970).

49. Again, the *Survey of Current Business*, January 1976, pt. 2, was used to provide the most up-to-date actual GNP series.

50. "Five"-year forecasts include forecasts for four- to six-year spans; "ten"-year forecasts include forecasts for eight- to twelve-year spans; and "fifteen"-year forecasts range from thirteen- to seventeen-year spans.

CHAPTER 5: ENERGY FORECASTING

1. "How Wrong Forecasts Hurt the Utilities," *Business Week*, 13 February 1971, pp. 44-45, offers a concise summary of the liabilities of stop-gap efforts to meet electric utility supply shortages.

2. Ibid., p. 44.

3. For example, the president of Humble Oil said in 1958: "As our domestic oil industry nears its centennial, some powerful voices are being raised in what sounds suspiciously like the premature preparation of an obituary. This is nothing new. The same cry that we are running out of oil has been raised many times before." Morgan J. Davis, "The Dynamics of Domestic Petroleum Resources," *Proceedings of the American Petroleum Institute* 38, no. 1 (1958): 22.

4. See U.S., Congress, Senate, Committee on Governmental Operations, *Energy Information Act, Hearings, Feb. 5, 6, 1974.* (Washington, D.C.: Government Printing Office, 1974). For another investigation that highlighted the level of recrimination, see U.S., Congress, Senate, Committee on the Judiciary, *Competition in the Energy Industry: Hearings, June 8, 11, 12, July 11, 27, 1973* (Washington, D.C.: Government Printing Office, 1974).

5. This distinction is explained and used in an excellent comparison of energy forecasts, Battelle Memorial Institute, Pacific Northwest Laboratories, *A Review and Comparison of Selected United States Energy Forecasts*, report prepared for the Executive Office of the President, Office of Science and Technology, Energy Policy Staff (Washington, D.C.: Government Printing Office, 1969), pp. 10-11.

6. For example, see U.S., Congress, House, Committee on Interior and Insular Affairs, *Energy "Demand" Studies: An Analysis and Appraisal* (Washington, D.C.: Government Printing Office, 1972), p. 52, which decries the use of the building-block construction; "The building-block method of projecting total energy consumption by making total energy consumption dependent upon projections of its components, fails to recognize inter-fuel substitutability, the influence of changes in relative fuel prices, and the derived nature of energy demand. . . . To the extent that the components of total energy consumption are growing at rates different from that of the total itself, forecasts of total energy consumption constructed by the building-block method will be subject to error, particularly for long-term forecasts."

7. A typical FPC report, published in December 1956, states that "it does not appear practicable to forecast loads merely on the basis of rates encountered in the past. . . . Assuming a doubling every 10 years in the future, as some estimators do, electric power use would reach astronomical

heights in a relatively short time." U.S., Federal Power Commission, *Estimated Future Power Requirements of the United States by Regions, 1955–1980* (Washington, D.C.: Government Printing Office, p. 5. Very similar reports were issued in June 1954, October 1955, April 1958, June 1959, and August 1960. The FPC (U.S., Federal Power Commission. *The National Power Survey, 1964* [Washington, D.C.: Government Printing Office, 1964], 1: 36) also assumes a slackening of growth, but overall it is characterized as an "extension of present trends" by the Battelle Memorial Institute study, *A Review and Comparison*, p. 10. The same study classifies the *1970 National Power Survey* forecasts in the same way. It should be noted that the FPC forecasts are actually the outcomes of interactions between the FPC staff and the regional advisory committees, which seek a consensus from separate forecasts established initially by the staff and the committees. A good survey and critique is offered in Thomas H. Burbank, "A Critique of Projections in the Electric Power Industry," *Edison Electric Institute Bulletin*, March/April 1973, pp. 64–70.

8. Because of the striking continuity in the methodology and format of *Electrical World* forecasts, each of the "Annual Electrical Industry Forecast" articles, which generally appear in the September 15 issue of *Electrical World*, faithfully illustrates the general approach.

9. Burbank, "A Critique of Projections," p. 67.

10. In each edition of the Edison Electric Institute, *Semi-Annual Electric Power Survey* (New York, various dates).

11. For example, see the American Petroleum Institute, *American Petroleum Industry, 1935* (New York, 1936); the analyses presented by Stewart Coleman of Standard Oil–New Jersey, Robert Wilson of Standard Oil–Indiana, and Robert Weidenhammer of the Department of Commerce, in U.S., Congress, Senate, Special Committee Investigating Petroleum Resources, *Petroleum Requirements—Postwar, Hearings, October 3, 4, 1945* (Washington, D.C.: Government Printing Office, 1946); and H. J. Barnett, *Energy Use and Supplies, 1939, 1947, 1965*, U.S. Bureau of Mines Information Circular no. 7582 (Washington, D.C.: Government Printing Office, 1950).

12. American Petroleum Institute, *American Petroleum Industry*, pp. 23–32.

13. See the *National Petroleum News* "Factbook" issue, mid-May, various years.

14. U.S., President's Materials Policy Commission, *Resources for Freedom* (Washington, D.C.: Government Printing Office, 1952), 2: 129.

15. U.S., supplies can be augmented by electricity produced in Canada, but only to a very limited extent.

16. For example, see Barnett, *Energy Use*, p. 6; and Perry D. Teitelbaum, *Nuclear Energy and the U.S. Fuel Economy, 1955–1980*, National Planning Association, Reports on the Productive Uses of Nuclear Energy, no. 8 (Washington, D.C., 1958), p. 35. This relationship generally does not hold for newly industrializing countries.

17. "How Wrong Forecasts Hurt the Utilities," *Business Week*, 13 February 1971, pp. 44–45.

18. Hasan Ozbekhan, *The Idea of a "Look-Out" Institution* (Santa Monica, Calif.: System Development Corporation, 1965), p. 1. See also Erich Jantsch, *Technological Forecasting in Perspective* (Paris: Organisation for Economic Cooperation and Development, 1967), annex A.5, for a list of such institutions.

19. U.S., President's Materials Policy Commission, *Resources for Freedom*.

20. U.S., Energy Study Group, in *Energy Research and Development and National Progress* (Washington, D.C.: Government Printing Office, 1965), p. 13, emphasizes the importance of detail: "A few detailed end-use projections that have been made in recent years are not necessarily more accurate than the simpler projections, but they are more useful. In particular, they provide a basis for discussion and criticism by experts in the energy field...."

21. For example, Warren E. Morrison, *An Energy Model for the United States Featuring Energy Balances for the Years 1947 to 1968 and Projections and Forecasts to the Years 1980 and 2000*, U.S. Bureau of Mines Information Circular no. 8324 (Washington, D.C.: Government Printing Office, 1968).

22. "How Wrong Forecasts Hurt the Utilities," *Business Week*, 13 February 1971.

23. U.S., House, Committee on Interior and Insular Affairs, *Energy "Demand" Studies*, p. 52.

24. Ibid.

25. Barnett, *Energy Use.*

26. Statements of Steward Coleman and Robert Wilson in U.S., Senate, Special Committee Investigating Petroleum Resources, *Petroleum Requirements.*

27. D. Belzer and C. Almon, *Forecasts of U.S. Petroleum Demand, 1972–1980, and Interindustry Analysis,* University of Maryland Inforum Research Report no. 4 (College Park, Md., 1972); Duane Chapman, Timothy Tyrrell, and Timothy Mount, "Electricity Demand Growth and the Energy Crisis." *Science* 178, no. 4062 (17 November 1972): 703–8.

28. For example, the Hudson and Jorgenson energy-modeling efforts have been carried out at Data Resources, Inc., which also maintains one of the country's most prominent full-scale econometric models.

29. See Milton F. Searl, ed., *Energy Modeling: Art, Science, Practice,* Resources for the Future Working Paper EN-1 (Washington, D.C., 1973), for descriptions of various energy models; and Dilip R. Limaye, R. Ciliano, and J. R. Sharko, *Quantitative Energy Studies and Models—A Review of the State of the Art,* final report to the Council on Environmental Quality (Washington, D.C.: Decision Sciences Corporation, 1973), for an analytical evaluation.

30. This is the formulation of Chapman, Tyrell, and Mount, "Electricity Demand Growth," p. 706.

31. For example, U.S., Congress, Senate, Committee on Finance, *Hearings on the Energy Conservation and Conversion Act of 1975, July 10–18, 1975,* statement of C. John Miller, president of the Independent Petroleum Association (Washington, D.C.: Government Printing Office, 1975), p. 581.

32. Forecasts compiled in Overly-Schell Associates, "Mineral Resources and the Environment: Appendix to Section IV, Report on Panel on Demand for Fuel and Mineral Resources," Washington, D.C., February 1975 (total energy and petroleum projections) (mimeographed); and in Robert T. Taussig, "Bibliography and Digest of U.S. Electric and Total Energy Forecasts, 1975–2050," Edison Electric Institute, New York, January 1974 (mimeographed).

33. Wallace F. Lovejoy and Paul T. Homan, *Methods of Estimating Reserves of Crude Oil, Natural Gas, and Natural Gas Liquids* (Baltimore: The Johns Hopkins Press for Resources for the Future, 1965), p. 84.

34. V. R. Garfias, "An Estimate of the World's Proven Oil Reserves," *American Institute of Mining and Metallurgical Engineers Transactions* 103 (1933): 1077.

35. U.S. National Resources Committee, *Energy Resources and National Policy* (Washington, D.C.: Governmental Printing Office, 1939), p. 292.

36. M. King Hubbert, *Energy Resources,* National Academy of Sciences, National Research Council Publication no. 1000-D (Washington, D.C., 1962), p. 50.

37. A typical critique is the statement of J.E. Pew (vice-president of Sun Oil Company and chairman of the API Committee on Petroleum Reserves) in U.S., Congress, Senate, Select Committee Investigating Petroleum Resources, *Petroleum Resources—Postwar, Hearings, June 19, 1945* (Washington, D.C.: Government Printing Office, 1946), pp. 5–22.

38. These early estimates are summarized in U.S., National Resources Committee, *Energy Resources,* p. 139.

39. Bruce Netschert, *The Future Supply of Oil and Gas* (Baltimore: The Johns Hopkins University Press for Resources for the Future, 1958) pp., 9–10.

40. Lovejoy and Homan, *Methods of Estimating Reserves,* pp., 79–80, point out the variations in definitions of "ultimate reserve."

41. National Petroleum Council, *Future Petroleum Provinces of the United States* (Washington, D.C., 1970), p. 25.

42. U.S., President's Materials Policy Commission, *Resources for Freedom,* 3: 4–5.

43. Hubbert, *Energy Resources,* p. 51.

44. A. D. Zapp, "World Petroleum Resources," in *Domestic and World Resources of Fossil Fuels, Radioactive Minerals, and Geothermal Energy,* U.S. Geological Survey, preliminary reports for the Natural Resources Subcommittee of the Federal Science Council (Washington, D.C.: Government Printing Office, 1961, p. 2.

45. U.S., Congress, Senate, Commerce and Government Operations Committees, *Hearings, May 10, 1974,* statement by M. King Hubbert (Washington, D.C., 1975), p. 88.

46. National Academy of Sciences, *Mineral Resources and the Environment* (Washington, D.C., 1975), p. 88.

47. Zapp, "World Petroleum Resources," p. 1.

48. Milton F. Searl, *Fossil Fuels in the Future* (Washington, D.C.: U.S. Atomic Energy Commission, 1960), p. 43.

49. U.S., President's Materials Policy Commission, *Resources for Freedom*, 4: 193–204. It is not clear whether Egloff was referring to "in-place" or recoverable petroleum.

50. National Academy of Sciences, *Mineral Resources*, p. 79.

51. V. E. McKelvey, "Mineral Resource Estimates and Public Policy," *American Scientist* 60 (January/February 1972): 32–40.

52. P. K. Theobald, S. P. Schweinfurth, and D. C. Duncan, *Energy Resources of the United States*, U.S. Geological Survey Circular no. 650 (Washington, D.C., 1972).

53. T. H. McCulloh, "1973 Oil and Gas," in *United States Mineral Resources*, ed. D. A. Brobst and W. P. Pratt, U.S. Geological Survey Prof. Paper no. 820 (Washington, D.C., 1973), pp. 477–96.

54. T. A. Hendricks, *Resources of Oil, Gas, and Natural Gas Liquids in the United States and the World*, U.S. Geological Survey Circular no. 522 (Washington, D.C., 1965), pp. 1–20; T. A. Hendricks and S. P. Schweinfurth, "The United States Resource Base of Petroleum," Department of Interior memorandum, 14 September 1966, cited in McCulloh, "1973 Oil and Gas," p. 491; Theobald, Schweinfurth, and Duncan, *Energy Resources*.

55. National Petroleum Council, *Future Petroleum Provinces*. Examples of estimates by experts in oil companies include: L. G. Weeks (Standard Oil of New Jersey), "Where Will Energy Come from in 2059?" *Petroleum Engineer* 31, no. 9 (August 1959); W. K. Link (Nelson Bunker Hunt International Petroleum Company), cited in *The Oil & Gas Journal* 64, no. 34 (22 August 1966): 150–51.

56. M. King Hubbert, "Nuclear Energy and the Fossil Fuels," in *Drilling and Production Practice* (New York: American Petroleum Institute, 1956), pp. 7–25; idem, *Energy Resources*, p. 50; idem, "M. King Hubbert's Reply to J. M. Ryan," *Journal of Petroleum Technology* 18 (February 1966): 284–86; idem, "Degree of Advancement of Petroleum Exploration in the United States," *Bulletin of the American Association of Petroleum Geologists* 51, no. 11 (1967): 2207–27; idem, "Energy Resources," *Resources and Man* (Washington, D.C.: National Academy of Sciences, National Research Council, 1969), pp. 157–242; idem, "The Energy Resources of the Earth," *Scientific American*, September 1971, pp., 61–70; U.S., Congress, Senate, Committee on Interior and Insular Affairs, *U.S. Energy Resources*, background paper prepared by M. King Hubbert (Washington, D.C.: Government Printing Office, 1974).

57. U.S. Department of Interior, Office of Oil and Gas, *Method for Evaluating United States Crude Oil Resources and Protecting Domestic Crude Oil Availability*, prepared by C. L. Moore (Washington, D.C.: Government Printing Office, 1966); C. L. Moore, "Analysis and Projection of Historic Patterns of U.S. Crude Oil and Natural Gas," in *Future Petroleum Provinces of the United States*, ed. I. H. Cram (Washington, D.C.: National Petroleum Council, 1970), pp., 133–38.

58. M. A. Elliot and H. R. Linden, "A New Analysis of U.S. Natural Gas Supplies," *Journal of Petroleum Technology* 20 (February 1968): 135–41.

59. Lovejoy and Homan, *Methods of Estimating Reserves*, p. 90.

60. As witnessed by the much lower 1974 estimate by V. E. McKelvey, "Revised U.S. Oil and Gas Resources Estimates," U.S. Geological Survey news release, 26 March 1974.

CHAPTER 6: TRANSPORTATION FORECASTING

1. For example, Wilfred Owen, *The Metropolitan Transportation Problem* (Washington, D.C.: Brookings Institution, 1956); idem, *Cities in the Motor Age* (New York: Viking, 1959).

2. U.S., Department of Commerce, Civil Aeronautics Administration, *1960, 1965, 1970 Civil Aviation and Federal Airways Forecasts* (Washington, D.C.: Government Printing Office, 1956), p. 35.

3. Forecast studies that express an explicit concern over the difficulties of forecasting saturation levels include: U.S. Department of Transportation, Federal Highway Administration, Office of Highway Planning, *Highway Travel Forecasts* (Washington, D.C.: Government Printing

Office, 1974), pp., 30–31; and The First Pennsylvania Banking and Trust Company, "Slower Auto Growth is Predicted for 1970s," cited in *Automotive News*, 8 May 1972.

4. These are forecasts of "active" civilian aircraft, as defined by the FAA and CAB. The FAA definition was altered in 1971 (see U.S., Department of Transportation, Federal Aviation Administration, *Aviation Forecasts: Fiscal Years 1971–1978* (Washington, D.C.: Government Printing Office, 1971), but FAA statistics for later years (i.e., 1971–1975) were readjusted to fit the former definition by multiplying the "new definition" figures by 1.0634, the ratio of "old definition" active aircraft (aircraft which have not necessarily been flown within a specified time) to "new definition" active aircraft (those which have). The ratio was determined by comparing figures for years included in studies using either definition. The FAA's own forecasts were evaluated separately from the others because its forecasts are targeted for fiscal years rather than calendar years, and therefore the actual levels for appraisal are somewhat different.

5. Caution is required when comparing overestimates with underestimates using this percentage error measure, because underestimates, even if extremely inaccurate, cannot exceed 100 percent inaccuracy, whereas overestimates can be much higher.

6. See U.S., Department of Transportation, Federal Aviation Administration, *Aviation Forecasts: Fiscal Years 1976–1987* (Washington, D.C.: Government Printing Office, 1975), pp. 59–70.

7. The problem of finding the level of "maturity" is mentioned in The Boeing Company, Boeing Commercial Airplane Company, Market Research Unit, *Domestic RPM Forecast: Trunks, Pan Am, and Local Service Carriers* (Renton, Wash., 1973), p. 54; and in the Air Transport Association of America, *Domestic Passenger Market Demand Forecast, 1973–2000* (Washington, D.C., 1973), p. 29.

8. U.S., Federal Power Commission, Bureau of Power, "Development of Electrically Powered Vehicles," in U.S., Congress, Senate, Committee on Commerce and Committee on Public Works, Subcommittee on Air and Water Pollution, *Joint Hearings*, 90th Cong., 1st sess., 4 March 1967, pp. 11–62, esp. pp. 37–38.

9. American Association of State Highway Officials, "A Progress Report to the Public Works Committee of the Congress of the United States on a Recommended Continuing Federal-Aid Program for the Period 1976 through 1985 ('After 75 Program'), as Developed by the Member State Highway Departments," in U.S., Congress, Senate, Committee on Public Works, Subcommittee on Roads, *Hearings on the Federal Highway Act of 1968*, 90th Cong., 2nd sess., 4 June 1968, p. 114.

10. U.S., Federal Power Commission, "Electrically Powered Vehicles," p. 34.

11. American Association of State Highway Officials, "Preliminary Report of AASHO on Federal-Aid Highway Needs after 1972," in U.S., Congress, House, Committee on Public Works, *Hearings*, 90th Cong., 1st sess., 7 June 1967.

12. Richard Vitek and Nawal Taneja, *The Impact of High Inflation Rates on the Demand for Air Passenger Transportation*, Massachusetts Institute of Technology, Flight Transportation Laboratory (Cambridge, Mass., 1975), pp., 15–16, 20–21.

CHAPTER 7: TECHNOLOGICAL FORECASTING

1. Marvin Cetron, "Using Technical Forecasts," *Science and Technology*, July 1968, p. 57.

2. Harold Linstone, "Editorial Comment," *Technological Forecasting and Social Change* 7, no. 1 (1975): 2.

3. This point was first made by S. C. Gilfillan in his *The Sociology of Invention* (Chicago: Follett, 1935), p. 12.

4. S. C. Gilfillan, "The Future Home Theater," *Independent* 73 (1912): 886–91.

5. Harold D. Lasswell, *Power and Personality* (New York: W. W. Norton, 1976), p. 207.

6. Harold D. Lasswell, "The Garrison State and Specialists on Violence," *American Journal of Sociology* 46 (1941): 455–68.

7. Eugene M. Grabbe and Donald L. Pyke, "An Evaluation of the Forecasting of Information Processing Technology and Applications," *Technological Forecasting and Social Change* 4 (1972): 143–50.

8. This figure was used by the Pacific Northwest Laboratories of the Battelle Memorial Institute in *A Review and Comparison of Selected United States Energy Forecasts*, report pre-

pared for the Executive Office of the President, Office of Science and Technology, Energy Policy Staff (Washington, D.C.: Government Printing Office, 1969), p. 19, for its conversions of installed-capacity estimates to generation estimates.

9. Eugene Ayres and Charles Scarlott, *Energy Sources—The Wealth of the World* (New York: McGraw-Hill, 1952), p. 171.

10. See John F. Hogerton, *Nuclear Power Today* (Cambridge, Mass.: Arthur D. Little, Inc., 1966), p. 23, for the mid-1960s lead-time estimate; and National Academy of Engineering, *U.S. Energy Prospects: An Engineering Viewpoint* (Washington, D.C., 1974), p. 92, for the 1970s lead-time estimate.

11. See chapter 2 of the present volume for a discussion of the component approach as applied to demographic forecasting.

12. James A. Lane, "Nuclear Fuel Requirements for Large-Scale Industrial Power," *Nucleonics* 12, no. 10 (October 1954): 65.

13. Richard Tarrice, "A Discussion of Future Nuclear Fuel Requirements," paper presented at the 1962 meeting of the American Institute of Mining Engineers, New York, 21 February 1962.

14. U.S. Atomic Energy Commission, Division of Operations Analysis and Forecasting, *Estimated Growth of Civilian Nuclear Power*, WASH-1055 (Washington, D.C.: Government Printing Office, 1965).

15. S. Golan, S. Siegel, and D. J. Stoker, "Uranium Utilization Patterns Based on Sodium-Cooled Reactors," in *Atom Forum 1962: Proceedings of the Annual Conference of the Atomic Industrial Forum* (Washington, D.C., 1962), pp. 101–11.

16. Karl Mayer, "Regional Aspects of Nuclear Power," app. 8 in Perry D. Teitelbaum, *Nuclear Energy and the U.S. Fuel Economy, 1955–1980*, National Planning Association, Reports on the Productive Uses of Nuclear Energy, no. 8 (Washington, D.C., 1958), pp. 153–68.

17. U.S., Atomic Energy Commission, *Estimated Growth;* U.S., Federal Power Commission, *The National Power Survey, 1964* (Washington, D.C.: Government Printing Office, 1964).

18. Robert U. Ayres, "Envelope Curve Forecasting," in *Technological Forecasting for Industry and Government*, ed. James R. Bright (Englewood Cliffs, N.J.: Prentice-Hall, 1968), pp. 79–80.

19. Joseph Martino, *Technological Forecasting for Decisionmaking* (New York: American Elsevier, 1972), pp. 140–41.

20. Willis Ware, *Limits in Computing Power*, Rand Corporation, Paper no. P-4710 (Santa Monica, Calif., 1971), pp. 15–17.

21. Ware estimates the development costs of a computer adequate for these tasks to be about $200–$300 million. Ibid., p. 17.

22. Kenneth E. Knight, "Application of Technological Forecasting to the Computer Industry," in *A Guide to Practical Technological Forecasting*, ed. James R. Bright and Milton E. F. Schoeman (Englewood Cliffs, N.J.: Prentice-Hall, 1973), p. 403.

23. This is the same standard used by Rein Turn in his book *Computers in the 1980s* (New York: Columbia University Press, 1974), which is the most comprehensive survey and forecast of computer capabilities.

24. John Diebold, "What's Ahead in Information Technology," *Harvard Business Review*, September/October 1965, pp. 76–82.

25. U.S., Naval Supply Systems Command, *Impact of Future Technology on Navy Business Management*, Report AD 824692 (Washington, D.C.: Government Printing Office, 1966); cited in Martino, *Technological Forecasting*, pp. 626–27.

26. George B. Bernstein and Lawrence A. Feidelman, *Data Processing: Forecast 80* (Westminster, Md.: Foundation Services, Inc., 1971), pp., 42–43.

27. Paul Armer, *Computer Aspects of Technological Change, Automation, and Economic Progress*, Rand Corporation, Paper no. P-3478 (Santa Monica, Calif., 1966), reprinted in *Technology and the American Economy*, report of the National Commission on Technology, Automation, and Economic Progress (Washington, D.C., 1966), app. vol. I, p. 1-211; Earl Joseph, "Computers: Trends toward the Future," in *Information Processing 68* (Amsterdam: North-

Holland Publishing Co., 1969), pp. 668–69. Joseph predicts capability in terms of "millions of instructions per second" (MIPS) which are comparable to the MIPS in Turn, *Computers*.

28. L. C. Hobbs, "The Impact of Hardward in the 1970s," *Datamation* 12, no. 3 (March 1966): 38; Hasan Ozbekhan, "Automation," *Science Journal*, October 1967, p. 70.

29. Turn, *Computers*, chaps. 1 and 2. Turn's forecasts are not evaluated here, even though some estimates of 1975 computer capabilities are included, because it is obvious that his emphasis is on long-range developments, such that the graphs and charts that include figures for 1975 are not meant to reflect accurate actual operational speeds for that year.

30. See, for example, Robert W. Keyes, "Physical Problems and Limits in Computer Logic," *IEEE Spectrum*, May 1969, pp. 36–45; and Ware, *Limits*, pp. 7–12.

31. The developers of the ILLIAC IV were promising as far back as 1968 that their machine would be capable of performing a billion operations per second. See George H. Barnes et al., "The ILLIAC IV Computer," *IEEE Transactions on Computers*, vol. c-17, no. 8 (August 1968), p. 746.

32. For example, Fred Gruenberger, "Speaking of Predictions," *Datamation* 14, no. 10 (October 1969): 141; and P. D. Hall, "Computer Systems," in *Technological Forecasting and Corporate Strategy*, ed. Gordon Wills et al. (New York: American Elsevier, 1969), p. 190.

33. See Marvin J. Cetron and Thomas I. Monahan, "An Evaluation and Appraisal of Various Approaches to Technological Forecasting," in Bright, ed., *Technological Forecasting*, p. 145.

34. "The Next Generation," *Datamation* 12, no. 1 (January 1967): 32, predicted that logic gate delays for 1972–73 would be as low as 0.5 nanoseconds; in fact, the minimum was about 0.55 nanoseconds.

35. Descriptions of the Delphi technique can be found in T. J. Gordon and Olaf Helmer, *Report on a Long-Range Forecasting Study*, Rand Corporation, Paper no. P-2982 (Santa Monica, Calif., 1964); and in Martino, *Technological Forecasting*, chap. 2.

36. "Legitimate" means that the convergence of opinions that occurs through the use of the Delphi technique in theory results from the fact that experts participating on the panels change their initial positions because they are genuinely convinced by the arguments of the other experts, and are not swayed by the personal forcefulness of the other experts or by other personality factors that do arise in face-to-face interactions.

37. Grabbe and Pyke, "An Evaluation," p. 146.

38. See William L. Hays, *Statistics for Psychologists* (New York: Rinehart & Winston, 1963), p. 182.

39. Gordon and Helmer, *Report*, p. 21. Two innovations have been left out of this discussion because their upper quartile is "never" rather than a specific year.

40. These studies are: ibid.; A. D. Bender et al., *A Delphic Study of the Future of Medicine* (Philadelphia: SK & F Laboratories, 1969); Oto Šulc, "A Methodological Approach to the Integration of Technological and Social Forecasts," *Technological Forecasting* 1 (1969): 105–8; Parsons & Williams, *Forecast 1968–2000 of Computer Developments and Applications*, (Copenhagen, 1968); Trans-Canada Telephone System, *Communications, Computers, and Data* (Ottawa, 1971). Other Delphi studies are available, but they generally lack information on interquartile ranges. For example, Bernstein and Feidelman, *Data Processing*, report ranges in terms of the dates chosen for 20 percent and 90 percent probability of the event's occurrence, a perfectly acceptable procedure, but one which is inappropriate for our specific purpose of calculating MTEs.

41. Martino, *Technological Forecasting*, pp. 42–43. In the following analysis, one study that was not included in Martino's analysis of absolute levels of minimum typical errors has been added—namely, the 1968 TRW study conducted by North and Pyke called "PROBE II." The "Probe" method is summarized in Harper Q. North and Donald L. Pyke, " 'Probes' of the Technological Future," *Harvard Business Review*, May/June 1969. Martino calculated the regression coefficients, but the median lengths and interquartile ranges are unavailable. Pyke has provided the identities of the topics as listed in Martino's table. The calculations for the Gordon and Helmer space exploration category were redone to eliminate the effects of forecasts for which the interquartile ranges included "never"; hence the figure for this panel is different from what

Martino reports. The Trans-Canada Telephone forecasts, which were not included in the Martino study, were added, but the Bernstein study included in Martino's table was deleted because it showed the relationship between forecast length and probability range rather than interquartile range.

42. Erich Jantsch, *Technological Forecasting in Perspective* (Paris: Organisation for Economic Cooperation and Development, 1967), pt. 2.

43. Cetron and Monahan, "An Evaluation," pp. 146–51.

44. Ibid., pp. 175–77.

45. Ibid., pp. 146–50, emphasis added.

46. Ibid., p. 150.

47. Ibid., p. 151.

48. Martino, *Technological Forecasting*, pp. 116–18.

49. Gilfillan, *The Sociology of Invention*.

50. See Kenneth E. Warner, "The Need for Some Innovative Concepts of Innovation: An Examination of Research on the Diffusion of Innovation," *Policy Sciences* 5, no. 4 (December 1974): 433–51, for a review of this literature.

CHAPTER 8: CONCLUSION

1. See the discussion of Pearl's method in Chapter 3 of this volume.

2. American Petroleum Institute, *American Petroleum Industry, 1935* (New York, 1936), pp. 26–27.

3. U.S., Department of Commerce, Business and Defense Services Administration, *Water Use in the United States, 1900–1980* (Washington, D.C.: Government Printing Office, 1960).

4. "How Wrong Forecasts Hurt the Utilities," *Business Week,* 13 February 1971, p. 44.

5. See, for example, Otis Dudley Duncan, "Social Forecasting: The State of the Art," *The Public Interest,* no. 17 (Fall 1969), pp. 88–118; Daniel Bell, "Twelve Modes of Prediction," in *Penguin Survey of the Social Sciences,* ed. J. Gould (Baltimore: Penguin Books, 1966); and Karl Popper, "Prediction and Prophecy in the Social Sciences," in *Theories of History,* ed. P. Gardner (Glencoe, Ill.: Free Press, 1959).

6. In fact, Duncan, "Social Forecasting," devotes a large part of his discussion to the record of *demographic* forecasts.

7. This terminology was developed in Harold D. Lasswell and Abraham Kaplan, *Power and Society* (New Haven: Yale University Press, 1950), pp. 55–57.

8. The same point with reference to developing interesting scenarios for learning and experimental games is found in Martin Shubik and Garry Brewer, "Methodological Advances in Gaming: The One-Person, Computer Interactive, Quasi-Rigid Rule Game," *Simulation & Games* 3, no. 3 (September 1972): 331–33.

9. U.S., Department of Health, Education, and Welfare, *Toward a Social Report* (Washington, D.C.: Government Printing Office, 1969).

10. Daniel Bell, "The Idea of a Social Report," *The Public Interest,* no. 15 (Spring 1969), p. 72.

11. Most notably, U.S., President's Research Committee on Social Trends, *Recent Social Trends* (New York: McGraw-Hill, 1933); and William F. Ogburn, *The Social Effects of Aviation* (Boston: Houghton-Mifflin, 1946).

12. Bell, "The Idea of a Social Report," p. 75.

13. Good examples are Eleanor Sheldon and Wilbert E. Moore, eds., *Indicators of Social Change* (New York: Russell Sage Foundation, 1968); and Raymond Bauer, ed., *Social Indicators* (Cambridge, Mass: MIT Press, 1966).

14. Duncan, "Social Forecasting," p. 111.

15. This term was developed principally in the discipline of technological forecasting. See H. W. Lanford, "A Penetration of the Technological Forecasting Jungle," *Technological Forecasting and Social Change* 4, no. 2 (1972): 207–25, esp. 209. However, the term is appropriate for goal-setting forecast efforts in any area.

16. Joseph Martino, *Technological Forecasting for Decisionmaking* (New York: American Elsevier, 1972), p. 287.

INDEX

LIBRARY OF CONGRESS CATALOGING IN PUBLICATION DATA

Ascher, William.

Forecasting.

Includes bibliographical references and index.
1. Forecasting. 2. Economic forecasting. 3. Population forecasting. 4. Technological forecasting. I. Title.
HB3730.A78   338.5'442   77-21423
ISBN 0-8018-2035-9 (hardcover)
ISBN 0-8018-2273-4 (paperback)

LIBRARY OF CONGRESS CATALOGING IN PUBLICATION DATA

Ascher, William.
  Forecasting.

  Includes bibliographical references and index.
  1. Forecasting.   2.   Economic forecasting.   3.   Population
forecasting.   4.   Technological forecasting.   I.   Title.
HB3730.A78   338.5'442   77-21423
ISBN 0-8018-2035-9 (hardcover)
ISBN 0-8018-2273-4 (paperback)